BLOOD · SWEAT
TRIUMPH & TEARS

BLOOD · SWEAT TRIUMPH & TEARS

TALES FROM THE GAA

JOHN SCALLY

BLACK & WHITE PUBLISHING

First published 2016
by Black & White Publishing Ltd
29 Ocean Drive, Edinburgh EH6 6JL

1 3 5 7 9 10 8 6 4 2   16 17 18 19

ISBN: 978 1 78530 073 8

A CIP catalogue record for this book is available from the British Library.

Typeset by Iolaire, Newtonmore
Printed and bound by CPI Group (UK) Ltd., Croydon, CR0 4YY

To John Jigger O'Connor

A man who put the class into classy

CONTENTS

Acknowledgements ix
Foreword by Ger Loughnane 1

Introduction 5
1. The Sunday Games 9
2. Tougher than the Rest 28
3. Magic Moments 56
4. The Curious Incidents of the GAA
    in the Daytime 125
5. Mischief Makers, Miscreants
    and Mad Hatters 166
6. Simply the Best 199
7. Wired for Sound 227
8. More than Words 250
Conclusion 275

ACKNOWLEDGEMENTS

Thanks to the many GAA greats of the past and present who generously gave me interviews down the years which form the heart of this book, including Joe McDonagh who died so tragically as this volume was being completed. Just as this book was going to press, the sad death occurred of the much-loved Tom Devine. He will be greatly missed by his devoted family. A great oak has fallen in the forest with the passing of Thomas O'Donnchadha. Roscommon will be poorer without him. My thoughts too are with Trish O'Brien on the sad passing of her father.

I wish to record my particular gratitude to Bernard Flynn for his characteristic generosity. Bernard is one of those people who put the big into the phrase 'big heart'. I am also profoundly grateful to the great Ger Loughnane for honouring me by writing the foreword to this book. My gratitude to Dermot Earley for his friendship and practical support.

I am grateful to the premier publication *The Connacht Tribune* for use of some of their photos. My particular thanks to national treasure Dave O'Connell for his assistance.

Special thanks to Karol Mannion for his help with photos. My gratitude also to John Boyle, Aidan Farrell, Teresa Scally and to Adam and Harry Minogue for help with photos.

As James Finneran and Orlaith Furey begin their new life

together, may they discover that love is all around.

Roscommon's greatest fan, Paddy Joe Burke, has had a year to remember. My best wishes to Maura and the wise man.

Thanks to Campbell Brown, Thomas Ross, Chris Kydd, Tom Maxwell, Daiden O'Regan and all at Black & White Publishing for their enthusiastic support of this book from day one.

Special thanks to Simon Hess who played a pivotal role behind the scenes in making this project a reality.

Thanks to Ian Brady and the Davy Group for their generous support of my previous book.

FOREWORD BY GER LOUGHNANE

I'll never forget our most thrilling victory. It was against Tipperary in Pairc Uí Chaoimh in 1997. We had set our sights on winning the All-Ireland in 1997. We had great days in '95 and beating Cork in the Championship in '97 was wonderful but, from a purely hurling point of view, and because of their great tradition and well-deserved reputation, to beat Tipperary was the day of days.

It was a beautiful sunny day. We had gone into the '95 All-Ireland in a relaxed frame of mind but there was no relaxation that day. We went to Cork with a sense of going on a mission that was only recaptured when we played Waterford in the Munster final replay the following year. Everybody was totally up for it. When we met the bus outside the Shamrock Hotel, Frank Lohan was dancing from foot to foot. When Fitzie (Davy Fitzgerald) arrived he was pale. There was none of the usual chatter. This was the day. There was an awful lot at stake.

As usual, the team went to bed after breakfast and the mentors and I went for a walk in the grounds of University College Cork. It was the first time I had been there. It's a really beautiful place but all the time the thought was flashing in our minds: this is the day.

We went for a puckout in the Mardyke. Afterwards, I called on the players and told them that they had done so much for Clare already but today we wanted a really special effort. I

1

said in a soft voice, 'Everything we've achieved is at stake today. Our entire reputation rests on the match.' We went on to the coach and, really, the bus didn't need an engine to power it. Everybody was totally geared up.

My last words to them were, 'Everything depends on today. Make every second of every minute count.'

I can't remember everything before the two All-Irelands but I can remember every second of that day. As soon as we went, we could feel the tension that was in the air. It wasn't a tension that drained you, it was a tension that enlivened you. For the first time when the names of each of the Clare players were read out, there was a massive cheer. The crowd was really up for it. There was an incredible sense of oneness between the team and the fans.

When the game began we were playing at 90 miles an hour. We made a brilliant start and led by 0-13 to 0-8 at the interval. Barely seven minutes after the re-start, Tipperary were level and playing with the wind. The Tipp supporters started singing 'Sliabh Na mBan'. I immediately leapt to my feet and shouted to each of the players, 'Is that the sound you want ringing in your ears all the way home?' Clare lifted their game and regained the lead almost immediately when Seánie McMahon scored a point from a free. Suddenly the tide had turned in our favour again. We brought on David Forde and he scored a wonder goal.

Clare were seemingly going to be beaten, after enjoying a huge lead. Then we came back, to lead again, with a magic goal. We were winning by three points. Then John Leahy broke through and Tipp almost scored a goal in the last minute to tie the match.

When the final whistle blew I just lost the head. I leapt out of the dugout and got a belt from a flag and my face was bleeding. Some lady jumped on me. I was ecstatic.

We won two All-Irelands and they were brilliant but this was unique. People outside Clare would find it very difficult to understand just how much it mattered. This was the dream for every Clare person for decades – to beat Tipperary in a Munster final. Forget about All-Irelands. Had we won six All-Irelands and hadn't beaten Tipp in a Munster final, it wouldn't have been as good, but to win that day and go into the dressing-room was sheer bliss.

I made sure, though, that the dressing-room was locked. The atmosphere inside was one of total and absolute contentment. We're not supposed to feel it in this lifetime. There was no need for a word to be said between each other. The downside was you knew that there would never be a day like that again but it is a feeling that will last forever.

You didn't even want to go out among the crowd afterwards. You wanted no patting on the back. We had all that when we won the All-Ireland in '95. We just wanted to sit back and share that among ourselves. We didn't want to leave the dressing-room because the magic was inside. It was great going out and meeting our relatives and everyone else in Clare but even though the fans felt brilliantly, they just hadn't felt what we felt in the dressing-room. Only those who were in there could ever understand what it was like. You just couldn't get it anywhere else and that was the magic that was Clare.

The '97 Munster final is the treasure of all treasures. You ask yourself, 'Did it ever really happen?' Everything that day was just bliss. It wasn't the All-Ireland final, but the Munster final was more important to us. That's what people don't understand. Munster is magic because of the local rivalries. Whatever changes are made in hurling, the Munster Cham-

3

pionship must stay. You look at the Munster Championship and see the passion it generates. Croke Park is business. There is something spiritual about the Munster Championship.

It took us four hours to get home that night. All the towns we went through, like Charleville and Buttevant, were thronged with Clare people and Limerick fans delighted for Clare. It was such a pleasure. No night coming home from any All-Ireland final could match it. The only night that matched it was coming home from the Munster final in '95. We felt we really had arrived as a major hurling power.

Great memories.

This is a book of great memories.

I hope you enjoy it.

Introduction

For many fans, the Gaelic Games are the Holy Grail. They are one of the few places left where the Corinthian spirit survives and where the stars are playing for the love of the game.

Listen to a small child imitating his father and mother's words, trying to get the sound right, the pitch and intonation, the vowels initially and eventually, after many a difficult battle, those elusive consonants. Deep grammar or not, what you are listening to is a young child trying to forge a link with generations past, present and future. Perhaps if there is one reason why so many adults with big brains remain fascinated with sport it is because we all start off as little creatures playing those games and, like salmon heading back from the sea, we never lose a sense of where the stream starts: in memories strung together which continue to mesmerise us.

Sport, unique in its evocative hold on identity, takes us back to that moment of initial fascination with the world when, as small, imitative children, we first swung a hurley or kicked a ball. I believe that the mystery of human selfhood is bound up with the mystery of sport: 'How are we conscious?' and 'how does sport affect us?' are probably parts of the same bigger question for many of us, but we don't answer the first unless we answer the second. Roddy Doyle famously remarked that it was only while watching Ireland play in the World Cup in Italy in 1990 that he first realised he loved his country.

No sociologist can ignore the power of Gaelic games in Ireland to harness the communal values of loyalty, self-discipline and sacrifice and all for the glory of the parish. They epitomise the importance of respect for place, memorably captured by Anthony Daly, the captain of the Clare hurling team, and his victory speech in 1997 when the Banner County emerged from decades in the wilderness to claim their second Munster title: 'We are no longer the Whipping Boys of Munster.'

As a boy growing up in Roscommon, Gaelic football was the battery that drove my imaginative life and dared me to see the county in a very different light. Football provided an escape from people's problems and anxieties. It allowed them to dream of better days to come. Success, albeit at a very modest level, increased our self-esteem. We walked that little bit taller, we talked just a little more boldly, and we wore our blue and gold caps with pride. When the county team was doing well, it did not seem to hurt as much if the price of cattle was abysmal or if the summer was wet and it was virtually impossible to save the hay or the turf.

Every year, the annual feast that is the championship unfolds, promising the usual mixture of the complete engagement of the senses, wild abandonment, heart-stopping elation, orgasmic bliss, the sheer toe-curling ecstasy of winning and the adrenalin rush of having the small hairs standing on the back of the neck.

Sport is agony and ecstasy. It does not lend itself to grey areas. Many fans though will also experience at first hand the slings and arrows of outrageous fortune and discover just how quickly glory becomes anguish. Fate can be far from kind in the unique roaring crucible of noise that is Croke Park.

May is the GAA version of Disneyland. Normal living is magically suspended for a state of communal bliss. It is a licence to thrill and be thrilled as each county sets out with a fresh slate hoping that the glory days in September will be theirs. The games are fast becoming the GAA fans' soap opera.

A Cork fan, with the sort of exuberant nasal hair that is difficult to escape one's gaze, remarks that he would prefer to see England win the All-Ireland rather than either the Kingdom or the Dubs. Kerry fans think they will have the power and the glory. The Blue Army are delirious.

Most fans though are destined for those terrible gut-wrenching days when their team loses. Elation can quickly yield to bitter disappointment. In this corner of the sporting world, fans experience more ups and downs than the Emperor Charlemagne. Spectating is no sport for the emotionally unfit. At best it leaves you shattered, at worst it could nearly kill you.

The rich wells of sentiment play a huge part in every corner of the GAA. Despite their tingles of anticipation throughout the four provinces, fans recall absent friends. The unique power of the GAA is its capacity to lift the shadows off the hearts of even its most troubled supporters. For many, the rain has fallen on their lives but this is a time to be happy.

Around the country, most teams and fans still have great expectations. It's sudden death in the qualifiers and teams are falling faster than horses in the Grand National. Some games, though, produce more twists and turns than a bad bog road. Not for the first time, there is a major controversy when an umpiring decision decides the match. Just ask Kildare fans! Every year it seems there is just one question in hurling: can anybody stop Kilkenny?

Sport is always inescapably intertwined with the wider culture. The old scourge of emigration returns with a vengeance to weaken teams. GAA fans in every county look to their players to inspire them, mostly for their exploits on the pitch, a rare few for their activities off it.

7

August comes with unseemly haste but often the summer continues to feel like a mild winter. Some county managers have to pay the price for their team's failure. For some counties, their manager will get his P45 after just one campaign as their fans are peeved again with an insipid championship. No supporters have suffered and mourned in the valley of tears that Croke Park can be for beaten teams with more depressing regularity than the green and red of Mayo.

These are the days of grace that fans live for – rendering sport what it truly is, life at its innocent best, the world as it ought to be, the ideal for a moment realised. Gaelic games are an expression of optimism. Such a victory enshrouds fans with a redemptive feeling, melting away depression, pain and bitter disappointment, hinting at a bygone age of innocence and values that are no longer obtained.

As he observes the sons of Ulster marching, Pat Spillane will be spitting fire.

Croke Park on All-Ireland final day is the best of times. Only two teams can reach the Promised Land. Then drama heaped upon drama. As Sweden's four most famous philosophers, Abba, famously sang: 'The winner takes it all.' Now only two sets of fans can be truly happy all winter – those with the Sam Maguire and Liam McCarthy trophy in their cabinets.

Regardless of what happened last year, thirty-four teams will begin the championship next year anew full of big dreams and high hopes. In many counties, history will be rewritten to the point of fiction. In the GAA, there are two elements that are never lacking – hope as hope, and as an incomplete recollection of the past. Next year will see a new beginning, which will bring new promise.

That is the magic of the GAA. This book seeks to capture some of that magic.

One

The Sunday Games

The Ireland of the 1840s was a vision of hell – the years of a tragedy beyond belief when more than a million people on this tiny island died from famine. Nothing prepared people for it. Nothing could prepare anyone for the sight and smell of death on a massive scale – bundles of corpses where once there had been life.

The mid 1840s saw the plagues of Ireland – hunger, disease and government neglect. Each plague compounded the other like a battleground of contending dooms. Fragile lifelines of aid reached only a minority of the population. In the first year there were barely enough potatoes, in the next only a trickle. Then nothing. Potato stalks withered and died. There was nothing for seed. Many people had nothing to live on and nothing to live for.

The death toll was seemingly unending in many districts. Everything had to be rationed. It would have taken too much land to bury the corpses individually so their relatives normally buried them in a mass grave. There were so many people dying it was impossible to make coffins for them all, or even have a coffin for each family. Timber was very scarce. Sometimes villagers decided to build one proper coffin with a sliding bottom. They solemnly put the corpses into the coffin, carried them up to the grave and slid back the bottom of the coffin and the body tumbled into the grave. The coffin was brought back to the village and passed on to the family of the next casualty.

Fear was the only real sign of life as people died slowly in agony. To the embattled, emotionally bankrupt and hopelessly disorganised, the ordinary joys and sorrows were an irrelevance. The chances of survival were slim. For many, death was a welcome escape from pain and heartache. The afterlife was the only dream they could still cherish. For the strong, life was a victory over death. Where possible, the corpses were buried under hawthorn trees – because of their alleged special favour in the eyes of God. These trees were long palls in a parched place. They sang a lament to the Angel of Death. The memories were too sad ever to be healed.

Ireland was a country of extremes, from the beginning to the end. It seemed simultaneously connected to the Garden of Eden in the landlords' palaces and to some foretaste of doomsday destruction where the peasants lived to die. Nowhere were the gardens more luxuriant or a people more miserable. The tragedy was a moral test that those with power failed.

Deep in their psychic memory the famine was still a painful experience for Irish people right through the nineteenth century and beyond. People used the words 'I'm famished' whenever they were cold or hungry. The frequent usage of these words was just one symptom of the lasting effect of the famine. Often Irish people buried their thoughts of the famine deep in their subconscious. The story of the famine years was so horrific they just wanted to erase it from their memory. There was great shame attached to failing to feed one's family. Parents always blamed themselves for their children's death. Succeeding generations had inherited their shame. Even in the twentieth century, some people in rural Ireland would not travel anywhere without bringing a piece of bread in their pocket because the fear of hunger was so strong.

Power To All Our Friends
Ireland had been governed from Westminster since the Act of Union in 1800. In the House of Commons there were about 100 members who represented Irish constituencies. The Viceregal Lodge in the Phoenix Park was home to the Queen's representatives. The Chief Secretary and his staff administered the daily routine of government from Dublin Castle.

One of the main problems faced by administrators in Ireland in the nineteenth century was to reconcile democratic principle with the continuation of ascendancy privilege. County grand juries were non-elective bodies drawn from the largest landholders in the county. Local government was in the hands of the grand juries, non-elective bodies dominated by landowners. The British Army had an important and visible presence throughout the country. The Royal Irish Constabulary was an armed body though the Dublin Metropolitan Police was not.

The close connection between Britain and Ireland made it natural to judge by English standards and, compared to England, Ireland was still a poor country. In the conventional portrait the most familiar figures are the greedy and tyrannical landlords squeezing every last penny of rent out of hungry peasants to finance their lives of debauchery.

While there were a number of such landlords, they were not all like that. The evil was not all on one side. Southern Protestants were slow to forget the stories they had been told of the fanatical fury waged against Protestants during the 1798 Wexford rising and the social intimidation of Protestants which had persisted for years afterwards. Until 1869, the Church of Ireland was the State church. Its disestablishment under an Act of Parliament made a major dent in the exclusiveness of Protestant ascendancy.

The second half of the nineteenth century saw the gradual extension of voting rights in both Britain and Ireland. For the first time, the demand for votes for women was being made with conviction. In the Irish context, an important milestone was the introduction of the secret ballot after 1872 since it relieved voters from pressure by landlords to vote according to their dictates.

The education system was imperialist rather than Irish with the prescribed reading books filled with Victorian values and designed to inculcate British loyalties. However, there were a number of counterbalancing forces at work, particularly the press. By 1860, national papers were available cheaply following the repeal of heavy taxes on the newspapers. *The Nation*, founded by Thomas Davis, carried on its national tradition in the 1860s. Songs formed an important agent of political evangelisation – notably 'God Save Ireland', which became virtually a national anthem in 1867.

The Irish national pulse was strengthening perceptibly. The demand for self-government was being made with more vigour. Political structures were not as secure as they had been. The old establishment was being challenged in various ways. In the countryside, the stirrings could be seen among the tenant farmers.

Throughout rural Ireland, agrarian unrest accelerated with increasing demands for tenant right reforms. Landlords were seen as a privileged minority, alienated from the majority of their tenants by differences in both religion and politics. Tenants normally held their holdings from year to year, thus having no security. In times of bad harvests, many could not afford to pay the rent. A high number of landlords were absentees living outside the country and leaving the management of their estates to agents. The great disaster of the famine was followed by mass evictions of tenants. The need for reform of the system became more obvious in the years that followed.

In 1870 a formal demand for Home Rule began when Isaac Butt, a lawyer and Member of Parliament, founded an association to campaign for a separate Irish parliament. However, the movement really only began in earnest when Butt was replaced as leader by Charles Stewart Parnell, a charismatic figure whose tactics brought increasing success to nationalist members of the House of Commons and eventually succeeded in making the 'Irish question' the central issue in British politics.

The Barrel of a Gun?

For a long time, people who talked about the origins of the Irish state did so in very simple terms. Nationhood was won through a barrel of a gun in a (virginal/pure) David and (dark/demonic) Goliath struggle. The 1919–21 War of Independence was the final episode in a whole series of attempts including: Grattan's volunteers in 1782; the bold Robert Emmet, 'the darling of Eireann', in 1803; the Young Ireland rising in 1848; the militant revolution of the Fenians in 1867; the 1916 Rising ('A terrible beauty is born') and the

War of Independence. In this perspective there was only one problem in Ireland – the British presence. The way to get rid of this presence was by violence.

By a supreme irony, the Act of Union, which so many Irish people considered anathema and fought so long and hard to abolish, was, step-by-step, turning Ireland into a modern state. Each of these important advances was achieved by an Act of parliament. Thus in the second half of the nineteenth century, on many different levels, change was driving Irish life like a great engine. All aspects of Irish culture could not but be affected by this dramatic transformation, including the national games. These games are steeped in Irish history.

The Whirr of the Sliotar

The founder of the GAA Michael Cusack said of hurling, 'When I reflect on the sublime simplicity of the game, the strength, the swiftness, of the players, their apparently angelic impetuosity, the apparent recklessness of life and limb, their magic skill, their marvellous escapes and the overwhelming pleasure they give their friends, I have no hesitation in saying that the game of hurling is in the front rank of the Fine Arts.'

Apart from the Irish language, nothing is more central and unique to Irish heritage than the game of hurling. In the popular imagination it can be traced back to folklore and stories of Cuchulainn. However, we have tangible historical proof that hurling has been an integral part of Irish life for over 1,000 years.

In recent years there has been a major debate in the GAA about 'the sin-bin'. However, in previous centuries players who committed a transgression faced a far more onerous punishment, such as two days' fasting or handing over a prize heifer. While top inter-county managers at the time, like Sean Boylan, fumed about their players having to cool their heels on the sidelines after serious fouls, their seventh century counterparts were fined cattle or denied food.

These unusual punishments have been discovered by Dr Angela Gleason, a young American academic based for a time at Trinity College Dublin, who has been researching the rules of the ancient stick and ball games which were a precursor to modern hurling and shinty.

'I have found a number of ancient texts that go into some detail about the penalty system associated with these ancient games,' she explains. 'From their inception, Gaelic games were always seen as "manly activities". However, there have always been sanctions when players stepped over the mark. There were penalties for injuries that resulted from play and, as was the norm in Brehon law, they were financial and could be expected to be paid in cattle.

'The texts are more vague on the precise nature and rules of the games, but it is believed that they involved teams several dozen strong and were violent affairs.

'These games are seen by many people as the predecessor of hurling, but in some texts they could be referring to hoop and ball games as well as stick and ball. These games should not be considered as in any way resembling the modern sport.

'Law texts dating from as early as the seventh century state that, while partaking in games, players had a degree of legal immunity from the Brehon laws. But they could be punished with special game-related fines. Penalties were graded according to the age of the player and the severity of the injury afflicted on an opponent.

'Adults who committed a foul during the play were judged

on whether they had set out to injure the other party inten-
tionally. If the offence was deemed intentional, the player
was expected to pay full sick maintenance to his victim. In
the case of death, not uncommon in these violent sports, the
full "honour price" of the victim had to be paid to his family.

'If the injury was unintentional and resulted from "fair
play" the penalty was half sick maintenance or one quarter
of honour price. The financial levy, usually a payment in
cattle, was calculated according to the status of the injured
person and whether they were "profitable or idle".

'Children were immune from paying penalties until they
reached a culpable age, usually about seven. But if their
offence was deemed to be deliberate they could expect to be
punished according to the rules applicable to an older age
bracket.'

So what did Angela uncover about the genesis of the game?

'In popular historical texts the first references to hurling
seem to have been written in approximately 1272 BC at the
battle of Moytura, near Cong in County Mayo. The Firbolgs
were rulers of Ireland and were protecting their position in
a battle against the Tuatha de Dannan. While they prepared
for battle, the Firbolgs challenged the invaders to a hurling
contest in which teams of 27-a-side took part. The Firbolgs
won the contest but lost the battle.

'There is no historical reference to Gaelic football until
1670 in a poem by Seamus MacCurta. The poem described a
game in Fennor – in which wrestling was allowed!'

The Clash of the Ash
In 1841 a book entitled *Ireland* was written by Samuel Carter
Hall and Anne Maria Hall and published shortly after. They
begin their section on sport by surprisingly claiming that the

great game in Kerry, and throughout the South, is the game of Hurley. The authors note: 'It is a fine manly exercise, with sufficient of danger to produce excitement; and is indeed, par excellence, the game of the peasantry of Ireland. To be an expert hurler, a man must possess athletic powers of no ordinary character; he must have a quick eye, a ready hand, and a strong arm; he must be a good runner, a skilful wrestler, and, withal, patient as well as resolute. In some respects it resembles cricket; but the rules, and the form of the bats, are altogether different; the bat of the cricketer being straight, and that of the hurler crooked.

'The forms of the games are these: the players, sometimes to the number of fifty or sixty, being chosen for each side, they are arranged (usually barefoot) in two opposing ranks, with their hurleys crossed, to await the tossing up of the ball, the wickets or goals being previously fixed at the extremities of the hurling green, which, from the nature of the play, is required to be a level extensive plain.

'Then there are two picked men chosen to keep the goal on each side, over whom the opposing party places equally tiered men as a counterpoise; the duty of these goalkeepers being to arrest the ball in case of its near approach to that station, and return it back towards that of the opposite party, while those placed over them exert all their energies to drive it through the wicket.

'All preliminaries being adjusted, the leaders take their places in the centre. A person is chosen to throw up the ball, which is done as straight as possible, when the whole party, withdrawing their hurleys, stand with them elevated, to receive and strike it in its descent. Now comes the crash of mimic war, hurleys rattle against hurleys – the ball is struck and re-struck, often for several minutes, without advancing much nearer to either goal; and when someone is lucky enough to get a clear "puck" at it, it is sent flying over the field. It is now followed by the entire party at their utmost speed; the men grapple, wrestle, and toss each other with amazing agility, neither victory nor vanquished waiting to take breath, but following the course of the rolling and flying prize.

'The best runners watch each other, and keep almost shoulder to shoulder through the play, and the best wrestlers keep as close on them as possible, to arrest or impede their progress. The ball must not be taken from the ground by the hand; and the tact and skill shown in taking it to the point of the hurley, and running with it half the length of the field, and (when too closely pressed) striking it towards the goal, is a matter of astonishment to those who are but slightly acquainted with the play.

'At the goal, is the chief brunt of the battle. The goalkeepers receive the prize, and are opposed by those set over them; the struggle is tremendous – every power of full speed to support their men engaged in the conflict; then tossing and straining is at its height; the men often lying in dozens side by side on the grass, while the ball is returned by some strong arm again, flying above their heads, towards the other goal. Thus for hours has the contention been carried on, and frequently the darkness of night arrests the game without giving victory to either side. It is often attended with dangerous, and sometimes with fateful, results.

'Matches are made, sometimes, between different townlands or parishes, sometimes by barony against barony, and not infrequently county against county; with the "crack men" from the most distant parts are selected, and the interest excited is proportionately great.'

———

The Halls then go on to describe the most famous match of them all – the clash between Munster and Leinster in the Phoenix Park in 1790. They write, 'It was got up by then Lord Lieutenant and other sporting noblemen, and was attended by all the nobility and gentry belonging to the Vice-Regal Court, and the beauty and fashion of the Irish capital and its vicinity.

'The victory was contended for a long time, with varied success; and at last it was decided in favour of the Munster men, by one of that party, Matt Healy, running with the ball on the point of his hurley, and striking it through the open windows of the Vice-Regal carriage and by that manoeuvre baffling the vigilance of the Leinster goals-men, and driving it in triumph through the goal.'

However, by the late nineteenth century Gaelic Games were in crisis. Remedial action was needed. One man stepped up to the plate.

The Magnificent Seven

For considerable time, Michael Cusack had been perturbed about the decline of native Irish games in the face of growing competition from British sports, like the garrison game soccer and also rugby. Initially Cusack sought to wrestle control, not only over field games, but athletics too and introduce a more egalitarian dimension to Irish sport. He said, 'No movement having for its object the social and political advancement of a nation from the tyranny of imported and enforced customs and manners, can be regarded as perfect, if it has not made adequate provision for the preservation and cultivation of the national pastimes of the people. Voluntary neglect of such times is a sure sign of National decay and of approaching dissolution . . .

19

'A so-called revival of athletics was inaugurated in Ireland. The new movement did not originate with those who have ever had any sympathy with Ireland or the Irish people. Accordingly, labourers, tradesmen, artisans, and even policemen and soldiers were excluded from the few competitions which constituted the lame and halting programme of the promoters . . .

'We tell the Irish people to take the management of their games into their own hands, to encourage and promote in every way, every form of athletics that is peculiarly Irish and to remove with one sweep everything that is foreign and iniquitous in the present system. The vast majority of the best athletes in Ireland are Nationalists. These gentlemen should take the matter in hand at once, and draft laws for the guidance of promoters of meetings in Ireland next year . . .

'It is only by such an arrangement that pure Irish athletics will be revived, and that the incomparable strength and physique of our race will be preserved.'

In the billiards room of Hayes's Hotel in Thurles on 1 November 1884, school teacher Michael Cusack met with athlete Maurice Davin (a world record holder in the hammer), stonemason John K. Bracken, District Inspector Thomas St George McCarthy, journalists John McKay and John Wyse Power and solicitor P.J. O'Ryan.

Two days later *The Cork Examiner* reported, 'A meeting of athletes and friends of athletics was held on Saturday at three o'clock in Miss Hayes's Commercial Hotel Thurles for the purpose of forming an association for the preservation and cultivation of our national pastimes.

'Mr Michael Cusack of Dublin and Mr Maurice Davin of Carrick-on-Suir had the meeting convened by the following circular: "You are earnestly requested to attend a meeting, which will be held in Thurles on 1st of November, to take steps for the formation of a Gaelic Association for the preservation and cultivation of our national pastimes, and for providing rational amusements for the Irish people during their leisure hours."

'Mr Davin was called to the chair and Mr Cusack read the circular convening the meeting . . . Mr Cusack then proposed that Mr Maurice Davin – an athlete who had distinguished himself much both in Ireland and in England – should be the president of the association.'

Patrons

The two most important political figures of nationalist Ireland, the leader of the Irish Party Charles Stewart Parnell Michael Davitt, the founder of the Land League, were quickly persuaded to act as patrons and, crucially, so too was the Archbishop of Cashel Thomas William Croke, to give an ecclesiastical imprimatur to the fledging body. This began the patronage of the Archbishop of Cashel at national level which continues to this day.

In the late nineteenth century, thanks in no small part to the work of Cardinal Paul Cullen, the Catholic Church exerted a massive cultural influence in Irish society. To have its blessing and, above all, to be *seen* to have its blessing was important for the GAA. Archbishop Croke was a shrewd choice. He was one of Parnell's most outspoken supporters among the hierarchy. In fact, he was summoned to Rome by Pope Leo XIII to explain his support for nationalist politicians. Croke's biases and prejudices were very clear in his letter of acceptance as patron: 'We are daily importing from England not only her manufactured goods . . . but together with her fashions, her accent, her vicious literature, her music, her dances and her manifold mannerisms, her games and also her pastimes, to the utter discredit of our own grand national sports, and to the sore humiliation, as I believe, of every genuine son and daughter of the old land.

'Ball-playing, hurling, football, kicking, according to Irish rules, "casting", leaping in various ways, wrestling, handy-grips, top-pegging, leap-frog, rounders, tip-in-the-heat, and all such favourite exercises and amusements among men and boys, may be said not only to be dead and buried, but in several localities to be entirely forgotten and unknown. And what have we got in their stead? We have got such foreign and fantastic field sports as lawn-tennis, croquet, cricket and the like – very excellent, I believe, and health-giving exercises in their way, still not racy of the soil, but rather alien, on the contrary, to it, as are indeed, for the most part, the men and women who first imported and still continue to patronise them . . .

'Indeed if we continue travelling for the next score of years in the same direction that we have been going in for some time past . . . we had better at once and publicly, adjure our nationality, clap hands for joy at the sight of the Union Jack, and place "England's bloody red" exultingly above "the green".'

We Irish are always happy to blame somebody else. Flann O'Brien claimed that he wrote *At Swim-Two-Birds* in order to become a millionaire, and he liked to complain that Hitler started a war a few weeks after publication just to frustrate this noble enterprise. Croke's fervent anti-English prejudices resonated strongly with Cusack and the other founders who saw themselves as actors in the age-old battle of good and evil. Accordingly, from its inception, the GAA had a two-fold objective of promoting Irish games and reducing the perceived malign influence of 'foreign games'.

Two further patrons came on board within months: the founder of the Irish Republican Brotherhood, John O'Leary, and the Nationalist MP William O'Brien.

From the outset, the GAA took on the parish organisation which had been so effectively deployed by Daniel O'Connell in the campaign to win Catholic Emancipation in 1829. The sense of parish identity was further copper fastened by the use of local patron saints or historical figures in the names taken by parish clubs. Davin drew up rules for four sports: football, hurling, athletics and handball. In reality, no serious attempt was made to regulate handball until the birth of a new organisation, the Irish Amateur Handball Union, in 1912.

Are You Right There Michael?
Like so many Irish organisations since, almost the first thing the GAA did was to have a split. From the beginning, the GAA has had a history of abrasive personalities, with the gift of rubbing people up the wrong way. Michael Cusack will always be remembered for his role in founding the GAA in 1884. Yet, having given birth to the Association, Cusack almost strangled it in its infancy because of his abrasive personality. People often miss out on the historical signifi-cance of the 'Athletic' in the title of the GAA. In the early years, it was envisaged that athletics would play a much greater role in the life of the GAA. One of the people trying to ensure this was John L. Dunbar. He wrote to Cusack in December 1885 suggesting that the GAA and the athletics organisation should meet 'with a view to a possible merger'. Cusack, an enthusiastic hurler, did not mince or waste his words in his response. The letter read as follows:

———————

GAA
4 Gardiners Place
Dublin

Dear Sir,
I received your letter this morning and burned it.
Yours faithfully,
Michael Cusack.

Cusack suffered from 'Irish bad memory' – which forgets everything but the grudge. He also alienated Archbishop Croke, who stated that he could not continue as patron, 'If Mr Michael Cusack is allowed to play the dictator in the GAA's counsels, to run a reckless tilt with impunity and without rebuke.'

Amongst Women?

Cusack claimed that the new organisation spread like a 'prairie fire'. However, women did not play a central role in the early years of the GAA. Although the tide of change was also impacting women, much of the establishment in Ireland continued to be male-dominated. It is instructive to consider the institutional Church's attitude to the newly established Ladies Land League as an indication of its attitude to women at the time. The organisation was set up in January 1881 and by May had 321 branches. The women became responsible for a detailed register known as 'the Book of the Kells'. This was a record of every estate, the number of tenants, the rent paid, the official valuations, the name of the landlord of the agent, the number of evictions that had taken place and the number that were still pending. The register was compiled from weekly reports sent in by the country branches. The

Ladies League was also active in relief work – when notice of a pending eviction was received, a member travelled to the area with money for assistance.

The League quickly fell foul of the institutional Church. This was not perhaps surprising given that involvement of women in such a political group was entirely new. Archbishop McCabe of Dublin denounced the organisation and, in the same breath, recalled the traditional modesty of Irish women and the splendid purity of St Brigid. He went on to state that the proper place for women was 'the seclusion of the home'. In a letter read at all Masses in the Archdiocese of Dublin in March 1881, he continued, 'But all this to be laid aside and the daughters of our Catholic people are called forth, under the flimsy pretext of charity, to take their stand in the noisy arena of public life. They are asked to forget the modesty of their sex and the high dignity of their womanhood by leaders who seem utterly reckless of consequences.'

The Broader Canvas

Declan Kiberd, one of Ireland's leading academics, draws attention to the need to situate the founding of the GAA in a wider context where cultural nationalism was flourishing: 'At the start of the last century, our people experienced a national revival epitomised by the self-help philosophies of various movements from the Gaelic League to the Co-ops, from the Abbey theatre to Sinn Féin. In the previous two generations, the Irish had achieved such mastery of English as the *lingua franca* of the modern world that they went on to produce one of the great experimental literatures in that tongue. A few years later, the process of global decolonisation was headed by men like Collins and de Valera, who managed to dislodge the greatest empire which the world until then had known . . . It might have been expected that the native elite which took over in 1922 would end old attitudes and rapidly develop a productive middle class; but no such thing happened.'

So why, then, did the country not make similar progress in successive decades? Kiberd advances three reasons: 'The sheer energy expended in removing British forces may be one reason. The Civil War is another. Both left people with very little energy with which to re-imagine a society. Instead, exhausted revolutionaries lapsed back into the inherited English forms. The Civil War induced a profound caution, making many distrustful of innovation. Fancy theories about a republic had, after all, cost hundreds of Irish lives.

'Many of those republicans who lost the Civil War could not bear to live on in a land which was a sore disappointment to their dreams. A number went to a real republic, the United States, where they made fortunes in business – and bootlegging. Even today if you walk the streets of New York, you see vans plying up and down with names like "P. J. Brennan, Est. 1926" inscribed on their doors. The republican idea has always been linked to entrepreneurship: after all, the French revolutionaries of 1789 were the first politically-organised businessmen of the modern world, keen to replace a parasitic upper-class with a society of "careers open to talents".

'The loss of such flair to Ireland in the mid-1920s was something which the fragile young state could ill afford. It became a mantra among commentators that the Irish were successful in the US in ways they never could be at home. One reason for this was that Irish-Americans continued to believe in their own culture, long after their "sophisticated" stay-at-home cousins seemed to have given it up. It is surely significant that the recent revivals of Irish dancing and fiddle-playing have been led by Irish-Americans like Michael Flatley and Eileen Ivers. For there is a demonstrable link between cultural self-belief and economic achievement.'

Shortly after she was elected president of Ireland in 1990, Mary Robinson coined the phrase 'the Irish diaspora' to describe the intrinsic link between Irish emigrants abroad and 'their native sod'. For the outset, Gaelic games have been one of the most formidable imaginative batteries which allow Irish exiles in the four corners of the earth to feel they continue to belong to 'home'.

The Power of One
Since its inception the power of the GAA has been built around great teams and great players. The next chapter tells the story of one such team through the eyes of one of its star players to give a window into the sort of passionate intensity that the GAA generates.

Two

Tougher than the Rest

Increasingly it seems that the GAA personalities of today live by the motto that while silence may often be misinterpreted, it can never be misquoted. Bernard Flynn is cast in a different mould. He knows the secrets of pain. Although he carries many physical scars from his efforts on the pitch, the mental toughness he acquired playing for Meath would equip him with the emotional resources for the big battles he would face off it.

'Gerry McEntee's brother Andy was on the Meath panel and, like me, he was very fiery. He was Meath minor manager and brought them to the All-Ireland final in 2012. But, with the greatest respect to him, he could be a bit dirty in training. He was by no means alone in that respect in the squad.

'One of the reasons I became a good player was that I generally marked Robbie O'Malley in training and those clashes with him brought me on so much. He was so good that I had to push myself to the very limits to match him. One night, Robbie wasn't able to train and I found myself marking Andy instead. He was anxious to get on the Meath team and wanted to make his mark and he hit me with a dirty belt in the ribs. We had words. Then he hit me a second time. I said to him, "Andy, if you do that again. I'll f**king bust you." So he hit me again and I did strike back.

'Sean Boylan was furious, not because we were hitting each other, but because we were doing it in a way that was disrupting what he wanted to get out of that session. He said, "That's it. Ye're going to do laps for the rest of the night." I'd say there were about 800 to 1,000 people watching us because we often had big crowds at our training sessions and this was going on in full view of everyone. Andy and I started running but we had only got to the corner when we started beating the heads off each other.

'Sean was so annoyed that he abandoned the training and ran over to us. What nobody realised was that he was ferociously strong and fit. Instead of stopping the fisticuffs, he hit me in the stomach with a belt and he said, "Ye think ye're so f**king hard I'll take both of ye on." Andy and I looked at each other. Sean was up on his toes and he was skipping like a real hard man and he was beckoning us forward with his fingers and he said: "Come on, ye think ye're hard come on and take me on. I'll f**king take both of ye on." We could do nothing because we were in such shock. If we threw a punch he was going to hit back and he had ferocious power in his arms. He cut the aggro stone dead. We didn't do it again. It was a masterclass in man management.'

From Small Acorns Grow Mighty Oaks
Flynn's inter-county career began when the county's fortunes were at a low ebb.

'In 1983 I played minor, under-21 and senior with Meath,' he says. 'I was a small, scrawny kid at that stage and a lot of people said I wouldn't make it because big powerful men were in vogue then and I was only five foot nine and ten-and-a-half stone.

'Sean Boylan had only come in the year before and the iconic names like Colm O'Rourke, Joe Cassells, Gerry McEntee, Mick Lyons and co were not iconic yet. Up to 1982, Meath had been all over the place but as soon as I arrived on the panel I could see what Sean was trying to do.

'He was and is an amazing man. He was brutally honest that hurling was his background and that he didn't know a massive amount about Gaelic football at the top level and that honesty really endeared him to everybody. He knew early on that he had four or five special men: Lyons, Cassells, McEntee, O'Rourke became his lieutenants and he kept them very close to him and rightly so because he knew what he had.

'Club football in Meath at the time was absolutely vicious. The clubs hated each other and that meant that there was no camaraderie but Boylan and the older players changed that culture within the squad.

'Organisationally, things had been a mess but pretty quickly you could see his organisational skills coming to the fore with the team bonding, the 'never say die' attitude, pulling people together – all of the things that were missing in Meath. He didn't have to be an expert to know that football was second. He had to get all the sideshows sorted first. He was excellent at that.'

Uneven Progress
Boylan's methods reaped a dividend almost immediately, says Flynn: 'We won the Centenary Cup in 1984. This was a big deal and meant a huge amount to us and for two years things were going great. We lost the Leinster final by two

points to Dublin that same year and we were delighted by how far we had come in the pecking order and that we were at the stage that we could compete.'

Flynn's Meath team were quickly to get a bruising awakening about their status in the hierarchy of Gaelic football: 'The biggest lesson that Meath team got came in 1985 when Laois beat us by ten points in the Leinster Championship in Tullamore. We were disgusted and to say it was a back-to-the-drawing-board moment was an understatement. We went to a quiet bar on the outskirts of Tullamore afterwards and we weren't able to eat. We didn't even sit on seats, we sat on the floor.'

It was time for a new approach, which was not going to be for the faint-hearted.

'It was then that Sean and the senior players recognised that we were nowhere near the level we needed to be,' says Flynn. 'From the autumn of 1985, we saw a huge change in terms of physical training and everyone upped the levels. The raw ambition in that team was relentless.'

The old warriors found talented and willing recruits to take their place in the unique torture chamber that constituted Meath training sessions.

Flynn says, 'The new players coming like Martin O'Connell, Brian Stafford, Robbie O'Malley, P. J. Gillick and David Beggy brought youth and flair but the change was the way they pushed themselves in training. We used to kill each other. The Laois defeat was the pivotal moment when everything changed. The effort the senior players put in training, especially for men of their age, was simply incredible. To this day I get goose pimples when I think of those remarkable men.

'Boylan learned as he went. We were lucky to have Noel Keating and Kepak by his side as sponsors. We went from

31

being fifteen years behind the times in 1985 to ten years ahead of the times by the late eighties. I would have heard about Kieran McGeeney and how driven he was with his Armagh team but I guarantee you they could not match what happened in our training sessions. We were nearly stupid and silly and it's only when you retire that you realise the belting that went on. It was unreal. I wouldn't go to training sessions in fear but I wouldn't know if I would come out safe at times. It was that vicious.

'My own experience was that the only time you missed training was on your deathbed. Boylan had instilled that culture into the squad. They were so true to each other, so honest with each other, and so committed to each other. They were committed to the cause to a fault because I believe some of the stuff that went on in training, while it made us, if we had managed it a bit more and released more of the creative spirit within us we could have won even more. It was madness beyond comprehension, the hitting, the thumping and the belting that went on but it was needed at the time.'

There were times, though, when it got very personal.

Flynn says, 'The day before one of the Leinster finals, there was a doubt if David Beggy was fit. I'm not sure what issue some of the lads had with him but they beat him up and down the field for about fifty minutes. I remember thinking that men shouldn't be able to play for a week but they were expecting him to play well in the Leinster final the next day. Nobody asked or said anything because we were afraid to but it was crazy the torture they put him through.'

The Lyons Den
Sport is a licence to thrill and be thrilled but elation can quickly yield to bitter disappointment. In the Meath squad

there were emotional swings and roundabouts – moments when friendships were put to the test because of the intensity of the gladiatorial combats. Flynn would experience this sensation with blood and sweat – but no tears.

He says, 'The only time I thought I was going to be killed and I really did fear for my life was in 1988. We got out of jail against Mayo in the All-Ireland semi-final because a number of us were not playing well. Training was not going well. Many of the older players had a lot of miles on the clock at that stage. The intensity and the ferocity wasn't what it should be and Mick Lyons, Joe Cassells and Gerry McEntee were stressing that we needed to up the intensity.

'Mick was an incredible captain. He never said much but when he did, you listened. At one session the hitting was unreal right across the pitch. When I was on the ball I was trying to watch out for the belts coming but at one stage Mick hit me a dirty belt. I said, "Mick, if you do that again I'll f**king split you." The next time I was heading into goal he hit me again. So I hit him with everything I had and split the bridge of his nose and the blood was pouring out of him. I have incredible regard for Mick and he is one of the most inspirational footballers of all time but there is no point in me saying otherwise – if he caught me again in that match he would have killed me.'

Would the punishment fit the crime? 'I was apprehensive going into the old dressing-room in Navan, which was like a scene from *Midnight Express*. It was like a dungeon and the steam was rising so you couldn't see anything and I was walking into that. Nothing was said but I was afraid that Mick was going to clock me. I remember showering and, as I held the shampoo in one hand, I had my other fist clenched ready to respond. My attitude was if someone was going to give me a box, I was going to give one back. There was no problem if you got sent off for hitting a lad but if a lad hit you and you didn't hit back there was a problem.

'Finally I saw Mick showering and I could see the shampoo mixing with the blood. I remember thinking he was going to clock me. He came over to me and put his arm on my shoulder and simply said, "Bernard, that's exactly what we need. We need more of that." There were no hard feelings.'

Humiliation

Flynn was to discover in a brutal way that there were severe consequences if you broke the code that drove the squad with the fervour of medieval monks.

He says, 'The training in Bettystown and the hill of Tara was savage. I hated the running up the hill of Tara sessions. I would always be at the back while fellas like Terry Ferguson, Cassells and McEntee would be up at the front. Even when I was vomiting down my top I kept going because you dared not stop.

'The biggest single lesson I got about Boylan's psyche came one night early in my career when he brought us over the sand dunes in Bettystown. It was minus four or five degrees and we were made to go into the water because he loved the healing and therapeutic powers of water and the whole spirituality of that but we were worried about getting hypothermia. Sean was way ahead of his time because he had a back-up team with him from early on. One of his first nights in Bettystown, he had his crew and they had jeeps with their lights on and they were providing the light in the sand dunes.

'It got so bad I was scared I was dying. I actually felt death was coming over me. I had never felt so bad before or since. I was at the back and I fell down and I got sick. I hid in the bush where it was pitch dark. When the lads came running around again I jumped into the middle and I thought I had got away with it. Sean had been watching me though. He saw what I was at and he stopped everybody. He knew I was a young lad and needed a bit of a reality check of what was expected and demanded of me. I was still wiping away the vomit from my top but he gave me such a lecture and a lesson that I never stopped again in my entire life.

'The lads were looking me in the eyes and some were shaking their heads and I knew they thought less of me because of that incident. It took me a lot of hard work to rebuild some of their trust after that. I felt I had let myself down and I had let them down but the one thing I learned was that you never give up. It wasn't a case of Sean putting his arm around my shoulder. He devoured me and tore strips off me and had me nearly crying. I got no sympathy from anybody else and that was the kind of thing that was needed. He has the image of being a lovely man but underneath he is a silent assassin in a way.'

The School of Hard Knocks
In case Flynn was to forget that lesson, there was another painful reminder of the etiquette that was required in the Meath camp, which put a premium on a widely shared sense of purpose and values.

'At one stage the All-Stars were going to play in the Skydome in Toronto,' he says. 'Robbie O'Malley, myself and a few players from other counties were asked to go over in advance to promote the games and generate the maximum level of interest. We ran it by Sean Boylan and somehow he said yes because we were going to be playing Dublin in the quarter-final of the National League, which was big for us at the time. When we arrived in Toronto we were met by a limousine and we were on the equivalent of *The Late Late Show* in Canada. There were three live television shows and three or four of the top radio shows. We were treated like royalty and we had never known anything like this. We got a few bob for it at a time when we had nothing.

'We had a great break and we were asked to extend the trip for an extra two days for more promotion. We managed to get the word back to Sean. We came back on a wet night and the quarter-final was the following Sunday and we went straight to training.

'As soon as we walked into the dressing-room the hatred we felt from the rest of the players because we had over-stepped the mark in their eyes or they were just plain jealous they didn't get to go and we had done something that was unacceptable for Meath players to do was unreal. I have no doubt but if it was Harnan or Lyons who had been asked to go to Toronto they would have said, "Go f**k off and get somebody else."

'We didn't think there was anything wrong in what we had done. What was done to me that night in training meant I physically couldn't walk at the end and stumbled into a car to get me home. I got thumped and belted all over the field that night. It was not the first time I got thumped but what was different that night was that nobody said anything to me. We were ignored because we had missed one training session and that was sacrosanct.'

A Misunderstood Man
Part of the problem for Flynn was that his colleagues made assumptions about him that did not reflect him in the best possible light.

'I was often underestimated within the Meath squad for my dedication,' he says. 'When I was going out with my wife, nearly all of our dates were spent just kicking the ball back to me. I knew there were many attributes of the game I didn't have but the one thing I could do was kick equally well with both feet which was not exactly commonplace at the time. I only got this skill with savage practice. There were some Meath players, though, who thought I liked to enjoy myself a bit more than the others because these guys were so serious and sure of themselves. Maybe I was just different in the dressing-room.

'I dressed a little differently. The boys never knew what gel was or creams were till I came into the dressing-room. I was a little different. They saw colours on me that they had never seen. They thought I was something from outer space. It was much later that I realised this and I wondered back then why they were kicking the sh*t out of me at times.'

On one occasion Flynn added fuel to that fire in Sean Boylan's eyes. Yet, like all great leaders, Boylan had the capacity for the counter-intuitive response and could understand the voice of resistance. He could change the rules of the game when he felt it was needed and find new possibilities and stay calm and engaged when there was a threat to his authority. Flynn also experienced this side of his manager at first hand.

'I know there was always a culture within the Dublin squad for example of going for a few drinks on the Monday night after a big match. I got into my head that one Monday night I would go out for a few drinks. Back then Bad Bobs was the place to go and I thought, as I was away from Meath, nobody would know. I had a great night and made it into work the next morning on time as I always did. That night I went to training having literally no sleep the night before and having had what might be nicely termed as "a rough night". It was one of the few times when I simply couldn't run and, a bit like that night in Bettystown, I was really scared that I was going to die because my head was spinning. Sean was running us up and down the hills and up the steps of the stand in Navan and he could see the way I was struggling badly. Normally he would pull up a fella in front of the whole squad but he knew I was a younger guy and there was a danger that he might push me over the edge. Although I had the height of respect for him, I was fiery. I would take him on the odd time and that was well known within the squad and he probably felt that if he started eating the face off me that night there could be a reaction and who knew where it would end? There was a bit of a rebel in me and some of the lads would say more than a bit.

'It was only afterwards that I realised how brilliantly Sean handled the situation that night. He pulled me up and he said to the lads, "Bernard is not feeling well. I chatted with him beforehand and I'm pulling him out." I knew that was not the case and I didn't know what was going on. He got me into a corner on my own and never discussed the incident with any other players. I know because I asked several of them about it subsequently. He said, "If you f**king ever do again what you did since Sunday evening you're finished." He then proceeded to go through all my movements from Monday evening to Tuesday morning: every pub and club I had been to and what time I came and left. He then said, "You are getting one chance. Now go home and rest."

'His psychology was brilliant. He weighed me up and felt that this was the best way to handle me because there could have been a major row and there were a few of those. I respected him and was a little in fear of him so there was no way I was going to try anything like that again. I didn't think he would be able to track my movements but he was letting me know he was. That was his genius. He knew the right card to play in nearly every situation.'

A Leader for All Seasons

The unique talent of great leaders is their ability to understand and work with the culture. When necessary, Boylan was a lion with a velvet paw.

'The other side of Sean Boylan is that I try to implement some of his brilliant man-management skills now as manager of Mullingar Shamrocks,' says Flynn. 'While he was incredibly strong and disciplined and this was reinforced by his lieutenants who put the fear of God into you, there was another side to him. He was very big into fun and craic and he also knew when to give you the benefit of the doubt and give you down time.'

Creating an intimate family unit was crucial to Boylan's project as it nurtured collaborative and collegial relationships, which in turn fed into a commitment to and sense of responsibility within the whole squad.

Flynn says, 'Our tradition was that every big match the wives, girlfriends and even parents were brought together with the players for a meal. It was a big bonding thing within the squad and families were made to feel very important. I should also say there was great bonding with the supporters at these sessions and I believe there is a huge disconnect in recent years between Meath players and the supporters. We had a huge rapport with them which Boylan nurtured.

'One thing I didn't realise about him in the early days was that he was incredibly astute. He was incredible at getting around to players' houses when they weren't there. I remember being very surprised one winter's evening that Sean Boylan had been to the house and of course both my parents were delighted to have him. He called two other times when I wasn't there and did that sort of thing regularly with the parents of the younger players especially. What he was doing was getting into their heads and pulling them into his way of thinking.'

Boylan could keep both the long- and short-term view and persevere with single-minded focus.

'The holidays we went on were brilliant,' says Flynn. 'Our girlfriends were treated like royalty. The steaks and the food were incredible. My parents would go to league matches in the mid-eighties and he would insist that they came in for the team meal. When I was a manager I would be pretty strict myself but what I learned from my days with Meath is that it is important to have a bit of craic. We would have a few drinks together when the time was right but once the drinking started Sean would be gone because things might be said when tongues were loosened that mightn't be easily forgotten or forgiven.'

The Demon Drink
Boylan played the long game in terms of creating a culture that reinforced commitment and motivation in a way that was consistent with his vision for the team. When discipline was breached in a major way, it was time to prepare for an earthquake. Flynn holds up his hands about his involvement in one of the most serious incidents in the camp.

He recalls, 'I would have to say that I was one of the ringleaders in this. Three weeks before the Championship he would take us away. Lads were very good at keeping off the drink, there were few who would need to be watched. People have no idea of the dedication and commitment of that squad. Sean put a massive amount of work into arranging a weekend away for us. We were going down to play Mayo to open a pitch on the Sunday in 1987 and we played Donegal in a challenge match on the Saturday. We were to stay with families in country houses outside Tuam and we are all paired off so, for example, Liam Harnan and Padraig Lyons were in one house and Robbie O'Malley and I were in another.

'The idea was that we would have breakfast with the families on the Sunday morning and it would be very different. On the Saturday there was an altercation in the Donegal match and Mattie McCabe had his jaw broken and that threw things out of synch. Understandably, Sean's priority was Mattie and he couldn't be with us that night. We had been training savagely hard and wanted to release the tension. Ten or twelve of us didn't go near the houses but ended up in a nightclub and we had craic like never before. Some of the lads went behind the counter to serve and others were dancing on the tables. I don't think any of us paid for anything. It went on till breakfast time. A few of us were brought to the houses we were supposed to be staying in in a garda car and we got to sleep for an hour or so. Meanwhile, Sean had heard what happened and he went ballistic.

'He called for a training session on the pitch at 11.30, just a few hours before we were due to be playing Mayo in front of four or five thousand people. He tortured us for an hour and a half until we couldn't stand and all of the drinkers were sick. Shortly afterwards he made us go out on the field to play Mayo and made to suffer a second time. We were beaten by more than twenty points. It was an embarrassment and we made a holy show of ourselves. On the drive home we were stopping cars because we were still getting sick. That was the end of it.

Instead of having a meeting, that was the way he handled it. There was no messing for the rest of the year and we won the All-Ireland. He really put manners on us because he had us eating out of the palm of his hand to a certain extent.'

Boylan, though, invested considerable time and reflection into the right time and circumstances when a different assessment of the situation was called for. He knew instinctively which elements supported the team's purpose and mission and which hindered it.

'We won the league in 1988 and, before the championship started, he was pushing us really hard,' says Flynn. 'We had trained nine nights out of twelve and some of the senior players had a lot of miles on the clock and things were a bit tetchy. You could feel the tension in training so we went into Navan one night and he said, "Lads, leave the bags in the corner." He brought us out to the Chinese and we had a great feed and then he brought us on to the pub and we all had a good few beers. I know for a fact he paid for everything himself. He even got some of us home when we were in no fit state to do it ourselves. That kind of thing was unheard of back then and we got weeks out of it in terms of craic and banter and of course he got so much more out of us in training for the next few weeks.'

Every Team Needs Bad Neighbours
The incredible sacrifices that the Meath players endured would reap a financial dividend.

'After we won the first All-Ireland, Sean looked in the car park one day and remarked that the cars were younger and better so football did help us in career terms,' says Flynn.

'I never thought I would get a job from football. I had been an electrician. It got to the stage that I felt dead from dust and abuse working in a cement factory with a boss who let's say didn't treat me very well. I dumped my toolbox with the tools and everything into the bottom of the river Boyne. I went to a night course in sales. I spoke with Sean Boylan and Noel Keating and they arranged for me to get an interview with Tennent's, who were employing a lot of high-profile players around the country like Nudie Hughes of Monaghan at the time as reps and they took me on too.'

Flynn's work and football commitments would literally clash in a dramatic way.

He says, 'Dublin's Davy Sinnott and I worked together. The week before the 1988 Leinster final, Davy and I were in the papers every day because we were going to be marking each other in the game. The hype was incredible and Tennent's milked it for all it was worth and had arranged a reception for sixty publicans after the match. On the match day, my wife was in the stand with Davy's wife Marie. Davy was a clean player and had burst on to the scene the previous few years and was a breath of fresh air.

'I got the first few balls and then he hit me. Then I got a score and he did it again. I said, "Davy, cop yourself f**king on. You've hit me twice and if you do it again I will bust you." The ball came out towards the middle of the field and I caught him with my elbow hard and burst his nose. The referee didn't see my elbow but did see Davy turning around and giving me a box. The game stopped. The crowd were going crazy. Davy was sent off. As he walked off he started to pump blood and the referee couldn't understand why. I remember him pleading with the referee that I hit him first.

'I was lying on the ground and thinking of my job, the first decent job I had in my life, my new Opel Ascona that made me feel that I was Don Johnson. I thought of my boss who was watching me playing and I was worried that I would lose my job and my car. I thought of the publicans who were going to be at our reception. I thought of Marie and Madeline together in the stand. All of these thoughts went through my head in seconds.

'There was a huge euphoria after we beat Dublin in the Leinster final but then I met Madeline and Marie was with her and she was inconsolable. She had a bit of a go at me. Then Davy didn't show up at the gig. Although it was one of Sean's big things that the team went together after the match I got the word back to him that I had to find Davy. I went back to the gig. Hours went by and still no Davy and Marie was very worried. My boss decided to have a party in his house in Swords and Davy arrived. After an hour of drinking and thrashing it out we made up.

'I crashed my lovely car late that night. I had to do a promotion in Gibney's in Malahide the next day. I was in a state. Who was the guy who put his arm around me and got me through it? Davy Sinnott. What did he do? The next day was a bank holiday Monday. Great man that he was, Davy drove me to the promotion and got all the stuff I needed and he helped me with my promotion in the pub. That's what the GAA is all about. I'll never forget him for that.'

Time to Say Goodbye
Injuries would eventually take their toll.

Flynn says, 'I had a lot of injuries and I retired from inter-county football in 1995 and club football in 1998. My knee had been severed. I had arthritis in my hip. I was getting cortisone injections – some that Sean Boylan knew about but many that he didn't. I always felt I needed to do more to be sure of holding my place on the team.'

As a defence mechanism against this insecurity, Flynn

overdid things and would pay a high price in later life. But then, answering questions that others would rather were not asked, he dragged up some hidden reserves of energy and determination to begin again like a surfer hitting a good wave.

He says, 'In 1990 I went to Australia with Eugene McGee to play in the Compromise Rules series. I had a dozen or so pain-killing injections on that trip. In 1995 I was getting an injection a week or at least every second week. There was somebody I was using that Sean knew nothing about because I was so afraid of losing my place. Apart from the injections I was also shovelling tablets. I was always looking over my shoulder with Sean and Pat Reynolds, one of his selectors, in particular. I have massive respect for them and we got on great but I think I mightn't have been their favourite son. I genuinely felt that if they got the chance they were going to drop me. That kept me on my toes but it probably knocked my confidence a few times and maybe I held back a bit more than I should have but I have to take responsibility for that because it was up to me to sort it out. We had so many great players like Mattie McCabe, Liam Smith and Finian Murtagh, who were waiting to take my place.'

Eventually, Flynn's creaking body was telling him loudly that he could no longer be reckless with his long-term health.

'I went to the former Dublin great, Dr Pat O'Neill,' he says. 'Gerry McEntee arranged it for me, and Pat told me very starkly that if I continued doing what I was doing I would be in a wheelchair before I was fifty. I think Sean was a bit miffed that I went to Pat without consulting him first because he thought he could have managed my condition using herbal medicine. I suffered a number of bad years after that. My whole knee was reconstructed and I was never the same again. I got a hip replacement and, although it was not a complete success, it has helped. The killing part was that, just a year after I retired, Sean won the All-Ireland again with a new Meath team. To miss out on that was heartbreaking. It was Sean's greatest achievement, winning that All-Ireland with a new team especially as, with all due respect, he did not have the glut of star players that Mick O'Dwyer had. It was unbelievable what he achieved with some of those players. The one thing I do regret is that I didn't mind myself.'

There remains a strong sense in Flynn that his Meath team, for all their success, did not achieve their potential.

'When we meet up I always contend that we underachieved,' he says. 'There is still strong debate about that among us. I believe what made us held us back. If we had managed ourselves a bit better we would have won at least one more All-Ireland. The last time we had the debate I told the lads: "If we had a little less f**king brawn and more f**king brain we would have won much more."'

Yet his abiding sense is the incredible bond he still feels for his band of brothers.

He says, 'When I meet a former Meath player there's no need to say a lot. We just look each other in the eye and know that we did what we did together. That connection will always be there and that is why it is so special.'

After his interview with me, Flynn was heading into the Mater Hospital to visit an 'unsung hero' of his Meath team, P. J. Gillick, who was recovering from a double heart bypass. Then a cup of tea had been arranged with Gerry McEntee.

Take Care of Business, Mr Businessman
Sport is agony and ecstasy. It does not lend itself to grey areas. It is adversity, which proves the true testing ground of

heroic status as only a true hero can smile through a veil of tears. Flynn would face his most severe character test away from the intimacy of the Meath dressing-room.

Socrates claimed that, 'If a man would move the world, he must first move himself'. Post inter-county football, Flynn decided it was time to make things happen.

'I got a poor-to-average Leaving Cert but I had the drive within me to make a go of myself,' he says. 'I went into business with Michael Dempsey who had been manager of the Laois hurling team for years before becoming Brian Cody's right-hand man. He was my best man and is my daughter's godfather.'

A Swedish proverb says, 'Don't throw away the old bucket until you know whether the new one holds water.' In business, Flynn did not have such caution.

He says, 'We went into the pub and nightclub business in Laois and what I made there allowed me to start my interior decor business in Mullingar. I gave up my good job after talking with my wife Madeline. We both wanted a fresh start. We met in a nightclub when I was in my late teens. She thought I was the most horrible man she had ever met. She genuinely didn't like me but I pursued her till she did.'

Great Expectations

Flynn's new venture began with high hopes and for a decade it looked as if no dream was too big.

'I always had an entrepreneurial mind,' he says. 'In 1995 I bought my first property and, until the crash in 2009, I developed a good portofolio with a really good business model. I would work in my retail busines by day and in the evening, with my own hands, would literally rip them apart. The value was in doing them up myself and then I would lease

47

them out and I built up a substantial rent portfolio while still running the retail business.

'I had no mortgage. I was proud to buy my own home for cash in 1999, a house my wife loved. When the crash started I didn't get out in time. I put up my last few properties I bought in 2005, 2006 and 2007 and my family home as equity and that was my big mistake. The bank called in their loans in 2010. My wife really rolled up her sleeves but there were three terrible years between 2009 and 2011.'

The financial problem morphed into a series of legal problems.

'I had twenty-four legal cases from small ones to big ones pending at one stage,' recalls Flynn. 'Myself and Madeline opened up the sitting room and we got files left, right and centre out. We had faced losing everything overnight. We would spend three or four hours a night, five nights a week, on paperwork when the kids had gone to bed. It was a nightmare. It took its toll. People were saying that I looked terribly bad.

'In 2010 they put in the receivers. It was when I got my hip replacement. My life was wiped and finished and, to add to everything, my retail business was gone as well. I was owed a fortune and couldn't carry it. My back was to the wall and it was traumatic. I went into some dark corners and it was hard to come out of them. My wife, Madeline, is a very strong woman and that is the only thing that saved me but I am a very resilient person. I had to be strong.

'I had no background in college. I had no-one to mentor me. Everything was on my own but I built a good business working with the bank. I have to hold my hand up and say I made mistakes but everything I did I ran it by the bank first. We did this together. Did I borrow money? Yes. Did I take a chance in business? Yes. I also employed ten or twelve people in my retail business and I reckon I spent over a million in the local area on renovations.

'The biggest resentment I have is that the bank sold all the properties I had worked so hard on. I had lost everything and all I asked the bank was that they would share in the mistake we had both made but they wouldn't do that.'

Flynn was caught up in a frazzle of anxiety.

'I didn't sleep much for two or three years because I would get up in the middle of the night and work on strategies to try to claw my way out of the hole I was in,' he says. 'At one stage I told Madeline and my parents that I was thinking of moving my family abroad for a fresh start.

'The darkest days were spent trying to cope with the debts. I spent a quarter of a million on legal fees till I could pay no more. Now Madeline and I run our own cases. We've got the debt down. I had a wife and three young kids to provide for. I was unemployable. My attitude was: do I lie down and die or do I fight back?

'I had no degree so I couldn't get a job. I had never gone to college because at that stage I only had one ambition – to play senior football for Meath. The only thing that put food on the table was that I did some media work. Every euro that came in was so important. I did some coaching with Nobber because the late Shane McEntee asked me and then with Westmeath at under-age level and now with Mullingar Shamrocks, but I never charged a penny for any of them. Now the big challenge is to try to save my house.'

In the Eye of the Storm
Flynn presents a brave face to the outside world, though the determination in his personality is a strong suit. What is

striking is the contrast between his language and its content: a cheerful voice relating a story of obstacles and disappointment. Any despair his story might generate is relieved by the spunk of the narrator. Nowhere is the truth of Hugh McIlvanney's observation more apparent: 'Sport at its finest is often poignant, if only because it is almost a caricature of the ephemerality of human achievements.'

There is a strong undercurrent of anger in Flynn's voice, though, as he describes the way the financial community has effectively washed its hands of the mess it had some responsibility for creating. Even at the start of his business career, he had some memorable clashes with the banks.

He says, 'I remember a bank manager in 1994. I was overtrading and my business was going under. He was overbearing, arrogant and disrespectful. He treated me like dirt and spoke to me in a very derogatory way and was refusing to support me. I grabbed him by the throat and pulled him across the table. I opened up an account elsewhere.'

Like an alien from outer space, Flynn and his wife Madeline would have to try to navigate themselves into a whole new world. The commercial court was a monument to broken hearts and foiled aspirations, to innumerable tales of sadness. Watching it was easy to imagine that the stench of fear would upset the stomach of a horse. All seemed soaked in a heavy despondency as if some totally melancholy spirit brooded over the place. It was difficult watching not to succumb to a great sense of the desolation of life, which swept all round like a tidal wave, drowning all in its blackness. It was then that the mental toughness nurtured in Meath training sessions in Bettystown really kicked in.

'The first time in commercial court was hard,' says Flynn.

'When the tsunami came and took everything, I wasn't siphoning off my money to the Cayman Islands. Did I think of doing something stupid? It would have flickered through my head. Have I stopped others from buying a rope? Yes.'

A New Shopping List

It would have been easy for Flynn to feel overwhelmed. This quiet, peaceful corner was home to tens of thousands who were trying to pick themselves from the mangled wreck of the Celtic tiger. Financial distress was sucking the vitality out of the country as a bee sucks nectar out of a flower: a monument to broken hearts and foiled aspirations, to innumerable tales of sadness and dawning shreds of hope. In this troubled terrain the sands of time shift slowly. There were many moments of indignity on the way.

'I was in with the bank at a time when I was in a bad place,' he says. 'My wife had sold her Jeep and I had sold my car to make a few bob and was hanging on by the fingertips. A junior official came in and he insulted me. He asked me how I spent my money down to the last euro. This cheeky pup was telling me I had to cut back on bread, milk and meat. It was the way that he spoke to me that really made me want to bust him but I knew it would cost me and I'd end up in court. So I tried a different tack and asked him how he spent his money. When he wouldn't say I pushed and said: 'I have told you everything about how I spend my money, now you tell me how much you earn and how you spend it.' But he wouldn't and was so dismissive of me. Eventually I was allowed enough to live on and to provide the basics for my wife and kids.

'That was the bleakest point of all. I will never forget walking out of that meeting because I had never felt so low. I was making every effort to tighten up and I had no problem with the idea, but to humiliate me in that way was just too much.'

With a Lack of a Little Help From My Friends

Murky memories scamper though the mists of his recent past. The code of loyalty he acquired with Meath would come back to bite Flynn's ass in financial terms.

'I could have finished a close friend's career if I disclosed some of his activities in some of my business dealings,' he says. 'My barrister told me if I was to do that I could have won the case. Against all advice I didn't because the person would have lost his pension and possibly his job. I thought so highly of this person, I just couldn't do it. I was loyal to a fault even though I knew it would cost me a lot in a time when I couldn't afford to be losing money. He held on to his job and his pension but I was very disappointed in his attitude thereafter. It hurt a lot.

'When I had money I gave it to friends. The big thing I learned was who my friends were. There were a few people who really disappointed me, but that's life.'

A Giant Among Men

The turning point was poignant, powerful and permanent.

Flynn says, 'Jim Stynes became a close friend of mine when I went to Australia with the Compromise Rules in 1990. I knew he was dying and I wanted to see him when I was right in the middle of my own crisis. A great friend of mine, Freddie Grehan, paid for myself and my son Billy to fly to Australia in December 2011. Jim and his family had probably spent seventeen out of the previous twenty Christmases with us. I can't adequately explain what I got out of that trip. It was life changing. He was very frail and had lost his peripheral vision and was broken into pieces in many ways. He cried and was a bit emotional as he hugged me. We went to a restaurant but he couldn't eat. He just sipped a whiskey. He kind of broke down and opened up about all the things he was going to miss out on, like seeing his kids growing up. As I said goodbye, he wrote a little note for me on a jersey and gave it to me. I have no pictures in my house of my football career but the one thing I have hung up is that jersey. When things were bad I just looked up at the jersey and his note. I had been struggling a bit but, all of a sudden, my problems seemed minor. After I came back from Australia, I was a new man and nothing fazed me.

'I mind myself better, have a great family and am in a good place, except financially. As Jim Stynes said to me: "It's only f**king money Flynner."'

A Helping Hand

In the final scene of the medieval epic *La Chanson de Roland*, the great Christian hero Charlemagne sat exhausted in Aix, his battles with the Moors over. According to the poem, he was more than 900 years old. An angel wakened the old man from his sleep and told him to get up again and return to battle because the work would not be finished until the end of time. Charlemagne sighed: '*Dieu, si penuse est ma vie.*' (O God, how hard is my life.) The work of the hero remains unfinished, but who will do it if not he or she?

Given the amount of pressure Flynn and his family have been under, he would have been forgiven for becoming insular but he has found new horizons of hope in his life through helping others. Behind the scenes he has been working busily but quietly in the corner of the world where there are no cameras, no press and there is no appearance fee. The objective is simple to state but more difficult to achieve: to try to rescue the GAA greats of the past and friends who have fallen into the abyss.

He says, 'I fractured both legs, had my knee severed, broke my collarbone and broke my sternum bone. Gerry McEntee told me, no matter what, I should keep up my VHI because I would have been banjaxed otherwise. My own experiences have given me a real feel for those players who are now in a bad way because of injuries but who can't afford to have them seen to. I started the GAA Legends and we had a golf event for charity. Overall, I helped raise a million euros for charity and I am proud of that.'

There is an air of expectation as he takes a familiar role – centre stage. He talks in his soft accent about issues with all the confidence and authority of a man firmly established as a leading figure on the national stage. Yet what struck me most forcefully was the way his eyes sparkled as he talked about the future. He exudes a decency and warmth not always associated with celebrities. His is the idealism of a youth and there was not the slightest trace of cynicism or disillusionment, though there were hints of a steely resolve behind the mild, almost innocent exterior. He is evangelical about a new venture, which is taking up a huge chunk of his time and energy.

'I resigned from the GAA's past players committee,' he says. 'I want to make a difference and one of my big passions is the Past Players Project. Sadly there are a number of former players who have fallen on hard times and if we could help even four or five of them a year I would be happy. It must be done.'

Flynn has managed to give a little hope to all the former

greats he cares for and a little hope is a powerful and precious commodity.

Where Do We Go From Here?

Flynn has taken Gandhi's advice to heart: 'Be the change you wish to see in the world.' He measures what he values rather than values what he measures.

'I'm fifty now and I have no pension,' he says. 'Two of my kids are in college now and my only priority is to secure their futures. My wife, who had believed in everything I did, has the threat of losing the home she loves constantly hanging over her.

'I see my glass as half-full. I look on it as half-time in a match. Now it is up to me to rescue the game in the second half. I'm enjoying life a little bit more with an awful lot less.'

Walking out from our interview, only a car radio punctured the silence. Tony Blair's favourite, 'Things Can Only Get Better', was blaring away a message of Micawber-like easy optimism. I could only reflect that a more appropriate soundtrack for Bernard Flynn would have been Labi Siffre's inspirational song – 'Something Inside So Strong'.

THREE

MAGIC MOMENTS

The GAA is made up of special days in a special history. This chapter covers some of them, which serve as a microcosm of the magic of the GAA.

The late RTE Gaelic Games Correspondent Mick Dunne spoke to me about the time when, to shamelessly steal from Paul Simon, the nation turned its lonely eyes to New York.

'In 1933, Cavan became the first Ulster team to win the All-Ireland,' he said. 'Further titles followed in 1935, '47, '48 and 1952. The most famous of them all was 'the Polo Grounds final' in 1947, when they were captained by "the Gallant" John Joe O'Reilly.

'In the 1930s the GAA entered a new era with the emergence of the greatest evangelist since Saint Paul. In 1938, Micheál O'Hehir made his first GAA commentary at the Galway–Monaghan All-Ireland football semi-final in Mullingar.

'Radio is the word. In the beginning was the word. Radio is essentially blind. Its images are a private treaty between commentator and listener. The audience must fill out the game with description and information. The commentator dabs words on to an aural canvas.

'Growing up there were few distractions apart from the wireless with the wet batteries and dry batteries and, of course, we listened to O'Hehir's commentaries religiously. Listening to the radio, we never saw those great players but Micheál, who really made the GAA, turned them into superheroes.

'Micheál O'Hehir was the man who brought Gaelic games in vivid form to the people of Ireland at a time when television was unknown and transistors unheard of. He showed that hurling and football and games like that are an art apart, its extent and depth perhaps not fully realised, rather merely accepted. He was a national institution. As we march, not always successfully, to the relentless demands of a faster, more superficial age, just to hear his voice was to know that all was well with the world. He painted pictures with words like a master craftsman. Young boys listening to him decided immediately they wanted to join the ranks of the football and hurling immortals. Irish sport is not the same without him. He was irreplaceable. Nobody ever did more for the GAA than him. Of all his commentaries, though, the stand-out one was the Polo Grounds final.'

Cavan's Fairytale of New York
Right half-back on that Cavan team was the late John Wilson, who went on to become Tanaiste in the Irish government in the 1980s, spoke with me about what is arguably the most iconic match in the long history of the GAA: 'The final was held in New York as a gesture of goodwill by the GAA to the Irish people in America. Once it was announced, it aroused great interest in every county. To get there was a great prize

in itself. The teams left Cobh together for a six-day trip on the *RMS Mauretania* to New York, after getting our vaccinations against smallpox, which were compulsory at the time. The fact that we were playing Kerry, the aristocrats of football, added to the occasion for us but the fact that it was the first final played abroad gave it a much more exotic quality so it really grabbed the public imagination.'

But what kind of machinations were going on behind the scenes in New York to make this event possible on the ground? The famous John Kerry O'Donnell, who for decades was 'Mr GAA' in New York, gave a breathtaking, hair-raising account of the real world of GAA politics behind closed doors involving moral blackmail, bribery of a kind, intimidation and blatant lie-telling which allowed this event to happen: 'Locating the 1947 All-Ireland final to the Big Apple was one of the great achievements of Canon Michael Hamilton's active career.

'Initially almost everyone seemed implacably opposed to the project.

'Machiavelli himself would have admired the "promptings" behind the scenes that finally persuaded a controversial Central Council meeting at Barry's Hotel that it was worth carrying through. Folklore abounds of how Miltown Malbay's Bob Fitzpatrick's passionate speech to congress, complemented by the prop of a tear-stained handkerchief, swung the vote as he read from a bogus "emigrant's letter".'

Meanwhile excitement was mounting in Kerry, as their former star full-back Joe Keohane told me many years ago: 'Before the final, Kerry, Cavan, Galway, Laois and Mayo had toured in New York. Mayo in particular could have clocked up frequent flyer credits, thanks to the clout and cash of a judge from Bohola, Bill O'Dwyer. After he was elected Mayor of New

York in 1946, the GAA had the cachet and the connections to locate its premier event in the world's most famous city.

'The decision gave new oxygen to the championship that year as every team in the country dreamed of a trip to New York. This was most apparent in the Munster final that year when we defeated Cork in the Athletic Grounds. With the clock ticking, Cork were awarded a penalty. I argued with the referee for two minutes, and helpfully stood on the ball and of course almost buried the ball into the mud. When Jim Ahearne struck the ball it dribbled weakly along the pitch.

'All the time I was arguing I could see the skyline of New York getting clearer and clearer.'

For Cavan, the trip to New York was particularly welcome because in previous years they had experienced many bitter disappointments as one of their biggest stars from that era, Mick Higgins, explained to me some years ago: 'Initially, most of our team would taste the bitter pill of defeat in three All-Ireland finals before getting their hands on the ultimate prize. We lost to Kerry in 1937, Roscommon in 1943 (after a replay) and Cork in 1945. The replay against Roscommon was mired in controversy because of our frustration with some of the refereeing decisions.

'What I remember most was the mayhem at the end. First, Cavan's Joe Stafford was sent off after having a go at Owensie Hoare. We got a point but Barney Culley didn't agree and put the umpire into the net with a box. Big Tom O'Reilly, our captain, came in to remonstrate and T. P. O'Reilly threw the referee in the air. After that game the GAA came down on us like a ton of bricks and imposed heavy suspensions on some of our greatest players. We felt there was an injustice done. The trip to New York was a great adventure for us all but we were there on a mission – redemption. We knew this was history in the making and that we would write our names into GAA immortality if we won. We wanted to show everybody at home as much as in New York that we were top-class footballers. From the outside it might have looked like this was a holiday, or as a "jolly" as some people call these trips, but we were there on a serious mission, which was to reclaim our reputation and it was going to take a great team to stop us. We knew Kerry would be good but they were going to have to be very, very good to beat us.'

There was a unique atmosphere in the city and in the grounds before the game. Mick Dunne recalled for me: 'Three thousand came in on an excursion train from Boston, and large contingents from Detroit, Pittsburgh and Chicago. There were specials from Hartford, Springfield and Newark. Lonely strangers were asking, anyone here from my county? This was much more than a football game. It was a rally of the scattered Irish, seeking friendship, warmth and renewal of the spirit. In a big way it was Galway races, Punchestown, Puck Fair.

'The players took the energy-sapping, twenty-nine-hour flight from Rineanna to New York via Santa Maria in the Azores, Gander and Boston, the Monday before the game. To compound the problems, the take-off was delayed by twenty-four hours, which led Kerry's Eddie Dowling to claim that he had thirty glasses of beer before boarding. Twenty-five officials and subs had already travelled by ocean liner, the *Mauretania*.

'A cavalcade of thirty cars, eighteen motorcycle cops escorting them with sirens screaming, drove the awe-stricken footballers through the famous avenues and streets. The Lord Mayor hosted a lavish reception at City Hall where no fewer than 5,000 people attended. On the morning of the match the Cardinal, his name was Spellman I believe, welcomed the team from the pulpit in Saint Patrick's Cathedral and was photographed with the team captains on the cathedral steps afterwards.

'This game was to become the stuff of myth. The New York Police Band played no fewer than three anthems: "Amhrán na bhFiann", "Faith of our Fathers" and "The Star-Spangled Banner".'

Joe Keohane offered an interesting perspective: 'Despite the hype at home, the game was poorly publicised and advertised in New York and this was reflected in the fact that only 34,491 attended. The pitch was too small and rock hard. In fact the surface had a crucial bearing on the outcome because Eddie Dowling was on fire that day and scored one of the goals that put Kerry in the lead and seemingly on course for victory, but he was knocked out cold when he fell on the ground and had to be carried off. This was the turning point of the game.'

Mick Higgins recalled his initial thoughts on the game: 'I knew we had a battle on our hands, but I noticed the Kerry fans were very jittery. The pitch was used for baseball and was much smaller than the usual Gaelic pitch. The grass was scorched and even bald in a few places and there was a mound in the playing area. The ground was rock hard and the weather was scorching hot. Kerry got off to a great start but Peter Donohoe was on fire for us that day. The American press described him as "the Babe Ruth" of Gaelic football after the greatest star in baseball of the era. We had a great leader and one of the all-time greats in Gaelic football in John Joe O'Reilly. We won by 2-11 to 2-7. By coincidence one of the biggest stars of our team Mick Higgins, who scored a goal and two points in that match, was born in New York.'

The event remains part of the fabric of the folk memory

in Cavan. The team was photographed with the Stars and Stripes. When the side arrived back, they were greeted on the outskirts of Cavan town by no fewer than fifteen bands.

The dizzy elation in Cavan did not last too long because, within four years, two of the greatest stars on the Cavan team that historic day had shockingly died as Mick Higgins explained: 'In 1950 P. J. Duke died suddenly from pleurisy in St Vincent's Hospital. Two years later, on 21 November 1952, Commandant John Joe O'Reilly, after being diagnosed with a kidney complaint, died unexpectedly in the Curragh Military Hospital. He was just thirty-four.

'Through the commentaries of Micheál O'Hehir, Cornafean's John Joe O'Reilly became one of the most famous names in Ireland in the 1940s. He won back-to-back All-Irelands in 1947 and 1948, National Leagues in 1948 and 1950 and four Railway Cup medals in 1942, '43, '47 and 1950. Born on a farm near Killeshandra in 1918, after receiving a scholarship to St Patrick's College in Cavan, he went on to the Army Cadet School at the Curragh, where he showed promise as a sprinter and as a basketball player. His career coincided with the most glorious era in Cavan football.

'It was very difficult for all of us to believe that those two great servants of Cavan football, who had played in the county's glory days, had gone to their eternal reward so prematurely. Whenever I talk to GAA fans there are always great arguments about who had the best half-back line of all time: the Roscommon half-back line of 1943–44 with Brendan Lynch, Bill Carlos and Phelim Murray or the Cavan back line of 1947–48. I can still hear Micheál O'Hehir calling them out, "On the right is P. J. Duke, in the centre Commandant John Joe O'Reilly and, on the left, Lieutenant Simon Deignan".

'It was a very traumatic time for the family when John Joe

died. His wife was left with four very young kids. They were very tough times. His wife was told she was not entitled to a widow's pension. Years later her son Brian investigated on her behalf and discovered that she had been. Brian played minor football for Cavan but it was hard to escape from his father's shadow. He retired from the game at a very young age.'

Jimmy Magee appraised the careers of the two fallen heroes: 'John Joe's status in the game is reflected as centre half-back on both the Team of the Century and the Team of the Millennium. It was such a shock to hear that he died – especially as we were still stunned from the death of P. J. Duke. I would rate P. J. as good a wing-back as we have ever seen. Two great oaks fell in the forest when those two great men drew their final breaths.'

Mick Dunne explained that it was not the end of the road for Cavan though: 'Mick Higgins captained Cavan to an All-Ireland final victory in 1952. The first match against Meath ended in a draw. It was the first time the GAA brought the two teams together for a meal after the game. When Mick and some of the Cavan boys got to the hotel they ordered drinks – just bottles of ale and a mineral. Mick went to pay for it but the barman said it was on the GAA. Mick double-checked if he had heard correctly. Quick as a flash once this was confirmed, one of his colleagues said, "Forget about the ales and get us brandies." For the replay, though, there was no free drink.

'Mick later took up coaching and found that management was a more frustrating experience than playing. He often told the story of taking charge of Cavan for a championship match against Armagh. As the match reached its climax, Cavan's dominance was threatened as Armagh took control over midfield. Corrective action was required urgently and Higgins decided to send on a sub, big Jim O'Donnell, whose high fielding prowess was just what Cavan needed. Jim, though, didn't seem to realise the urgency of the situation. After going on to the pitch, he strolled back to the sideline seeking a slip of paper with his name on it for the referee. Moments later, O'Donnell was back again seeking a pair of gloves. Higgins forcefully told him to get back to his position immediately and not to mind about the gloves. A minute or two later he was back a third time to ask, "Mick, would you ever mind my false teeth?" As he calmly handed the manager his molars, Mick's blood pressure hit record levels.'

Longford Leaders

A turning point in Longford's fortunes came when three time All-Ireland winner Mick Higgins of Cavan agreed to become county trainer in 1965.

Jimmy Flynn was at the centre of the most successful period of Longford's history. Longford's only previous successes at national level had been the All-Ireland Junior Championship of 1937. In 1968, Flynn helped Longford to take their only Leinster senior title. His towering performances in midfield helped his county to beat the famous three-in-a-row All-Ireland-winning Galway team in the National League final in 1966.

Flynn first made his mark with his native Clonguish. The most formative influence on his career was one of the most famous personalities in the history of Longford football, Bertie Allen.

'He was the greatest character I ever came across in football,' says Flynn. 'I remember playing a nine-a-side juvenile match in Longford. Eamon Barden and I were in the half-back line and were pretty strong so we were winning a lot of ball and sending it in to the forwards but they couldn't score. Bertie said that the four forwards were like Khrushchev, Eisenhower, Macmillan and De Gaulle – they were so far apart. He had a great turn of phrase and all kinds of comments were attributed to him, though I'm not sure if all of them were true.'

Success quickly came at schoolboys, juvenile and minor level with his club. That trend accelerated when he began his career in St Mel's. In 1961 he helped them reach the All-Ireland Colleges final. Flynn made his senior debut for Offaly in 1963 as a nineteen-year-old marking Larry Coughlan. Longford had earlier reached their first Leinster final in 1965, losing out to Dublin by 3-6 to 0-9 after missing a penalty at a crucial stage. That September they won their first senior tournament of note when they defeated Kildare to take the O'Byrne Cup.

Jimmy Flynn recalls Longford's progression: 'We had a great county chairman in Jimmy Flynn (no relation). He had a very cool head and was a very astute man. Another key figure was Father Phil McGee (brother of Eugene). He had a great love for the game. It was much more a passion than an interest for him and you need people like that behind you. In 1966 we were invited to go to America. I well remember Fr Phil making a statement, which I think he regretted afterwards. He said, "We'll go to America when we're All-Ireland champions." We never got there.

'There were hardly 5,000 people left in the county the day of the final. When we got home on the Monday evening, we hopped on a truck. I'll always remember Larry Cunningham, who was at the height of his fame, got up with us and sang a song. Particularly as it was the first time we won a national title, there were ecstatic celebrations in the county. Although we didn't become Longford's answer to The Beatles, at least when any of us went to a dance in Rooskey after that we were recognised.

'The best team I saw in terms of excitement was the Down team of the early sixties.

'My father worshipped the ground Seán Purcell walked on. When I was young, my father often brought me to see him play and he was a colossus. He was definitely the best natural footballer I ever saw play. His Galway team of the fifties were a great team. I'd be doing Longford a disservice if I didn't say the Galway three-in-a-row side weren't a great team too. The great thing about all Galway teams was that they were always very clean and fair. Mind you, they had a couple of hard men but I'm not going to mention any names. After I retired the great Kerry team were, of course, something special.

'To win the league was a great achievement for a small county like Longford and although there was a lot of dedication on the part of the players, I think Mick Higgins has to take a lot of the credit for it. He was never a hard taskmaster in training or anything but he grew into the job with us. There was always great local rivalry between us and Cavan but Longford people up to then had never much to shout about in comparison with our northern neighbours, but we changed that. He gave us the confidence to do it.

'One of the other great memories I have of that league campaign was of playing Sligo, who had a very strong team that year. They were a bit like ourselves in that they could have made the breakthrough, especially as they had Mickey Kearins –a fantastic footballer. When Sligo wanted to beat you they dragged you into Ballymote, which was a fairly remote part of the country. Our sub goalie was the late Michael "Smiler" Fay but on that day he was doing the sideline. At one stage John Donnellan got the ball towards the end of the game and ballooned the ball over the line. It was as clear as the nose on your face it was a line ball to Sligo, but Smiler gave it to us. Afterwards we got a point and stole the match. The Sligo crowd were incensed by that and rightly so. When the game was over the crowd were baying for Smiler's blood. Smiler saved a fair few goals for Longford in his playing career but he saved that match for us and I believe that was the day we won the league.'

Galway at the time looked invincible but an indication that they did not regard Longford as pushovers came when they flew their outstanding half-back Martin Newell back from Frankfurt, where he was attending university.

Flynn retains a great admiration for that Galway team. 'They had great players individually but we were also a great unit,' he says. 'The great teams like that Galway side, and later Mick O'Dwyer's Kerry, were a team with all the roles. Having said that about the Kerry lads, the first man I would have on a team of all-time greats would be Galway's Seán Purcell. The teams that are most successful are the teams that mould as a team. If a team has one or two great players you can always blot them out and you can take them but you can't blot out six class forwards. You couldn't single out any one player on either that Galway or Kerry side. They were a team of stars, from the great Johnny Geraghty in goal, to Enda Colleran, Noel Tierney and Martin Newell in the backs right through to John Keenan at top of the left. If we kept Mattie McDonagh quiet, someone like the young Liam Sammon would pop up to get the scores.

'The final was one of those days when you are up for it and the game went well for me. The one incident I remember most from the game was Martin Newell coming up the field with the ball and hitting a diagonal pass to Cyril Dunne. I intercepted it and there was nobody between me and the goal – which was about seventy yards away. We were two points up at the time. There was about ten minutes to go and I was very tired. I soloed through and had nobody to beat but the goalie but I shaved the post and put it wide. I fell on the ground with exhaustion and I can still hear Jackie Devine saying to me, "Why didn't you f**king pass the ball to me?" It made for an agonising finish because Galway were throwing everything at us but our backs held out well.

'The memory that stays with me to this day, though, is of the joy on the faces of the Longford crowd. We had a hell of a night in Power's Hotel afterwards and a hell of a day the following day. The party finished on Tuesday – but I'm not saying which Tuesday! We came down to earth with a bang, though, when we lost in the first round of the Leinster Championship against Louth, but I thought it was unfair to us to have to play a championship match just two weeks after winning the league final.

'After we won the league we had to play a two-header with New York: one in Croke Park and the second game a week later in Longford. The Croke Park match was a fiasco and ended in an absolute shambles. The Longford fans were livid with the referee because they felt that he let the New York lads get away with murder. Murder is too strong to describe what they were up to but they were very, very physical. I talked to journalists after the match and they told me we should refuse to play them in the second game. A lot of the Longford crowd came on to the pitch to try to get at the New York fellas afterwards. When we played them in Longford, it was the first time they had to put barbed wire around the pitch.

'There were a number of us based in Dublin at the time and sometimes we had two carloads of us travelling down to training.

———————

'There were stories told about fellas coming out of various towns at night with maybe too many on board. I remember a situation one night where a few of the lads, who shall remain nameless, headed off to the Fleadh Ceol in Clones but made a detour into a bog. There was no such thing as foreign holidays then. You were lucky if you got to stay in a good hotel before a big match.

'We should have won the Leinster final in 1965. We were a far better team than Dublin on the day but we hadn't the experience or the confidence. We didn't drive home our advantage. I was marking Des Foley that day and I remember talking to him about it and he pointed out that they had got two very soft goals from speculative balls that went into the square.

'I never saw myself on television. I think there was a little bit of coverage on television of one of our Leinster Championship games.

'We would be training in Longford once a week. I don't think training then was anything like as intensive as it is now. Maybe we did a bit more ball play though.

'Winning the Leinster title against Laois in 1968 was a big thrill, though I got a knee injury. I was injured and missed out on the All-Ireland semi-final against Kerry. It was a big disappointment to have to miss out but what really killed me was losing out on the opportunity to mark Mick O'Connell. I was on the sideline and we lost by two points. One of the problems of Longford and weaker counties generally is that we didn't have strength in depth and that told against us against Kerry. We had good players when we were all free from injury but couldn't afford to be short of anyone.

'I played on Mick O'Connell twice. I especially recall a match down in Killarney. We both caught the ball together and, whatever way it happened, I kind of dragged him down and landed on his backside. The next time we clashed I was picking up the ball off the ground and he came in and pulled on me. I said, "Now listen, Mick. That's not the way the game is played." But because of the previous incident he said, "Well it's better than pulling and hauling." I remember that remark well and I kind of laughed. He took football very seriously. I thought he was a purist. He was a complete footballer in that he had all the skills: he could strike the ball off the ground, had a great catch, was a great athlete and could kick with both feet. I don't regard him, though, as a match-winner in the same way as I would have seen Jack O'Shea or Eoin Liston. I had huge time for the Bomber. I would have a question mark about O'Connell's temperament. It wasn't as strong as other parts of his game. It was possible to psyche him out of a match and the Offaly boys were pretty adept at that.

'If you're talking about great footballers, one of the lads I would have to mention is Willie Bryan. We had some great tussles. I met him a few years after we retired and he said, "I've a great photograph of you and me up in the air catching the ball and we both have our hands around the ball." And then he said, "But I have mine on the inside." I thought it was a great remark. He had a great sense of humour and was a lovely footballer.

'I played for Ireland against Australia in Croke Park – the first time Ireland had played Australia. I was marking a famous Australian player called Ron Barrazzi. We put together a team with the likes of Jimmy Keaveney, Tony Hanahoe and Paddy Cullen. We were a motley crew. In fairness, I think it was more a question of who was available than who was the best.

'They wore sleeveless black singlets and all of them were

tanned and bronzed. We were wearing white vests and were all as white as sheets. I reckon there was about seven or eight thousand in the crowd that day and when we trotted out the crowd started laughing at us because we looked anaemic. My only specific memory of the game was Jim Eivers getting the oval ball and trying to solo it at one stage.'

Galway Boys Hurrah
'People of Galway we love you.'

The final words in the most memorable speech in the history of the GAA, when Joe Connolly accepted the Liam McCarthy Cup after leading Galway to only their second All-Ireland final victory in 1980. The emotional frenzy his speech provoked will never be forgotten.

Galway's victory did not come from nowhere. The first sign Noel Lane received that he had potential as a hurler came in National School when any time a new batch of hurleys came to the school, 'the Master' gave him first pick. His club form was rewarded with a call-up to the county panel for the 1977–78 league campaign, making his debut against Clare in Tulla. His build-up to the game was unusual.

He says, 'I was overawed going into the dressing-room with all my heroes from the National League win in 1975. There were some great characters like John Connolly and Joe McDonagh who went out of their way to give me confidence. P. J. Molloy was preparing for the game by rubbing poitín on to his legs. Poitín was hard enough to get at the time so it didn't seem a good use of it to me. I asked him for the bottle and said, "Better value to slug it than to rub it." So I had a sup. It didn't do me any harm. I was marking Johnny McMahon who was an All-Star and I was thrilled with my performance. I held my place after that.'

After suffering a heavy defeat to Tipperary in the 1979 National League final, a shake-up of the team was necessary and Lane was one of the casualties and dropped from the panel. Breaking the news sensitively to him was not a priority for the Galway management.

'I got a letter in an envelope which was handed to me in the dressing-room in a club game,' he recalls. 'I smelled a rat. No reason was given for my omission. It was just, "We regret to inform you . . . " I felt it was severe to drop me like that.'

The opportunity for redemption came quickly.

'Babs Keating was training Galway at the time,' says Lane. 'He spearheaded a delegation that came down to see me to ask me back. I replied, "Not a chance." I was just playing hard to get. I was the first one in Athenry for training that evening.

'Babs was an excellent manager. As I was moved into full-forward, he gave me a lot of his time and attention coaching me on how to approach forward play and working on my solo and my passing. He gave me a lot of confidence in my own game. I really admired him as a player for Tipp. We had thought of ourselves as inferior to the big powers like Cork and Tipperary but he was one of them and I suppose, to our surprise, he was a normal guy. He gave us a lot of confidence. Babs was "let go" after we lost the 1979 All-Ireland but I believe the belief he gave us was a significant factor in our breakthrough the following year.'

Lane also has a high opinion of Keating's successor: 'Cyril Farrell was a brilliant manager. His talent was shown especially in the way he managed players who were that bit more difficult to manage like Tony Keady and Brendan Lynskey. Cyril had a different strategy for each player.'

One incident illustrates this capacity. The week before an

All-Ireland final, the team was training in Ballinasloe on the night the team was due to be announced for the final. There was a terrible storm that evening with thunder, lightning and incredible rain. Lynskey and Keady did not travel down from Dublin. Farrell felt like shooting the two miscreants but knew he could not win the final without them. Things were tense for a while, especially as he never picked a team until the squad were there to hear it first. He arranged a training session for the next evening and this time the two stars were back and victory was secured.

'Cyril always preached that we were better than everybody else,' says Lane. 'He had great passion and would get us to see the opposition in terms of what they didn't have more than what they did have. He inherited Babs' team in 1979 but really showed his skills with his "second team" from 1985–90. He would have worked with most of that team at minor and under-21 level. He knew everything about them: what they ate and drank, who they slept with and their strengths and weaknesses.'

Lane's first All-Ireland came in 1980.

'We won that day because our leaders, especially Joe Connolly, stood up and were counted,' he says. 'We were a powerful team and that side should have won more than one All-Ireland. It suited us that day that we were playing Limerick rather than Cork or Kilkenny and that gave us confidence. It felt like it was for us that day, though Limerick could have considered themselves unlucky.

'It was a proud time to be from Galway but I don't know if we were ready for the celebrations that came afterwards. For six months afterwards we were touring schools and clubs. Every night we could have been out if we wanted to. I was very lucky in that my wife Carmel kept me on the straight and narrow and gave me great support in the low points of my career and that my daughter Aoife was born that year. Likewise, my sons Mark and Patrick helped me to keep my focus. All that 1980 team were very lucky in that respect also. I can't give enough credit to the wives and partners who supported us but I can understand how that kind of absence from home has destroyed relationships and marriages for some players on other teams.'

Galway's triumph that year did create one of the funniest memories from Lane's time with Galway.

'We went to America on the All-Star trip and brought a big contingent of Galway supporters with us,' says Lane. 'We visited Disneyland and a gang of us went on the Space Mountain roller coaster. I was sharing a carriage with Steve Mahon and some of the lads like Finbarr Gantley were behind us. Two of the most "mature" members of the group, John Connolly's dad, Pat, and Mick Sylver were behind them. After we came down we were all petrified and just glad to have got out of there alive. We went to a little bar nearby to catch our breath. Just as we started to relax, who did we see in the queue to go back up Space Mountain but Pat and Mick.'

The most famous quote in the hurling vernacular is Micheál O'Muircheartaigh's observation: 'A mighty poc from the hurl of Seán Og O'Halpín . . . his father was from Fermanagh, his mother from Fiji, neither a hurling stronghold.'

However, a good contender for runner–up must be, 'Sylvie Linnane: The man who drives a JCB on a Monday and turns into one on a Sunday.'

His fire and brimstone approach to the game was legendary. He says, 'For me, the colour of a jersey, especially the Kilkenny one, was all I needed to get up for a game. I always had a passion for beating them. Everyone likes to take their scalp. I was never one to say anything to an opponent but I did believe they should know I was there. One time we were playing Kilkenny, I received an uppercut from Harry Ryan before the national anthem. I couldn't see after it but I still let fly at him.

'The other thing I remember was the incredible reception we got when we won the All-Ireland in 1980. It was clear how much it meant to people. The great thing was they were all there again when we lost the next year.'

Linnane has spent half a lifetime denying some of the dramas attributed to him on the pitch. However, it is a little known fact that he once created a drama off the pitch.

'We were in Dublin the night before that All-Ireland final and, as always, we were sent to bed early,' he recalls. 'The problem is that it's very hard to sleep the night before an All-Ireland. I was rooming with Steve Mahon and we heard a massive row going on in the street underneath. So I went to investigate and saw this fella beating up his wife or his girlfriend. I ran into the bathroom, got the waste-paper basket, filled it with water and ran over to the window and threw the water over the man. It did the trick and he stopped and the woman ran away. A happy ending or so I thought, until the man recovered from the shock and got really, really angry and started to climb up the drainpipe to pay back the person who threw the water on him. I didn't think the night before the All-Ireland was the best time to get involved in a brawl – especially as this guy looked like a pure psycho and I decided discretion was the better part of valour. I turned off the light so he wouldn't know where to find me. I went quietly back to bed and listened attentively to see what would happen. What I hadn't known at the time was that the light immediately below my room was on. The room belonged to the former Galway great Inky Flaherty. Inky was not a man to mess with and, a few minutes later, I heard him forcefully eject the intruder out the window – which was not the typical way to prepare for an All-Ireland.'

Money, Money, Money

Many Kerry folk believed they were cast-iron certainties to win the 1982 All-Ireland. A song to celebrate the victory had already been written. Then Offaly's super sub Seamus Darby intervened with the winning goal and the Kingdom were deprived of history. Before the game, a Kerry entrepreneur had invested a small fortune in making a large number of Kerry five-in-a-row T-shirts. His money would surely go to waste. Not a bit of it. With exceptional cunning, even by Kerry standards, he made an even bigger fortune by writing 'RIP' on each of them and selling them all in Offaly.

The Famine Days Are Over

'It was one of the days of our lives. You could cut the atmosphere with a knife.'

Babs Keating glows as if he is transmitting electricity while he recalls the 1987 Munster final replay, when his Tipperary team defeated Cork in one of the most memorable matches between the two old rivals. Nothing captures the unique magic and tribalism of the GAA more vividly than that Munster final.

Michael Lowry has been one of the most controversial figures in recent Irish political life but he was to play a significant role in the revival of Tipperary's hurling fortunes in 1986. His meeting with Babs Keating would change hurling history.

'When Michael became county chairman, he asked to

meet me,' says Keating. 'We met in a private house, the late Seamus Maher's home, because I wanted to meet in secret knowing the stories that would go around. To be fair to him, he could give me the power to pick my own selectors. I'll always remember he said, "You have the job but we have no money." The County Board was broke after hosting the Centenary All-Ireland in '84 and the economic situation was very bleak. I got the idea to start the Supporters Club. Then I decided we would raffle a racehorse and Christy Roche bought an ideal horse for us. I got everyone I ever knew to buy a ticket, like Charlie Haughey and Jack Lynch. I remember being at home one morning and getting a call from Niall Quinn when he was at Arsenal. He told me he had sold seven tickets for me and listed a who's who of Arsenal greats who had bought one.

'My back-up team was Donie Nealon and Theo English. They had played for the county for about twelve years and I don't think Cork ever beat them. They couldn't understand why there was such fear of Cork and they transferred that attitude. Our captain Richie Stakelum would always say that Tipperary had such fear of Cork at that stage.

'People talk about the great team Tipperary had in the '84 Munster final but that team brought Tipp into Division Two. We played our first league game away against Antrim and won it fairly impressively. The great thing that happened to us was that, in our second league match, we played Laois and they beat us by ten points in Thurles. We got rid of six or seven players and went in a different direction. If that defeat had come later in the campaign, it would have been much harder to regroup. As with everything in life you need a bit of luck. We got it with that game in Laois.

'One thing I did every January was to take out the two

selectors and their wives for a meal and told them to pick the team they would play in the All-Ireland that year. The three of us had thirteen identical choices that night in '87 so we only had to find two players.

'We had huge confidence going into the Munster final even though Cork were 3-1 to on. We had come from nowhere in Division Two and had twelve new personnel. We had money behind us. When we travelled away for big matches we stayed in five-star hotels. I will never forget the first game we played against Cork. Both of us got to the ground at the same time. Our bus was in the Tipperary colours. The Cork players were in their jeans and jumpers. Our lads looked like film stars in their blazers. Richie Stakelum said it was worth five points to us.'

Nicky English won six All-Stars in seven years and was hurler of the year in 1989. He is ideally placed to give an insider's guide to the game.

'When I came on the scene, Tipperary changed managers almost every year because we weren't winning Munster Championships,' he says. 'It is a bit like what has been happening in Galway in the last decade. In a county where you have a lot of hurlers, there is a massive turnover of players with each new manager, and that means there is little or no continuity and a lot of good players are thrown out in the wash before they have the chance to develop. We came close in a high-scoring Munster final that we should have won in 1984 when Seánie O'Leary scored a late goal to win for Cork.

'Things changed when Babs came on board. He did things differently. He raised a lot of money and arranged things in what was a radically different way back then, though county players take it for granted. He got us blazers and we stayed in hotels before matches. Things were tight economically in the 1980s. There was no money around. The Tipperary County Board were putting all their money into upgrading Semple Stadium. All their financial focus was on infrastructure, not on looking after players. Up to then, we would drive through the traffic on the day and be stuck in it. Anything we needed in terms of gear or hurleys was got for us. Before that you got your own hurleys and handed in receipts and often there was a long delay before you got your money back. Sometimes you wouldn't get your money back at all. It is hard to quantify how much all this helped us on the field of play but it did make an impact. Babs blazed the trail and every football and hurling team followed to a greater or lesser extent. He brought a whole new attitude and confidence. Babs believed and we believed because of him.

'Winning the 1987 Munster final was my greatest day in hurling. The fact that we beat Cork after extra time in a replay added to it. Tipperary hadn't won a Munster final since 1971 so that's why Richie Stakelum's comment that the "famine days are over" struck such a chord. The emotion our victory unleashed was unreal. Nothing has ever matched that feeling.'

The Glens of Antrim
One of the biggest shocks in the history of the GAA came when Antrim defeated Offaly in the 1989 All-Ireland hurling semi-final. It also saw one of the greatest displays of sportsmanship when the Offaly team gave the Antrim players a guard of honour as they left the pitch.

The Donnelly clan, from beautiful Ballycastle, are the most famous dynasty in Antrim hurling and were at the heart of that victory. In 1978 the pride of Derry, The Undertones, were singing about 'Teenage Kicks'. Dessie Donnelly's teenage kicks revolved around hurling.

He says, 'In 1977, when I was still a minor, I made my senior debut for Antrim when I came on as a sub in a league match against Westmeath in Mullingar. I scored a point and held my place after that.'

A momentous day in Antrim's history came in 1983 when Lougheil Shamrocks won the All-Ireland senior hurling club title by defeating St Ryanagh's of Offaly after a replay at Casement Park. Three years earlier, Ballycastle had lost the final to Castlegar of Galway. Twenty years on, the game remains a very vivid memory for Dessie Donnelly.

'That was the biggest disappointment of my career – even more so than losing the All-Ireland to Tipperary because no-one really expected us to win in 1989,' he says. 'It was very different in 1980. The match was billed as the clash between the Connollys and the Donnellys – because there were seven Connollys playing for Castlegar and seven Donnellys playing for us. We really thought we could do it and it was a crushing blow when we lost.'

That year, 1989, would provide Dessie with his most satisfying moment on a personal level.

'I was first nominated for the All-Stars in 1986,' he says. 'Although I didn't get selected, I was chosen as a replacement for the trip to America in 1987, which is the nicest consolation prize I ever got for anything. To be selected on the actual team in 1989 was, I'd say, the biggest thrill I ever got in hurling. I can't explain just how much it meant.'

That year also presented Donnelly with his sole opportunity to play on the highest stage within the game. Everyone was expecting the day of the All-Ireland hurling semi-finals to produce high drama – mainly because the second semi-final was between old rivals Galway and Tipperary. Eleven days previously, Galway had hammered Antrim in a challenge match, suggesting to neutrals that the Northerners would be like lambs to the slaughter against Offaly.

Antrim's confidence, though, was high because they had already beaten Offaly twice that year. Although it was an All-Ireland semi-final, the Antrim team did not think of it like that. They were conditioned to think of it just as a match against Offaly. Although Offaly were the form team in Leinster in the eighties, the men in saffron and white would have been more nervous if they had been playing Kilkenny and they were mentally right for it.

It was Offaly who made the better start and their half-time lead was 1-10 to 1-6.

It was a different story in the second half as Dessie Donnelly marshalled the Antrim defence superbly and Antrim ran out 4-15 to 1-15 winners. Ciaran Barr assumed the playmaker role to provide ample scoring opportunities for Olcan 'Cloot' McFetridge (who, with Donnelly, won an All-Star in 1989), Aidan 'Beaver' McCarry and Donal Armstrong. It was fitting that Armstrong should be part of Antrim's finest hour as his late father, dual star Kevin and Antrim GAA's most famous son – left half-forward on the team of the century of greatest players never to have won an All-Ireland medal had starred in the last Antrim team to reach the All-Ireland final back in 1943. After beating Galway by 7-0 to 6-2 in the quarter-final, they shocked Kilkenny in the semi-final, only to lose to Cork in the final.

During the Troubles, Donnelly came to regard the abnormality of that situation as normal.

'Thankfully the Troubles never had a major impact on me,' he says. 'The only time it was an issue for me was when we were travelling for some of the Antrim matches. Of course you have to be particularly careful when times are especially tense, like the marching season. There are quite a few places in Antrim that you wouldn't walk down the road on your own, or even in company, with a hurley stick in your hand – especially around 12 July.

'Back in the 1970s our changing rooms were bombed. The damage was superficial. I'd say that was more a matter of luck than because of careful management on the part of the bombers. There were a lot of theories floating around about who did it as you can imagine, but I can't tell you who was responsible.'

Donnelly has a special place in his heart for his teammates: 'In 1989 after we won the All-Ireland semi-final we were training hard coming up to the All-Ireland final. To get a bit of a break Paul McKillen and I went to see the All-Ireland football semi-final between Cork and Dublin. We were having a great chat before the game and as the players were coming on to the field I kind of noticed the big screen for the first time and I said to him, "This should be a great game today." Paul looked up at the big screen and then he turned around and asked me, "Is this game live?" I nearly died laughing.'

The Homes of Donegal

Seamus Bonner first played for Donegal when he was only eighteen in 1970 and had an unbroken record of service with Donegal until 1985. For the first eight years he was a star midfielder but, as he got a bit older, he got moved closer to the goal and the latter part of his career was as a full-forward. Football is obviously in his genes as his son Kevin has played with the Dublin senior team.

In 1989, Brian McEniff took charge of training Donegal again and he invited Bonner to be a selector. The offer was readily accepted despite the fact that it committed him to extensive travelling up and down to Donegal from his Dublin base. McEniff's Midas touch was soon in evidence again as Donegal won the Ulster title the following year. What's the secret of McEniff's success and what was he like as a player?

'As a forward he's the sort of guy I would really hate to have marking me,' says Bonner. 'He was very tough and tenacious. He'd be standing on your toes almost and wouldn't give you much time on the ball.

'His dedication is total. He's got his own business but, if he heard a Donegal man was playing football in Cork, he'd drop everything and travel down to Cork to see him play and it wouldn't cost him a thought. He never missed a single training session in the 1992 campaign and this encouraged the players to do the same. His willpower rubbed off on the players. He's also got incredible enthusiasm and that's infectious.'

The Bonner-McEniff double act had their finest hour in 1992 when they masterminded Donegal's All-Ireland 0-18 to 0-14 triumph over red-hot favourites Dublin. Before they reached that stage, controversy had erupted about Padraig Brogan's appearance in the All-Ireland semi-final.

'Padraig had made his name with Mayo but had declared for us a couple of years previously and played for us,' says Bonner. 'Then he switched back to Mayo and a year or so later Mayo brought him on against us in an All-Ireland semi-final. Mayo would consider themselves unlucky not to have won the match but when they brought on Padraig, instead of lifting Mayo, it lifted our lads. The feeling among our lads was that Padraig had left Donegal because he had a better chance of winning an All-Ireland medal with Mayo. Although we were playing poorly, when our boys saw him coming on, it made them more determined than ever not to lose the game. The sight of Padraig coming on the pitch caused them to move up a gear.'

In conversation with this writer, Padraig Brogan candidly admitted that his arrival on the pitch had the opposite effect to the one intended and in fact inspired Donegal players and fans alike and was a serious tactical blunder. His reason, though, for transferring back to Mayo was that, 'blood is thicker than water'.

In the Bonner household, tension was high for a different reason before the semi-final as Seamus's wife Cathy is from Achill Island. Bonner's inside knowledge of the Dublin players was to prove invaluable in the final.

'Having played club football so long in Dublin, I knew the Dublin players better than McEniff did,' he says. 'One of the highlights of my career had been captaining Civil Service to the Dublin championship in 1980.

'Basically I was keen that we would do two things in the All-Ireland. Firstly, that we would keep very tight on Vinny Murphy. I knew he was their target man and if we kept him quiet the other Dublin forwards would struggle. It was also vital that we curbed the Dublin half-back line because we didn't want the likes of Keith Barr running at our defence with the ball. We took steps to do both and after we got over their penalty miss we were always holding our own.

'We had been so unimpressive in the All-Ireland semi-final against Mayo that nobody gave us a chance against Dublin. I think that gave the Dublin players a false sense of security. The media really built them up and I think the Dubs started to believe their own publicity. That's a dangerous game. I think something similar happened to Kildare in 1998. In contrast, there was no hype about us because we hadn't done anything to deserve it. None of

84

our fellas were going on radio shows blowing their own trumpet.'

Although the excitement was unprecedented, Donegal's marvellous victory came with a price tag attached for Bonner.

'The hardest part of my time as a selector came in the run-up to the final,' he says. 'Tommy Ryan had played for us in the All-Ireland semi-final but we felt that Manus Boyle could do a job for us on the day. He scored nine points in the final so our judgement was vindicated but nobody wants to miss out on the chance to play in an All-Ireland final so it was incredibly tough to have to tell Tommy that he was going to miss out.'

McEniff and Bonner gave leadership from the sideline, but who were the Donegal leaders on the pitch?

'You can't win an All-Ireland without leaders on the pitch and we had four of them in 1992: Anthony Molloy, Martin McHugh at centre-forward, Tony Boyle at full-forward and Martin Gavigan at centre-back were all leaders in different ways. Molloy was a superb leader. He could catch a ball in the clouds and that would lift the team. If you could get past Martin Gavigan you were doing well. Tony and Martin could get you a score from nowhere.

'To win an All-Ireland at any time is special but to win the first one is simply magical. Nobody will ever forget the colour Donegal brought to Croke Park that day. People had never seen anything like it before. The celebrations in the county seemed to go on forever. It had such a massive impact on the psychology of the county – the way we thought and felt about ourselves. It put a smile on everybody's face in the county.'

No Ordinary Joe
When Derry succeeded Donegal as All-Ireland champions in 1993, Joe Brolly was fast becoming a star name in Gaelic football.

'I always wanted to play for Derry because of the great team of the 1970s that won back-to-back Ulster titles,' he says. 'It was very clear from an early stage that the team was going somewhere. We had a lot of very strong characters on the team. An important catalyst for our success was Lavey winning the All-Ireland club title in 1991. Our captain was Henry Downey from Lavey and he was driving us on. He would tell us we were not training enough. So when Lavey won the All-Ireland club title we all bought into the belief that the Downey way is the right way. We were training five nights a week.

'Our manager Eamonn Coleman was also crucial. He was jolly and a great character. He always played cards with the lads down the back of the bus. He was a teetotaller himself and didn't understand drink. Eamonn was a small man so it was a sight to see him berating a giant like Brian McGilligan about drinking. The most enthusiastic drinker in the squad was Johnny McGurk. Eamonn would say to him, "Wee man, wee men can't drink." The boys would be laughing because Johnny could drink any member of the squad under the table.

'Eamonn was a rogue but his heart was in the right place. He wasn't a great tactician but he was a real leader 'cos the boys loved him very dearly because he was a man's man. He once told me I needed to do weight training, saying, "Brolly, you're like a girl." This was before advanced training methods or anything. We often started with ten 400-metre runs. It was masochistic stuff.

'Then Mickey Moran came in. He is a quiet man who is a terrific coach and a football fanatic. He worked very well with Eamonn. The broad-brush stroke man who had the philosophy behind everything was Eamonn – while Mickey was the nuts and bolts man. I know in hindsight that Eamonn was not a good trainer but when Mickey came in all of a sudden everything was right.

'The other thing that was important to us was Down winning the All-Ireland in '91. We had nearly beaten them that year in a titanic game in the Athletic Grounds. We were a point up at the end when they got a free sixty yards out. I was close to the ball at the time and I heard Ross Carr saying to Enda Gormley, "I'm going to drive this over the bar." Enda told him, "Wise up you f**king eejit." But Ross sent it over the bar and they went through instead of us but when they won the All-Ireland it inspired us because it made us realise how close we were.

'I've never seen either the 1993 semi-final or All-Ireland final but anyone who has tells me they never had the slightest worry that we would win either although it was very close against Dublin in the semi-final and, even though Cork got a whirlwind start scoring 1-2 in the first five minutes in the final, we beat them without any problems.

'The strange thing for me was the sense of anti-climax. I thought to myself, "Is this what it's like?" I thought it would open up some promised land. We went to the Cat and Cage and nobody knew what to do. That was before the time sponsors looked after everything. The reward was the fulfillment of a lifetime's ambition.

'It was a massive thing for the people. Derry is a huge football county. So, when we won the All-Ireland, people were delirious. To this day people speak about that time – by talking about winning the All-Ireland to fix other things by. I especially recall people queuing for the Credit Union because nobody worked for two weeks. We had a banquet in the Guild Hall. It was organised by people who wouldn't know if a football was pumped or stuffed. It was like the end of the world. The spiritual side was very important. To Kerry, winning an All-Ireland is just routine but to Derry it was cathartic. At last we could take our place among the football counties with self-respect.'

It can be exclusively revealed that, despite the amateur ethos, the Derry squad were the first to engage in pay for play when they got an unexpected reward for their achievements.

'Eamonn brought us to Ballymaguigan one night and said, "Lads, there's someone who wants to speak to you." In comes Phil Coulter. He was wearing a lemon suit and a lime tie. He presented each of us with a signed photo of himself and a commemorative copy of *The Town I Loved So Well*. The reason he gave us that was that when *The Sunday Game* came to film our celebration the night of the final we sang that song for them. On the cover of the record, Phil had his arm outstretched in a Liberace pose. It was ghastly. It is gathering cobwebs somewhere in my house. There are few signs in my home that I was ever a footballer. My mother has my All-Ireland medal and three National League medals.'

Derry's first All-Ireland win in 1993 was a source of great pride for Jim McKeever, their legendary player from the 1950s.

'It was very emotional when the full-time whistle went,' he says. 'The magnificent players on that team personified not only their own accomplishments, but the sacrifices of generations of Derry people who made that moment possible. I was very conscious of all the people who organised games and travelling arrangements down through the years, regardless of personal inconvenience or harsh weather. Without those people, the sequence that led to Derry's historic success would not have started. The fact that all the years of disappointment have been wiped out with the 1993 side gave me a certain amount of pleasure. It was a unique occasion. The first time that something great happens is special, because there can never be another first time.'

Like so many others, Joe Brolly expected more great things from that Derry team.

'I remember John O'Keeffe wrote in *The Irish Times* that, "This Derry team will dominate Gaelic football for the next ten years,"' he says. 'We had a lot of advantages like our midfield. Brian McGilligan was astonishing. There was never a tougher or better athlete than him. He never did weights but he was like granite. Brian was as tough as they come. His big break in football came from Kevin Heffernan. Hurling is big in Derry and Brian started out as a hurler. After he was appointed manager of the Irish Compromise Rules side, Heffo saw him playing hurling one day in Dublin and was very taken by his physical presence and said, "Can you play football, son?" Brian replied, "I'll give it a try, sir." The rest is history.

'Anthony Tohill loved playing with him because Brian did all the donkey work while Anthony played all the football. Tohill was a brilliant finisher. He always wanted to be a professional athlete. He is a huge physical specimen. As a teenager he had gone to Australia to try his luck at Aussie rules but came back when Derry started to motor. I think Eamonn Coleman was keen to get him back. When he was twenty-four or twenty-five he went on trial to Manchester United. At one stage he was playing in a training match with the United squad. Although there was a hundred million pounds' worth of talent on display, Anthony was doing sliding tackles and bashing into people. Andrei Kanchelskis went to Alex Ferguson and said, "Take that f**ker off before he kills someone." Fergie went over to him and said, "Son, I think we've just got to you a bit late in life."

'Anthony was a very popular and respected member of the squad. At one stage we were all in a bar when Anthony got his results from university. When we heard he got first class honours someone piped up, "The bastard's got no chink in his armour."'

After the high of 1993, Derry made an early exit in the Championship in 1994.

'Down beat us in an epic game in Celtic Park,' says Brolly. 'Eamonn Coleman took them for granted because we had beaten them by eighteen or twenty points the year before. Eamonn positively laughed at the notion that Down could beat Derry in Celtic Park. Mickey Linden kept them in it in the first half. Then in a classic smash and grab, they beat us with a late goal. After one game we were gone.

'There had been a lot of discomfort in Derry about Eamonn. He was a players' man, not a County Board man. He would have literally told them to f**k off and there was a lot of jealousy. All of a sudden he was sacked. In his first year he won a National League. Derry's previous league title was in 1947. In his second year he won an All-Ireland. He had won a minor All-Ireland himself as a player and had coached Derry to an All-Ireland minor title, with his son Gary as captain. He had coached an All-Ireland under-21 team. When he was sacked it killed the spirit within the team. It had been a very special group but Eamonn's sacking spread a poison through the team. It is a fact that three or four members of the County Board undid all the good work. It is also a fact that they weren't the slightest bit interested in winning All-Ireland titles or having success because that put them under the spotlight. They were only interested in running things and getting tickets. That was their mentality. They screwed him. It was impossible to pick up the pieces. Mickey Moran stood on in controversial circumstances. He never had the team with him. We won the National League the following year on auto-pilot. The interest was gone.'

Lovely Leitrim

Leitrim for Croke Park. Mayo for Croagh Patrick. (Sign outside a church in Leitrim after their Connacht title in 1994.)

Gaelic football needs every nostalgic prop it can muster and, when many of the controversies of today are forgotten, the powerful grip Leitrim's Connacht final triumph exerted on the popular imagination will never vanish. In his radio commentary, Micheál O'Muircheartaigh said it was easy to imagine the Leitrim fans that had gone on to their eternal reward leaning over the banisters in heaven watching the drama unfold. The images leaned against their thoughts until they could no longer resist giving themselves up to their embrace.

At the centre of that famous victory was Mickey Quinn, who played under-age football for Leitrim for five years, twenty years for the senior team (1978-1997) and nine years with the over-40s. He made his senior inter-county debut in 1978.

Glamour was alien to much of Quinn's own career.

He says, 'One day we were playing Mayo in Charlestown and there was such a gale blowing that, at one stage, when the Mayo goalie kicked out the ball it got caught in the wind and blew back over the inline for a forty-five.'

Throughout the 1980s, Leitrim experienced nothing but disappointment.

'In 1983 Galway beat us by a point in injury time,' recalls Quinn. 'I was sick the night before the All-Ireland final when

Galway were preparing to meet Dublin knowing we could have and should have beat them, but we hadn't the confidence and lacked quality in the full-forward line.'

Things changed for the better for Quinn personally and Leitrim when P. J. Carroll became manager.

'We went on a fourteen- or fifteen-game unbeaten game run which was very unusual for Leitrim and won an All-Ireland B final in 1990,' says Quinn. 'I won an All-Star that year and, as it was the first one in Leitrim, it caused a lot of excitement in the county and gave me a new lease of life even though I had two or three trips with them as replacements at that stage. It meant everything to me because it was always my burning ambition. Winning an All-Ireland with Leitrim was too much to hope for. We were playing Leinster in the 1984 Railway Cup in Ballinalsoe when the journalist David Walsh told me that I had missed out on an All-Star the year before by just one vote.'

The year 1994 was one that was never to be forgotten for Leitrim. Their nearest neighbours had to be dealt with first.

'Roscommon had been the biggest bogey team for us,' says Quinn. 'We had great battles with them in previous years but, no matter what we threw at them, they always seemed to have the upper hand. That spring, though, we relegated Roscommon from our division in the National League in Carrick-on-Shannon. We knew then we could beat them and we did in the Connacht Championship. In previous years we should have beaten them but that year they should have beaten us. We went on to take Mayo in the Connacht final. Although we made a dreadful start, we had great belief and that was in large measure due to our manager.'

From the outset, Quinn and Declan Darcy had almost a mutual admiration society.

Quinn says, 'Declan was playing in a Connacht trial and was marking Tomás Tierney. By that stage Tierney was a household name and Declan was just a whippersnapper that nobody had heard of outside Leitrim. At one stage Declan went into him like an express train and sent him sprawling. I said to him afterwards, "Did you know who you were doing that to?" I think though it showed everybody that reputations meant nothing to Declan and he was going to hold his own in any company.'

Aughawillan, like Leitrim, linked Darcy with Quinn. Quinn admits to playing a leading role in the infamous 'Battle of the Fog'.

'Aughawillan were playing Clann na Gael in the Connacht club championship but the match shouldn't have gone ahead,' he says. 'The fog was so bad you couldn't see the goalie kicking out the ball. Things heated up when two of our players were hit. I think it was me who really started it off. I "had a go" at Jimmy McManus and soon the whole set of players, subs and supporters were involved. The referee had a hard time getting law and order back but the game was a great battle in every sense.'

The match did have an amusing postscript though.

'Jerome Quinn played for Aughawillan against Clann na Gael that day and really dished it out to some of the Clann lads and developed a reputation as a hard nut. That was one of the reasons why Aughawillan versus Clann was renamed "the Provos versus the Guards". We were playing Roscommon in the Connacht Championship in 1990 and, before the match, P. J. Carroll had an unusual mind game planned. He said, "Jerome Quinn, they all think you're f**king mad in Roscommon. What you need to do is pick up a clump of grass, stick it in your mouth and eat it in front of your marker's face. He'll sh*t himself." Jerome was wing half-back and was marking a lovely, skilful player. Sure enough, Jerome did as he was told and you could see the Roscommon player's legs turn to jelly.'

Declan Darcy should have been another Ross O'Carroll-Kelly. Growing up in Sandymount in the heart of Dublin 4, an inhospitable even barren hinterland for the GAA, it was difficult to have foreseen in his childhood that he would become the face of Leitrim football's finest hour. The fact that both his parents were from Leitrim was the catalyst for his immersion into club football in the county, though initially the move was shrouded in controversy.

'I was playing illegally with Aughawillan,' says Darcy. 'I was not living or working there but I put my father's home place down as my address. Some people in other clubs didn't want me because I was giving Aughawillan an advantage but it was arranged by the club for me to play with Leitrim and that certainly made things easier.'

Darcy soon learned an important footballing lesson.

'I was marking Greg Blaney in a Railway Cup,' he says. 'I was just a nipper and, because I respected him so much, I was marking him very tightly and hanging on to him for dear life. Eventually he lifted me with an elbow and it was lights out. I couldn't see a thing. Greg is a dentist but he knocked out two or three of my back teeth. He remembers the incident well and we've often laughed about it since. It taught me an invaluable lesson that when you are marking a top player you can't be hanging out of him. Finbarr Cullen famously found out the same thing marking Paul Curran. I learned that day that you don't cross the line and the next time I played on Greg, I marked him very differently.'

Things moved up another gear for Darcy when John O'Mahony became county manager.

Darcy says, 'The first thing was that he came. Before he did so he had seen us play when he was Mayo boss and we beat them out the gate in Carrick-on-Shannon so he knew what we could do. When he agreed to manage us we knew that he was coming because he believed something was going to happen.'

O'Mahony's Midas touch worked its unique magic in 1994. Mickey Quinn believes that a major catalyst for Leitrim's taste of glory was the management of John O'Mahony: 'He is a very tough trainer. He took everybody back because he drove us so hard.

'There were evenings that we would turn up for training in Kells that would be so wet that you wouldn't let your dog out in it. We'd be wondering if he would send us out in the absolute deluge but he would be out just in a T-shirt and tracksuit setting up the bollards. We'd be thinking, "This guy is off his rocker", but he was setting us an example. Then he stood in the corner and blew the whistle and we came out. There was always method to his madness. He brought us to train on the biggest sand dunes in Sligo and often there would be no hot showers afterwards but that toughened us up and then we were ready to move on to the next phase.

'One thing is attention to detail. He had music for us on the bus to games, like Queen's 'We Will Rock You'. I remember the All-Ireland semi-final against Dublin in 1994. Every line on the pitch I looked at that day John had a water carrier, so that any time I wanted water I always had at least one in my vision.

'What it took for us to win a Connacht Championship was massive. Winning an All-Ireland is nothing to Kerry because they are used to it but winning a Connacht title was a huge burden for us mentally because we had never won one. John

O'Mahony brought a psychologist on board, Frank Cogan. He started off by getting us to set goals. Then before our first game, in his distinctive Scottish accent, he asked what score we would concede. We said seven points. He asked, "Why not no goal and no point?" When we started to giggle he asked again, "Why not?" Each time we came up with a reason he came back and asked, "Why not?" Then when he asked us how much we would score we said, "2-10". He asked us, "Why not 7-24?" We all laughed and again he came back with, "Why not?" Then each time we offered a reason he again replied, "Why not?" Eventually we started to think, "Why not?" Then he split the defenders into one group, the forwards into another and got us to come up with our individual goals. The psychologist would then board the team bus about twenty minutes before we reached the ground on match days and that reinforced the messages he was putting across.

'John was brilliant at getting into the head of individual players. Colm McGlynn was a great full-forward for us but he always liked to think he was a bit special. He told John one night that he could not train one evening.

'"Why?"

'"I have exams in college. I can't train Thursday either."

'"Why?"

'"I have exams in college."

'"Well when are you free?"

'"Ten o'clock on Wednesday night."

'"Okay I will meet you in Ringsend at ten o'clock."

'John traveled all the way to Dublin and ran the sh*te out of him. Colm never asked for special treatment again. That's the way John was. What he did for Leitrim was priceless.'

Declan Darcy also believes O'Mahony was crucial: 'One

thing is his man management and the belief that he gives you. He was very good at talking to players. In 1994 he told me that he didn't want to see me in a chipper, not that I was into that anyway. After we won the Connacht final he told me he didn't want to see me drinking because I was the public face of the team and had to project the right image for the lads.

'I remember a very tight game against Galway in Carrick-on-Shannon and we got a potentially decisive free about forty yards out. Two or three of our lads ran over to take it but John came running to the sideline and roared at the top of his voice, "Dec, I want you to take it." He believed in me to score this vital kick and, because he believed in me, I had confidence that I would. To an outsider it looked a pressure kick but I felt totally calm because of what Johnno had said. It was very emotional when John left – both for us and for Johnno.'

One of the iconic images of the year was Declan Darcy, as captain of the Connacht champions, holding the Nestor Cup with Tom Gannon who captained Leitrim to their only previous Connacht title in 1927. That was the start of an unforgettable adventure for Darcy.

'I stayed in the Bush Hotel in Carrick the night after the game,' he says. 'The next morning the receptionist apologetically rang me and said she was being hounded by somebody who wanted to speak with me on the phone. "Who is it?" I asked. "Pat Kenny."

'I thought somebody was winding me up, but, sure enough, it was Pat who came on the line and asked, "Where are you?" I said, "I'm in bed." He asked, "With who?" I said, "With the Nestor Cup."

'After the interview I went out on the main street and was surprised at how quiet it was. I had expected a bit of a buzz. I went across the road to the pub and when I opened the door it was like a nightclub. The place was jammed and hyper and it was only ten-thirty in the morning. Shannonside radio were broadcasting live in the corner.

'My abiding memory of the whole thing came that day in Ballinamore. When my father was asked where he was from he had always said, "West of the Shannon" rather than Leitrim. We did a tour of the county and it was very special. All the players went to their own clubs. The emotion was unbelievable but, as someone who grew up in Dublin 4, I didn't have that local base. I found myself on the stage in Ballinamore not sure what to do when my father ran on, grabbed the cup and threw it in the air like a mad lunatic. It was raw and real. It was about passion and pride. It meant so much to him. It is an unbelievable memory that will stay with me forever.'

Although Leitrim were to lose the All-Ireland semi-final, Darcy was literally to leave his mark.

He recalls, 'As captain when I shook hands with John O'Leary, as the photo shows, I was so fired up I nearly squashed John's hand. He told me afterwards that I nearly broke two or three of his fingers and that he thought I had done it deliberately but it was just because I was pumped up.

'It was a fantastic achievement for the team and when I led them out on to Croke Park and, although it meant a lot to the county, I was really thinking about all those training sessions we had suffered in Strand Hill. This was the reward for the sacrifices, the endless travel to training sessions and the blood, sweat and tears.

'For Leitrim people, just to be in Croke Park one day in their lives was such a proud moment for them. That's the magic of the GAA. It is so much more than football.

———————

'We didn't do ourselves justice in the semi-final and the next year we left the game against Galway behind us in the Connacht Championship. If we had won I believe we would have retained the Connacht final and given a much better showing in the All-Ireland semi-final. I know Armagh's Enda McNulty and he often says that they should have won more than one All-Ireland. I tell him that they were lucky to win one because it is so hard to make a breakthrough when you have no tradition of winning.'

Although Leitrim were not to reach those dizzy heights again, they did find themselves in the headlines once more.

Darcy says, 'We were playing Mayo on a live game for RTE and a melee broke out and the Mayo manager John Maughan came running on to the pitch in his shorts. He passed a comment to Gerry Flanagan and Gerry floored him. In our view, Maughan definitely deserved it but it's probably not the thing to do on live TV. Pat Spillane and the pundits were outraged but it did Flanagan's reputation no harm in Leitrim.'

The Clare Champions

Some Roman warriors who knew they were about to lose a battle killed themselves rather than be condemned to defeat: *damnata iam luce ferox* – 'furious by daylight, having been condemned.' This intense desire to win was replicated by Ger Loughnane – a man born under the sign of contradiction.

When you meet him for the first time you have preconceptions because you've been watching him for years walking up and down the sideline. The fist is clenched and he has that look on his face that says, 'You mess me with me and I'll split your head open.' When I was a boy, Neil Diamond had a song called 'What A Beautiful Noise'. In recent years, my favourite sound has become Ger's big, hearty, belly laugh. He's a man who laughs hard and laughs often. It is a shock to find how relaxed he can be. There are times when you think that behind it all he's just a pussycat, but in his time as Clare and Galway managers Ger had a 'few scrapes' and, as soon as he starts to talk about them, the lion roars again. In fact, there were many stories Ger told me that had the hairs standing on the back of my head. But the biggest shock I got was to discover that this man was once an altar boy. Is it any wonder the Catholic Church has had so many problems in recent years?

During a game, communication is almost impossible on the field because of the noise. Loughnane had to rely on his players for leadership on the field. Anthony Daly was the natural choice to be the team's spokesman and captain. As a player, he deserved all the plaudits heaped upon him with a string of performances as captivating as the sport can offer. Daly had to be what he was: an excellent craftsman with a superb fighting spirit and the stamina of body and mind to cope with the long haul. While his famous speeches and innate media skills might have seemed to be his obvious credentials, Loughnane chose him for his ability in the dressing-room, given his flair to help players cope with frus-tration and disappointment. 'Dalo' was adept at deflecting any anger by giving his team-mates a chance to air their complaints.

Early in 1995, Clare fans were anything but optimistic. Even when one major disappointment followed another, hope and dream always lived side by side in Clare. In '95 Daly's team was poised to react hungrily to a disappointing first half of the year.

'I think that after the League final in 1995, ninety per cent of Clare followers felt that is it – we can't take any more trouncings,' he says. 'You couldn't blame them. Although we hadn't been trounced on the scoreboard, in hurling terms we were. Coming out after the game one supporter said, "Kilkenny were a different class." This massacre came on the back of major defeats in the two previous years in Munster finals. When Ger Loughnane spoke about us winning the Munster final none of the fans believed him.

'There were fewer than 15,000 fans at our first game in the championship and most of them were from Cork. Even when we beat Cork and the Munster final was jammed, it was mostly filled with Limerick people.'

Never was Daly's role as captain more clearly illustrated than the Munster final in '95.

'Everybody in Clare was convinced that we had no chance of winning that game because, two weeks before, we had played Galway in a challenge match in Shannon and we bombed,' he says. 'On the day of the final we stopped in the hotel in Cashel for a cup of tea. We were on the way into Thurles and just when we came to the bridge, the place was crowded with supporters wearing the Limerick colours. A few of them shouted at us, "What a waste of time." They were sure they were going back to the All-Ireland final. Straight away I said, "We'll show ye whether it's a waste of time or not." A small thing like that can make a big difference. Some of the lads afterwards said it made a difference. I'm not so sure.

'The scenes when we won the Munster final in 1995 were something to treasure. Although there weren't that many Clare people there, they were absolutely fanatical.

'Bringing home the cup was absolutely incredible. There was a wonderful feeling of achievement and togetherness.

We came over the bridge in Limerick and that was fantastic but we were on our own because there wasn't a Clare person in sight. We thought it would be just a bit of a celebration in Ennis.

'When we got to Cratloe we couldn't get through the crowds. It was such a scene of celebration and sporting hysteria. We couldn't even get to Shannon because we were a mile late getting to Ennis but they had bonfires for us and everything. Clare FM was well established and it was putting out bulletins of our progress, so everybody knew where we were.

'In 1992 the Clare footballers had won the Munster title and that generated great celebrations, but hurling was the game that had produced all the disappointments. This was a real break away from all that. You have to remember that, when people talked about winning in Clare, all they meant was winning the Munster final. The All-Ireland final wasn't even contemplated because the Munster final had always been such a stumbling block.

'For myself personally, it was winning the Munster final and the satisfaction out of that. The boys often talk about how unprepared the Clare people were for our win. We got back to Clarecastle and there was no podium. I had to stand on the top of the bus. My mother was an avid bingo goer to Ennis on Sunday nights and all I said was it must be a very special night when my mother wasn't away to bingo.'

Daly's team-mate Seánie McMahon echoes this sentiment.

'Personally, the memory that will stand out was when we won the Munster final,' he says. 'I never dreamt of All-Irelands, just the Munster final and I remember when we won I just went down on my knees and said, "Thank You, God." It was such a relief. There were lots of tears shed – but

102

for once Clare people were crying tears of joy. It brought a huge uplifting of Clare people.'

Clare's 1995 triumph was hurling's equivalent of the ugly duckling who turned into a swan. To gain an insight into the inner secrets of this transformation, I trekked the famous hill of Shannon in the company of ace forward Jamesie O'Connor.

'On a typical Tuesday or Thursday night we would meet in Wolfe Tones,' he says. 'Mike (McNamara) would do some upper-body exercises with us like sit-ups. Then we would don the woolly hats and head here to the hill. We would park in front of the school where the two Lohans went. Generally you would approach the session with a sense of absolute dread. You could sense the lethargy and you would troop from the cars practically crying. Everybody felt equally the same way. Mike Mac would then break your heart by saying, "Right lads – we've forty to do" and you would sink even deeper into your boots. I would be one of the guys that would be in reasonably good shape and I would be better equipped to run up the hill than Sparrow or Liam Doyle or fellas that dreaded physical training. Mike was psychologically trying to break you even before the session started, by telling you how many you had to do.

'Mike was on top of the hill with the whistle, Tony Considine was standing in the middle and Ger was on the bottom starting us off. When we reached the top of the hill you would be gasping for oxygen. I don't know what altitude training is like but at the top of the hill the air always seemed to be that bit thinner. It was a mental thing and a physical thing. By the last four or five rounds there would be water on top of the hill but you would be unable to take it. On some occasions you would be literally incapable of starting the car. Your head would be spinning and your mind was gone.

That training was very important to us, particularly coming into the last ten/fifteen minutes of big games – when most matches are won.

'We set out to take the league seriously and won our first five games and qualified for the league semi-final. We went for a weekend down to Killarney for a kind of bonding session and I think that might have been the making of us. We had a really great weekend. I remember speaking with Brian Lohan and at three or four in the morning lying awake talking to him and asking him, "Did you ever think you'd be like Cyril Lyons and play for ten years and win nothing?" His response was, "Jesus, we'll win something," and I remember rolling over thinking he was dead right.

'People were in euphoria after we won the Munster final. Sixty-three years was a long wait. People couldn't believe it was actually happening. I remember towards the end of the game, as people started climbing in towards the pitch, thinking, "Jesus, get off the pitch or he'll abandon it." I thought some catastrophe was in store for us.

'With that win, a massive weight was lifted off the county. Clare people had travelled to so many Munster finals: minor, under-21 and senior, and always come home with their tails between their legs. I had the cup the next week and I brought it to Don Ryan, who lived just around the corner from my parents' shop in Ennis. He was a diehard Clare fan, who had been the first fan to every match for years and years. I said that he might like to take a look at that. He just broke down in tears and I said, "I will call back later." That's what it meant to the guy.'

So how important does Jamesie feel Loughnane was to Clare's success?

'He was looking for a particular type of player – a player

who wouldn't roll over. If a guy was going to roll over here in Shannon then he wouldn't survive in Croke Park. Much of the training was psychological. They were testing you and looking for a certain reaction. They were looking for a type of guy who would bite his lip and grit his teeth and say, "I'll prove you wrong." Ger would have said tough things to me. The guy who used to mark me in training was Christy Rusty Chaplain and I would have awful battles with him. I remember one wet evening he was cleaning me out and Loughnane would let out this roar, "Good man, Christy – you have him cleaned." I'm saying under my breath, "You bollox", but at the same time gritting my teeth to win the next ball. That's what he was doing. If you sunk down in your boots you were going to be no good to him in Croke Park. That was part of his psychological approach.

'I used to live in Galway and, ten days before the All-Ireland final, I went down to a summer camp in Woodford. One of the men running it was Paddy Kirwan from Offaly. Paddy is a fierce hurling man but I just got a sense from him that he didn't rate us. Ger said to us a week before the game that, if we made a battle out of it, nobody was going to beat us and I remember thinking he was dead right.

'Another thing that was crucial to his contribution was in driving us on to get the hunger back two years later to win the second All-Ireland. I always think that first one was for the county. The second one was for the team.'

Clare's Brian Lohan is the greatest full-back of all time. Loughnane's summation of him is just three words: 'Simply the best.' Does Lohan reciprocate the compliment?

'Loughnane on the training field was a brute. He just dictated everything that you had to do and you did it or else you stood outside and watched other people doing it. So it was very simple – his way or no way. Nobody would have dared question it. Loughnane constantly did things that were to the benefit of the players and everything was for the benefit of the team. He was brutal but he was very honest.

'He didn't allow you to have feelings for him. You did what he asked you to do out of pure respect for him. When we did what he asked us to do we were winning matches – so that's why we kept doing what he said.'

Anthony Daly identifies one moment when Loughnane's contribution was particularly significant.

'No-one will ever forget the night the training was bad and Stephen McNamara had complained of a stomach bug and Loughnane brought us all back into the dressing-room because we were so lethargic in training,' he says. 'He gave a tyranny of a speech and began with me. "It starts with the captain." He lambasted me and then everybody else and eventually he came around to Stephen Mac and he hit him a kind of belt in the stomach and said, "Sick, Mac. Sick is coming out of Croke Park beaten." I think that was a turning point because we weren't going to settle for winning Munster – we were going to go all the way.'

Although it was only one step in a long climb which the team must make if there was any chance of surviving among the best in the country, Clare's Munster final victory was more feverishly acclaimed than any other in recent decades. Even when the small hairs stood on the back of his neck and the war-whoops of victory echoed all round him, Anthony Daly never imagined the attendant fanfare that might accompany it. It quickly became evident, though, that they had to forget about that game if they were to capture the All-Ireland title from the holders, Offaly.

'We were different people and there was a swagger in our

steps going into work and thus we were nearly like new men.

'The Sparrow and myself went for a swim the day before the final and I asked him what he thought and he said he thought we were going to win. I said I felt the same. I had bought in to the theory that it was our year. There was a bit of magic in the air in Croke Park that day. It just seemed the way things fell into place. I just felt that, on the day, Offaly got two fortunate goals but we never dropped our heads. We came out and hurled away and got the break with the goal two minutes from the end. Offaly got the goal just before half-time and everyone says that's a great time to get a goal but it is probably a better time to get one with two minutes to go.

'When the All-Ireland started, everything was going grand. Seánie McMahon scored two great points to set us off. We were doing everything we planned. It was a war of attrition. We were blocking them and hooking them.

'Then just before half-time disaster struck. Michael Duignan came along under the Cusack Stand and he seemed to try to lob the ball over the bar but it fell short. Fitzie (Clare's goalie David Fitzgerald) tried to control the ball with his hurley, which was unusual for him, but the sliotar skidded off his hurley and into the net. It looked like the classic sucker punch that could destroy us. If there was any fragile area in our make-up, that would undo us.'

This gifted team were suddenly buzzing and Clare were on their way to victory.

Croke Park takes you like no other place but add in Anthony Daly's famous victory speech to the emotional mix and it's a recipe for emotional release: 'There's been a missing person in Clare for eighty-one long years. Well, today that person has been found alive and that person's name is Liam McCarthy.'

Daly saw how much it meant to Clare people.

'I will never forget the colour the Clare fans brought to the game,' he says. 'That's when it all really took off. Donegal had brought it first in 1992 but in '95 it really took off. We take it for granted now.

'It was great going to the schools, just to witness the magic, the awe and the wonder but, to me, the most special part was meeting the older people. I remember meeting my brother's father-in-law crying in Thurles after we won. He could remember back to '55 and all the catalogue of Clare's heartbreaks. At the time I was so wound up and drained from games that I didn't fully appreciate it until later.'

Ger Loughnane saw Clare's victory in 1995 in spiritual terms.

He says, 'The win was for all those who wore the saffron and blue with pride down through eighty-one barren years, who gave their best for Clare with no reward in terms of medals, but who passed on the torch that lit the flame that burned so brightly on 3 September 1995.

'Every now and again something happens that brings the memories of '95 flooding back: memories of the colour, joy and excitement the Clare supporters brought, especially on the way home after victories in Croke Park with the flags hanging out of the windows. When I think back, it was seeing in their eyes how much it meant for Clare to win and in latter years to hearing people talk about those who had passed on that they were glad they were there to see Clare winning an All-Ireland. That was the great thrill of it and worth more than any medals. That was what brought such great contentment – that I think will last a lifetime. It showed to everybody that hurling was more than a game. It was a movement of people, a liberation of people in Clare.

'To misquote William Wordsworth, I would sum up it up like this:

> *For oft, when on my couch I lie*
> *In vacant or in pensive mood,*
> *They flash upon that inward eye*
> *Which is the bliss of solitude;*
> *And then my heart with pleasure fills,*
> *And dances with the Croke Park thrills.'*

Dancing at the Crossroads

The joy in Clare in 1995 was replicated by Wexford fans in 1996. After he retired from playing, Martin Quigley immediately took charge of piloting Wexford's fortunes. His new role was no bed of roses.

'Managing is not nearly as enjoyable as playing,' he says. 'When you are playing you only have to worry about your own job but, when you're the manager, you have to worry about everybody else. There are so many things outside your control as a manager, from players getting injured to bad refereeing decisions that can cost you a game, that you can feel things are outside your control. Once I retired as a player, I missed the buzz of it and I got involved in managing Wexford almost immediately. With the benefit of hindsight, I should have taken a break from the game and turned to management later but, while hindsight is great, it's not any good when you have to make a decision. I should have given myself a bit of distance from the switch to playing and managing. It's hard to have a clear perspective when emotionally you're too close to the centre of things.'

How would he assess his own term in charge of Wexford?

'I'm not the best person to judge. Ultimately a manager is

judged by results. In my three years in charge we got to two league finals but we won nothing. I suppose, though, any manager is only as good as the players he has at his disposal.'

Quigley was replaced as Wexford manager by Christy Keogh. Among Keogh's innovations was to enlist the services of Cyril Farrell to assist the team in their preparations for the Leinster Championship, particularly the clash with old rivals Kilkenny. The move did not have the desired impact as Kilkenny inflicted a heavy defeat on the Slaneysiders. How does Quigley react to the criticism that was aired at the time that, instead of rallying Wexford, Farrell's mere presence inspired Kilkenny?

'I wouldn't pay any heed to that sort of talk. Anyone who thinks that Kilkenny need Cyril Farrell's involvement to be fully motivated to beat Wexford in the championship knows nothing about hurling, and Kilkenny hurling in particular. Kilkenny had a strong team and beat us badly. I don't think it would have made much difference who was managing us that particular year. The one thing that Cyril's involvement did achieve was to dramatically heighten the expectations within the county. Not for the first time, though, they were to be cruelly dashed.'

In 1996, Wexford became the home of the Riverdance of Sport and the story of paradise regained. Why did they win the All-Ireland that year and not earlier?

'Expectations were low in 1996 because we had been beaten in the league semi-final. To me, the key match in 1996 was not the All-Ireland final but beating Offaly in the Leinster final. That really set them up as a team of winners. I think the supporters played a huge part in Wexford's win – almost as much as the team itself. It was fascinating to see the way the support snowballed in the county throughout the championship. It was said there were 8,000 Wexford fans at the Kilkenny match, but there were 40,000 there for the final.

'I think there were two crucial factors to explain why Wexford won that year. Firstly, there was Liam Griffin and the passion, motivation, organisation and leadership he gave to the team. Secondly, there was Damien Fitzhenry. I don't want to cast any aspersions on anybody but Wexford had been waiting for a long time for a goalie up to that standard. He was the best goalie in Ireland in my opinion. If I had to pinpoint one player on the pitch who meant the difference between victory and defeat in 1996, it would be him.'

The Boys From the County of Armagh

Armagh's 2002 All-Ireland final triumph was memorable. John Evans, trainer of leading Carlow club team Eire Og, famously said some of his team he wouldn't insult by sending them to a sports psychologist and others he wouldn't insult the sporting psychologist with by sending them to him. One of Ireland's leading sports psychologists, Enda McNulty, was crucial to the 'orange revolution'.

He says, 'I started playing for Armagh in 1996. Myself and Aidan O'Rourke and Barry Duffy were asked on to the Armagh panel at the same time. I remember we got a phone call to the house and the two boys were out on the drink and arrived back at the house at three or four in the morning in very good form to say the least. So let's say I had a struggle to make them believe me that we were really on the panel. There was a bit too much partying done after that. There was a door broken and a window broken. The next morning I had to break the news to the two boys that we were required to go to training that night. A phone call was made that afternoon saying we had a prior engagement because the two boys were in a very bad way and we started off the following Thursday night.

'Brian McAlinden and Brian Canavan were coaching at the time and they probably haven't got due credit for what they have done. They did a massive job between 1996 and 2001. They took us from been the whipping boys of Ulster football to a side that was a year away from winning an All-Ireland. Brian McAlinden, in particular, deserves a lot of credit: the discipline, the ethos, the work ethic he created is probably still in the squad. I think he should have got a lot of credit.

'We won an Ulster title in '99, beating Down who had defeated us so often. I wouldn't even say we were second-class citizens – we were third-class citizens when compared with Down because of all their titles. It was much more special to win the Ulster that year than it was in '08 for Armagh because we had won it so often at that stage.'

The year 2000, though, would bring heartbreak for Armagh when they lost an All-Ireland semi-final replay to eventual champions Kerry.

'We knew we were good enough to beat Kerry that time but I'd say we just weren't smart enough,' says McNulty. 'I think if we had a bit more cuteness on the pitch we would have won either of those games. The master Maurice Fitz created all sorts of havoc when he came on as sub in both games. Looking back, if he had been there in 2002 he could have done something special, either a score or a pass, to win the game for Kerry. Losing in extra-time in a replay was shattering but, on reflection, it was a positive thing. It made us stronger as individuals and as a team.

'In 2001 we were playing Galway in the All-Ireland quarter-final. We were doing a warm-up in Na Fianna's pitch and were due to get a garda motorcycle to lead us to Croke

Park. We were waiting on the coach for over half an hour, maybe forty minutes, when the motorcycle finally came. We got to Croke Park ten minutes before the match. We had no time for a warm-up or a team talk. I remember pulling on my shorts and socks very quickly and, as I ran on to the pitch, I saw Barry O'Hagan coming out and he was still in his jeans. I remember thinking, "How are we going to win an All-Ireland? This fella isn't even togged out here." We had to spring out into the tunnel and I remember thinking, "There's something not right here." We gave Galway a seven-point lead and only lost by a point and Galway went on to win an All-Ireland. If only we had a bit more composure, we would have taken our time and realised that the match couldn't have started without us. Had we had that bit of composure and experience, we would have won that game.'

Joe Kernan would bring Armagh to football's top table when he was appointed Armagh manager.

'The biggest thing that Joe brought to the table was belief,' says McNulty. 'When Joe walked into the Canal Court Hotel in December 2001 for his first team meeting with us, he had already won All-Irelands with Crossmaglen. So when he sat down with us you knew you were in the presence of a winner in Croke Park. Allied to that he had already played for Armagh in an All-Ireland final. Of course, when Joe walks into the room he brings a great presence because of his physique. All he said was, "Get me to Croke Park and I'll ensure ye win." You believed him. We knew we were on the edge of winning an All-Ireland and believed that Joe was the final piece of the jigsaw – and he was.

'We played Louth in the league in 2002 and Louth are always tough to play against in the league. I think we were level at half-time. I remember vividly Joe saying to us at the break, "Do you think that just because I have won an All-Ireland with Crossmaglen that I have a magic wand? Boys, there's no magic wand. You have to make more blocks than you have ever made in your life. You have to kick the ball in to the forwards better than you ever have in your life. It's not about anything that I can say or weave. It's about what ye do. It has to do with what ye do in the middle of the game." That struck a chord with me.'

McNulty feels that it was a variety of factors coming together, like converging lines, that paved the way for the team's ultimate success.

'I believe sport is the kaleidoscope of a whole range of small things made perfect,' he says. 'I think that is the road Armagh went down.

'In 2002 Armagh started to get more of all the small things right than all the other teams. We got some unbelievable guys in from a mental sessions point of view. We worked on team cohesion and did some good bonding sessions. The other thing we did was to bring in Darren Campbell from basketball for statistical analysis – which was on a different level because of his basketball background. I remember him handing me a sheet before we played Tyrone in the 2002 Ulster Championship with a diagram showing me exactly where Peter Canavan received every ball on the pitch in the previous five games. From a mental preparation point of view, that was great for me. Not only that it was pinpointing to me when he liked to get the balls in those positions – so as the game went on did he like to move out or in. That was invaluable. Then we went on a training week in the sun – which was very innovative then, though everybody knows it now. Apart from the bonding, it was a very serious trip. Not only was there no alcohol or nights out, there wasn't even a discussion about nights out or alcohol. It was very tough training and the mental resolve that trip gave us was important.

'We were walking up the hill in Clones like an army before the Tyrone game. Everyone knew we had been on the trip to the sun and one of the Tyrone fans shouted at us, "I don't see any suntan, lads." When Joe got us in the dressing-room he used that incident and said, "We'll show them a f**king suntan before the end of the match." That was the spark we needed.

'There were numerous small things. A nutritionist was brought in. Physical conditioning was brought to a new level, which probably reflected how driven the lads were. Joe brought a good team all around him. Every little detail was sorted out.'

Like the Clare hurlers in 1995, myths abound about the obsessiveness of Kieran McGeeney.

'There was a bit of a legend about Armagh that we got our motivation from Joe or Kieran,' says McNulty. 'I believe that motivation is something that comes from within and that all our boys were incredibly driven and didn't need anybody else to motivate them. They all have the Michael Jordan concept of "driven from within". That was there before Joe came. Joe nurtured that and it took a smart man to do that but Brian McAlinden had already inculcated that discipline before Joe came in. When Joe brought in a nutritionist, the Paul McGranes of this world are going to lap up everything that gives them an edge or anything that would make him a leaner, fitter or meaner athlete.

'Kieran is a leader. When he walks into a dressing-room and talks about dedication, players know that nobody is more dedicated than him but Kieran would be the first to admit that there would be other leaders like Paul McGrane, Diarmaid Marsden, the McEntees and guys who would have got very little credit like Andrew McCann, who drove to training every single night from Armagh to Dublin on his own. Andy was a leader in actions rather than words.

'Kieran is a great friend but, more than anything, he has a desire for excellence and is unwilling to settle for mediocrity in anything he does, from weight training, to nutrition, to skills training and you always know that, even when a game looks as if its gone, he's not going to throw in the towel.

'We were trailing by seven points to nil in that match against Galway in 2001 and they were on fire. I remember I was out of breath and Kieran was out of breath as we were both trying to tame the waves of Galway attacks. I can still hear in my ears Kieran saying, as he was out of breath, "Weather the storm, weather the storm, weather the storm." I'm sure he said this to the other boys too and we did, and very nearly hauled them back.

'We fancied ourselves, not in a joking way, as a band of brothers. We knew each other better than some of our own brothers because we spent so much time together. One of the things that encapsulate him is that in every one of the big games, when he talked to us in the circle before the game, he'd be nearly crying and that's how emotional he would be. He was very focused. After we won the Ulster finals he'd say, "Boys take a good look at the cup. That's the last time ye're going to look at it. The next cup we want to see is the All-Ireland." He was very good at bringing guys down to earth. He would be very good at calling a spade a spade. If one of the guys was not pulling his weight he'd say, "What the f**k is going on here? You're dossing, Enda", or "Oisín, you're not up to your own high standards. I'm disappointed in you." Because he was able to walk the walk you could never argue with that.

'Towards the end of my career I was club training with Kieran at Na Fianna. Paul Grimley was taking the session and he was doing a blocking session with us. Kieran, at thirty-six years of age, was throwing himself at every ball, so that his teeth and nose were literally on top of it. There were no half measures. Every single ball with him was all or nothing. Every single ball that night was like the famous block he made against Dara O Cinnéide in the 2002 All-Ireland final. That's something I sought to learn from him. I tried to lead the boys too much in a verbal sense during a match whereas all Kiernan's communication on the pitch would be through actions. Kieran would only ever say a few words on the pitch. I learned from him to taper down my words and to try to taper up my actions. He was a master of leading by actions on the pitch and by words off the pitch.

'Myself and my brother Justin and Kieran would have trained every Christmas Day since we were about fifteen, no matter what we would have done the night before. One Christmas Day Justin, my younger brother Patrick, myself, Kieran McKeever, Kieran and Kieran's brother Declan trained on the local pitch at home. We all had a good breakfast and some of the boys had a few beers the night before. We played a match: three on three. At this stage Kieran was the Kildare manager. I left the pitch that day totally physically drained and, with absolutely no exaggeration, having being hit harder than I would in a championship match. The three lads were giving everything in body and mind to be better than the three other fellas and Kieran was literally boxing the head of boys to get a ball. Even though he had retired, even though it was Christmas Day, he was unbelievably fit, unbelievably driven to win every f**king ball. It was Kieran who set up the game, with the pitch only twenty metres and small goals. Just to see the fella who wanted to be that good in that game, even though it had no consequences, more than anything else exemplifies his ethos, his attitude and his drive.'

McNulty is keen to pay tribute to the lesser lights of Armagh football.

'My own brother, Justin, never got very much credit,' he says. 'Yet he got his hands to three balls in the last fifteen minutes of the 2002 All-Ireland final and had a Kerry forward got possession even one of those times they could have scored and we would have been beaten. In the 2002 All-Ireland semi-final, when Ray Cosgrave's free struck the post, four Armagh backs jumped for it but only Dessie Farrell jumped for it in the Dublin side. It was Justin who got his hands to it and cleared it.'

Things came to a happy ending for Armagh in the All-Ireland final against Kerry in 2002.

'We knew we could win if we played to our potential and most of our team performed but didn't know we would win,' says McNulty. 'We knew our conditioning was better than Kerry's. We knew we were a tougher team than Kerry, despite what anybody said. There was bit of a myth about how good that Kerry team were and the press had built them up the way they'd built up Dublin in recent years. We weren't under any illusions, though, that it was going to be easy. We knew it would probably go down to one kick of a ball and that's what happened.

'It hadn't gone well in the first half but what hasn't gone into folklore is that we started off well. Then Kerry had a period of dominance and Oisín (McConville) missed a penalty and we

Goalmouth scramble: (from left) Mayo's Tom Acton and Cavan's Bill Doonan, Brian O'Reilly and Des Benson in the 1953 All-Ireland final.

Goalmouth action: (left to right) Umpire Nicky Rackard watches Sean Duggan (on his knees) and Mick Burke on the defence against Cork's Christy Ring and Liam Dowling in the 1953 All Ireland.

The clash of the ash: The rivalry between Tipperary and Galway illuminated hurling in the 1980s.

The Glens of Antrim: Dessie Donnelly showcases his skills.

Queen of the Ash: Kilkenny legend Angela Downey.

Lovely Leitrim: As Leitrim win an historic Connacht tie in 1994 Joe Honeyman keeps a close eye on Mayo's Anthony McGarry.

Jeepers Keepers: Down's Neil Collins saves Charlie Redmond's penalty in the 1994 All-Ireland final.

Simply the Best: Mayo legend Cora Staunton is closely marked by the Cork defence.

Rock DJ: DJ Carey confront's 'the Rock' Diarmuid O'Sullivan in the 1999 All-Ireland final.

It Started with a Kiss: Paul Flynn shows his affectionate side to
Kevin McManamon after Dublin's victory over Kerry in 2016.

© PAUL MOHAN / SPORTSFILE

Hat-trick hero: Clare's Brendan Bulger, left,
and Shane O'Donnell celebrates Shane's three
goals in the 2013 All-Ireland final replay.

© DAVID MAHER / SPORTSFILE

Magic Moments: Aidan O'Shea celebrates his goal against Donegal in the 2016 All-Ireland quarter-final.

Glad All Over: James McCarthy and Michael Fitzsimons rejoice after Dublin's victory over old rivals Kerry in the 2015 All-Ireland final.

Checkpoint: Kilkenny's Conor Fogarty gets close attention from Galway's David Burke, Cathal Mannion and Joe Canning in the 2015 All-Ireland final.

Master McGrath: Tipperary's John McGrath scores a goal against the Kilkenny in the 2016 All-Ireland final.

sort of went off the rails after that, but we finished well and went in at half-time trailing by only four points. I remember I personally went in at half-time, having slipped a few times on the pitch because I changed to studs rather than blades on my boots before the match, knowing I had to pick my game up. I started on Gooch Cooper and then moved on to Mike Frank Russell. I changed my boots at the break and that made a big difference in the second half. I remember looking around the dressing-room and thinking the mood in the team wasn't unbelievably spirited and the body language wasn't very strong. Joe came in and he started talking, "Listen boys, we weren't playing well. I played in the 1977 All-Ireland final and I remember going home on the bus crying and with all the boys crying. Do ye want to f**king be like me?" It wasn't really what he said next, but the impact of him physically throwing his loser's medal from that game against the shower and it rattling all over the wall, shattering into little pieces and the plastic breaking and the coin, or whatever it was, rolling all over the floor. I again vividly remember looking around and seeing the body language change immediately. Before that, everybody was sitting kind of slumped and suddenly everybody was sitting up as if we were all saying, "That's not going to be us." To use a term from sports psychology, we all went up into a "peak state". It was as if we were all saying to each other, "Jesus boys, we're going to win this." Then Kieran (McGeeney) brought us into a circle and you knew by looking into the boys' eyes that everybody was ready for a battle. There were other games when you'd look into the boys' eyes and you'd see a bit of uncertainty, but there was none at that stage.

'It was total euphoria when we won. The first thing that happens is hundreds of supporters jumping on top of you. I remember my little brother Patrick coming into the dressing-room afterwards and that was very important to myself and my brother Justin. It wasn't about realising my lifetime ambition, it was more about seeing the impact it had on the fans. I also remember the next morning it wasn't, "We're the men here." It was: "How can we win another one?" I remember feeling this drive to become the first Ulster team to win back-to-back All-Irelands since the great team of the 1960s. Going on a tour in south Armagh with all the bonfires lit was very powerful. The disappointing thing was that we only had one chat as a team without any hangers-on on the Wednesday afternoon, in Paddy McKeever's bar in Portadown. There had been a bottle of whiskey which had not been open since 1953 – when Armagh had been beaten in the All-Ireland final and we all had a drink out of it. It was very powerful because it was just us. There is a time to meet the supporters, family and friends but we had too many of those and not enough with just ourselves. Again there were too many hangers-on when we were presented with our All-Ireland medals. Any team I am ever involved with in the future, I will always get the boys together on their own, whether it's a win or a loss, have a few drinks and decide what happens next and have closure.'

The glory of 2002 was not to be repeated the following year.

'There's a lot of regrets about 2003,' says McNulty. 'Probably, on reflection, we played better football in 2003 than we did in 2002 but we made a big mistake. Two weeks before the All-Ireland final, we changed a few critical things. We changed the way we played the whole year, which was a critical mistake. We picked some players in different positions, which was a big mistake in hindsight. Not only the game plan and the positional changes, and I have spoken to

Kieran about this many times, but even more importantly was the change in our attitude. In all the games up to the final we had a "take no sh*t" attitude. We got stuck in and used our physical capacities, not in any dirty way, but harnessed the physical strength of the team: Francie Bellew, Kieran, the McEntees, Paul McGrane. In the run-up to the final there were a lot of articles in the press saying that not only were Armagh a dirty team, but over-the-top dirty. One of the articles stated that somebody was going to be left in a wheelchair because of the way we played. I remember reading that article, which was written by a Fermanagh player, and thinking to myself, "Oh dear. What's going to happen if some of our players are affected by this?" We probably subconsciously decided not to be as physical as we were in the previous games, which was an absolute disaster. Armagh's game was built on our physical nature and in a lot of games in 2002 we crushed teams just by our physical exertions and because we were so well conditioned we could easily deal with anyone else in that respect. Against Tyrone in 2003, we decided we were going to show the whole country that we could win by playing nice football. We tried to play less tough football and more champagne football. We needed to marry the skills with the physical dimension. We could also have been more intelligent on the day on the pitch – I'm not talking about management. For example, I was marking Canavan, who wasn't fit to walk and I marked him man to man. I should have come out in front of him and covered off Eoin Mulligan as well. So I am taking the blame for my own performance. The player I always knew I had to be unbelievably focused on when I was marking him was Peter Canavan. You knew you had to be incredibly switched on for every single ball because, if you even blinked, he would stick the ball in the net.

———————

'We must all shoulder the blame. I wouldn't blame the management for any of our defeats.

'We don't despise Tyrone though we have a great rivalry with them. You have to respect any team that wins All-Irelands. They were probably smarter than us in the games they beat us. I think the media have not picked up on the fact that winning Ulster so often has been a big disadvantage. We have won way more Ulsters but Tyrone have won more All-Irelands. Playing in the qualifiers gives them more games and, above all, the opportunity to iron out their weaknesses when they lose. When we lost we were knocked out and learned our weaknesses too late. It's not the only reason Tyrone have won more All-Irelands, but it has been an advantage to them. I would say the rivalry has been a positive thing for football.'

Westmeath Wonder

After his reluctant resignation as Kerry manager in October 2003, Páidí O'Sé said, 'I wouldn't rule anything in or out, but I couldn't see myself at the present time having the bottle to go in and train another team against the green and gold jersey.'

A week later, after taking over as Westmeath manager, he said, 'I now want to transfer all my professional allegiance to Westmeath and will endeavour to coach and improve the team and achieve success in the future.'

After an inauspicious league campaign, Pat Spillane was skeptical of Westmeath's chances in the league. On 18 April 2004, in his column in *The Sunday World*, he divided counties into various categories. One of his five no-hopers was Westmeath. He wrote, 'One would not normally expect a team who managed to avoid relegation from Division One to be parked here. But Westmeath's Houdini-like escape from relegation had precious little to do with their own ability and more to do with other counties shooting themselves in the foot, notably Longford, who would have stayed up and put Westmeath down had they managed to beat Fermanagh at home. This is looking like a temporary little management arrangement for Páidí.'

Spillane had no doubts before the championship but Westmeath were going nowhere. He may often be wrong but he never has any doubts!

To add insult to injury, Westmeath beat Dublin comfortably in the Leinster quarter-final. He had confidently slotted the Dubs in as number two, behind Laois, on his list of 'Glory Hunters'.

Flying High

Given the desire for success in Westmeath, people were not surprised when their County Board pulled out all the stops and, according to popular belief, their cheque book. Obviously, under GAA rules, it can only be for expenses and we all know how strictly they adhere to that rule, to lure Páidí to the county.

There were loads of rumours about all the money Páidí was getting from Westmeath for doing the job. Fans were reminded of the story of the rich GAA manager, the poor GAA manager and the tooth fairy, who are in a room with a £100 pound note on the table when the lights go out. When the light comes back on, the money is gone. So who took it? It's got to be the rich GAA manager, because the other two are figments of the imagination.

Páidí raised the profile of the game within the county, really putting Westmeath on the football map by taking them to the Leinster final in his first season and creating a buzz within the county and a feeling of togetherness and identity. More and more youngsters were wearing the Westmeath jersey.

The other story was that Páidí was supposed to be getting a helicopter to fly him from Kerry to Westmeath for training sessions. During his days on the Kerry team, Páidí had an amazing fear of flying. Paudie Lynch shared that fear and when they were travelling on trips abroad, the way the two of them coped was to get totally inebriated before the trip.

Someone had said, 'Look here Páidí, if it's your day to go, it's your day to go.'

Páidí turned around to him and said, 'But if it's the f**king pilot's day to go, he's going to bring me down with him.'

Westmeath's first Leinster title that year generated unrivalled excitement for fans of the maroon and white. Not surprisingly, the win generated some memorable stories. Páidí's nephew and All-Star footballer Tomás recalled his uncle's excitement each time the team bus would get close to Croke Park. He cited the example of a day when he was managing Westmeath. When they got into the dressing-room, Páidí sat down beside one of the lads and said, 'Jesus, you have to get out in front of your man quicker than the last day. The ball was going in fast and you were hanging back. You weren't coming out.'

His conversation partner looked at him stoically and said, 'Páidí, I'm the physio.'

Four

The Curious Incidents of the GAA in the Daytime

The bittersweet history of the GAA has produced many stories down the generations. This mixed grill goes behind the scenes to offer a unique perspective of the human and sporting episodes of glories, disappointments and dramatic deeds through a series of significant snapshots that help to illustrate the wide canvas that is the GAA.

For Whom the Bell Tolls

Gaelic football has a great history going back to the origins of the GAA, when Ballylongford were playing Tarbert. The match began on the first bell of the Angelus at twelve noon and they kicked the ball between the two parishes until six o'clock in the evening and when the second bell rang for the second Angelus. Whatever parish the ball was in, that parish lost the game. It was wonderfully ironic, because now whoever gets acquisition of the ball is the team that has the advantage.

Thy Kingdom Come

Although Limerick won the first All-Ireland in 1887, Gaelic football really came of age in 1903, when Kerry won their first All-Ireland. They beat Kildare in a three-game saga that grabbed the public imagination. Kerry won the first game but the match was replayed because Kerry had been awarded a controversial goal. So intense was the second game, which finished in a draw, that the referee collapsed at the end. On the third occasion, Kerry were comprehensive winners by 0-8 to 0-2.

The following year saw the first taster of what would become one of the great rivalries in the GAA, when Kerry beat Dublin to claim their second All-Ireland. By now Dick Fitzgerald, the first true star of Gaelic football, had emerged. He won five All-Ireland medals, captaining the team to All-Irelands in 1913 and 1914. Like many men of the time, Fitzgerald was active in the IRA, as the movement for Irish independence gathered momentum. After the 1916 Rising, he found himself interned with Michael Collins in Wales.

The Fab Four

In a time when marriage was for richer or poorer – or the land, Wexford became the first county to win the All-Ireland Senior Championship for a fourth successive year in 1918. In 1925 the National League was introduced, with Cork winning the hurling title and Laois winning the football title.

Desperately Seeking Sam

Kildare became the first winners of the Sam Maguire Cup in 1928. The new trophy was presented by friends of a Cork man, Sam Maguire, who had died the previous year and who had been a prominent figure in both the GAA and the Irish Republican Brotherhood.

Healing Hands

Gaelic football and hurling were always about more than sport in rural Ireland and in Kerry in particular. Professor Liam Ryan has pointed out that the GAA played a greater part than the Catholic Church in healing the many rifts which have threatened to rupture families and communities throughout Irish history in the last century.

Neighbours, for example who had shot at one another in the Civil War, displayed a greater desire to forgive and forget when gathered around the goalposts than when gathered around the altar.

A Load of Balls

Traditionally in Kerry there are three things that matter – football, sex and Mass with Mass and sex a distant second in the championship season.

In Kerry, football was called 'CAID' as it referred to the type of ball used. The ball was made from dried farm animal skins with an inflated natural animal bladder inside. They take football very seriously in Kerry but they also take politics very seriously. Sometimes their twin passions collide. This was probably most clearly illustrated in 1935, when Kerry refused to take part in the football championship because of the ongoing detention of prisoners in the Curragh.

Is There a Doctor in the House?

The famous Dr Eamon O'Sullivan trained Kerry on and off from the 1920s to the 1960s. He was a firm believer in all players keeping their positions. He actually wrote a book about his ideas called *The Art and Science of Gaelic Football*. He pointed out that for Gaelic football to be seen at its very best, all players should keep to their positions and that every tussle for the ball should be between just two players. He also said that good kicking and fielding would win out in the end. In the book are sentences like, 'There is no justification for finding a right-handed midfielder over on the left.' He took it to an extreme but he did win a lot of All-Irelands with Kerry.

Poetry in Motion

Brendan Kennelly is perhaps Ireland's best-loved poet. He was born in 1936 in Ballylongford. As a boy in one of his first matches, he found himself marking Pata Spring. Brendan knew he was good and as he lined up at the half-way line before the throw-in to mark Pata, he was really psyched up. Just before the ref threw in the ball Pata said, 'Do you know anything about sex?'

Brendan replied, 'I don't, Pata.'

Spring replied, 'Well I'll tell you about it now. It's like Kelly's bull and Sullivan's cow and that's how it happens and that's how you were born. Would you ever think about that now?'

The ball was thrown in and Brendan was left standing looking at Pata with his mouth open, pondering on the mysteries of the origins of life. It was a deliberate ploy to throw him. Pata had gone up the field with the ball while Brendan was rooted to the spot, burdened with the big questions of life.

Brendan's All-Ireland memories are not those of the standard Kerry footballer.

He claims the dubious privilege of losing an All-Ireland

minor final for Kerry in 1954. The referee, Bill Jackson from Roscommon, pulled him up for a foul on the left half-forward of the Dublin team – and he swears to God he never fouled him. They got a goal from it and then another goal from the kick-out. Kerry had been five points up with three minutes to go but they got two goals and Brendan was the cause of the first one. That has been the cause of many a nightmare for Brendan down the years.

The Keane Edge

Another famous Kerry writer, John B. Keane, was also a footballer of note.

As a child, John B. was enthralled by the thought of lifting the Sam Maguire Cup and captaining the Kerry team to win the All-Ireland. So much was he exercised by this that when his mother brought him to Mass one Sunday, as the priest lifted the chalice during the consecration, John B. turned to her and whispered, 'Why does he get to win the cup every Sunday?'

John B. always made the point that the most dangerous animal on the planet was a forty-year-old junior footballer with varicose veins. One of his many stories was about a Kerry County Junior Football final. By the time the final was played, most of the better players had returned to college as it was delayed due to the usual quota of objections. John B. claimed he was drafted in to play at corner forward, even though he was only about fifteen years of age. He gave a vivid description of his increasing trepidation as he went to take up his position and saw a 'seasoned' corner-back advancing to meet him. John B. was getting more intimidated with each step but was puzzled when the corner-back veered off at the last moment and went back towards his goalkeeper. He took out his false teeth and loudly told his keeper, 'Paddy, mind these in case I forget myself and eat someone.'

Last Man Standing
It is claimed that Skinny Meara from Toomevara, one of Tipperary's greatest-ever goalkeepers, trained in the summertime by opening the doors of his barn, standing in the great gap and stopping swallows from flying in and out.

The Curse
After Mayo won the All-Ireland in 1951, legend has it that it was then that the seeds of Mayo's woes were sown for decades to come. People tell it slightly differently but the core story is that, when they returned with the Sam Maguire Cup, they interrupted either a Mass or a funeral and the priest was so enraged that he put a curse on the team that they would never win another All-Ireland while any of that team were still alive.

The Man from Valentia
The most obvious reason for Kerry's success has been a phenomenal array of fantastic footballers, from Dick Fitzgerald to Paddy Kennedy to Gooch Cooper.

At the top of the footballing hierarchy in Kerry is Mick O'Connell, who is reputed to have left the dressing-room immediately after captaining Kerry to win the All-Ireland in 1959 and headed straight home for Kerry. Asked why he had to forgo the celebrations, he is said to have replied, 'I had to go home to milk the cows.'

Breaking Balls
In emphasising O'Connell's ability to strike a ball, John B.

Keane told a story which showed how ecumenical his appeal was for both the sacred and the profane.

'Mick was rowing from Valentia to the mainland and decided to practise his striking by taking a free from the boat. He hit it so hard that the ball burst on its journey. The cover of the ball landed outside the presbytery in Lisdoon-varna. The bladder landed outside a hoor house in Buenos Aires.'

A Woman's Heart

Throughout his long life, Mayo legend Paddy Prendergast has always been given interesting advice. As a teenager, he was told by his Latin and Irish teacher, 'Treat women like Kerry men do. Get them young, treat them rough and tell them nothing.'

Fingers

Dermot O'Brien, one of Gaelic football's great gentlemen and characters, captained Louth to their third senior All-Ireland title in 1957. Of course, he was equally famous for his powers on the accordion and his singing and, as one of Ireland's best-loved show business personalities, he was responsible for hits like 'The Merry Ploughboy'.

One of Dermot's favourite stories was about the Louth player of the 1950s who, on a visit to America, was chatted up by a woman in a bar. To put it very charitably, she was less than pretty and was as heavy as the combined weight of Louth's two midfielders. At first the Louth player was immune to the woman's charms. His attention, though, was captured when she told him that her mother had only two months to live and the dying widow had inherited a multi-million dollar fortune from her husband. Now the daughter stood to inherit everything. The Louth player was moved to action.

Two weeks later he was married . . . to the mother.

Father and Son

In his role as an analyst on RTE Joe Brolly defers to nobody, especially not to Colm O'Rourke. Away from the cameras, the only man Brolly defers to is his father, Francie.

'I played half-forward for Derry in the 1960s,' he says. 'Anyone who saw both of us play would agree that I was always a much better player than Joe ever was! The 1958 team had crumbled at that stage although Jim McKeever was in charge of us and he was both a wonderful man and coach. Although we had a star player in Seán O'Connell, we would never emulate the '58 side. I think that although Derry lost the final in 1958 it was important for the county to know that we could legitimately dream of eventually winning that elusive All-Ireland. At the time, though, we didn't think we'd have to wait so long to have that dream realised.'

Brief Encounters

Mayo have a great tradition of producing top-class characters and players. It has become a cliché for journalists and broadcasters to refer to a particular player's 'cultured left foot'. Yet every cliché has its truth and from the days when he first sprang to prominence with St Jarlath's College, Tuam, where he won All-Ireland Colleges' senior medals in both 1960 and 1961, there was never any doubt that John Morley's left foot merited this sobriquet. John was always getting slagged about his right leg but he always defended it by saying that, without it, he couldn't use his left.

The most famous incident in his illustrious career came

in the 1970 League final clash when Mayo defeated Down. John was playing at centre-half back, when a Down player grabbed him and tore his shorts. Just as he was about to put his foot into a new pair, the ball came close by, he abandoned his shorts and in his briefs fielded the ball and cleared it heroically down the field, to the adulation of the crowd.

Supreme Scout

Tadhg Jennings has a unique claim to fame. He is Kevin Heffernan's godson and, in 1974, Dublin were struggling to find a free taker. Tadhg was only eight at the time and he said to Kevin, 'I've seen a man up in Marino and he never misses a free.' Heffo was intrigued and went to see for himself. The rest is history. So Tadhg has been heard to say, 'I'm the man who discovered Jimmy Keaveney.'

Revealing Talent

A lot of strange things happen in club games. The strangest story must be about a camogie club match in Westmeath when, about twenty-five years ago, Cullion had a man on their team. What was stranger was that nobody noticed the difference until after the match. The headline in the local paper was, 'When is a girl not a girl?'

This is not a unique situation. In 1936, in the run-up to the Berlin Olympics, the Germans were very confident that Dora Ratjen was going to win the gold medal in the women's high jump. She finished fourth. In 1957, the reason for their confidence was finally revealed when it emerged that she was a he. In 1992, before the Olympic Games in Barcelona, the 2,400 female athletes were tested. It was discovered that five of them were men. Four years later in Atlanta, a similar number of athletes were tested. This time eight of them were found, on closer inspection, to be men.

Hello Darkness My Old Friend

Tragedy seems to have a special fondness for Mayo football. In 1975, Ted Webb was 'the great white hope' of Mayo football – having starred in the county's All-Ireland under-21 winning side the previous year. In the final, he scored what Micheál O'Hehir described as one of the greatest goals he had ever seen in Croke Park. Webb was physically a bit of a John Travolta lookalike – which added to his iconic status.

On 26 February 1976, John O'Mahony dropped Ted and his brother Michael, also a Mayo player, home from a county training session. Later that night, Ted got a call to collect his uncle from a pub. As he drove to collect him, he passed the spot where the road was dissected by the Westport–Dublin railway track at a time when a poorly lit carriage train ploughed into the car, smashed it 500 yards down the track and killed Ted.

Up Down

The Down team of the 1960s won three All-Irelands. One of their stars was James McCartan. He was a fantastic player, like his brother Dan and, years later, wee James, and was a great character. He was once playing in a club match and was harshly sent off. A formidable woman came in from the sideline and put her foot on the ball, so outraged was she that her hero had been wronged. Nobody could persuade her to move so the match had to be abandoned.

Fans Forum

Of course the GAA has attracted its share of famous fans. Eamon de Valera attended every All-Ireland final during his presidency – even though by the end of his reign he was almost totally blind. One of his latter day All-Irelands had a number of controversial refereeing decisions. The losing manager was asked for his thoughts afterwards. He observed, 'Dev saw more of the game than the ref did.'

The Wicklow Way

Tommy Docherty once remarked, 'After the match, an official asked for two of my players to take a dope test. I offered him a referee.' It sums up the lack of esteem most people have for referees. In Wicklow, though, they take things to a different level.

Club football in Wicklow is not for the faint-hearted, especially for faint-hearted referees. One of the most famous incidents in its history was when a group of disaffected fans, after losing a club match, locked a referee in the boot of his car. In the return fixture, the nervous referee brought the two teams together and pointed to his whistle and said, 'Do ye see this yoke, lads? I'm going to blow it now and blow it again at the finish and whatever happens in between ye can sort out yerselves.'

Have a Break

It has been said that junior club football in Wicklow has produced so many injuries that it has generated more breaks than Kit Kat.

Eyesore

A referee's lot in such an environment is not a happy one. It is the only occupation where a man has to be perfect on the first day on the job and then improve over the years. One spectator at a club match in Wicklow was complaining bitterly all through the game about the referee's poor eyesight. At one stage, though, the fan was responsible for a 'Colemanball' when he shouted, 'Ah ref, where are your testicles?'

Bless Me Father

Kerry football has produced many great characters, like Jackie Lyne. Jackie was a great player himself and produced three fine sons who all played for the local club team: Dinny, Jackie and one who was just ordained to the priesthood. Jackie referred to him as 'His Reverence.' Jackie always, always wore his hat. The only time the hat came off his head was during the consecration at Mass. After a club match Jackie was holding court in the pub, reliving the crucial moment in the match: 'Dinny kicked the ball out. Jackie caught it and kicked it in to His Reverence . . . ' He paused his dramatic narrative to lift his hat at the mention of 'His Reverence'. The religious aura though was quickly dissipated as he came to the climax, ' . . . and he kicked it into the f***king goal.'

A Papal Blessing

The Spillane family played a role in Irish sporting history but they were also involved in one of Ireland's greatest religious occasions. Early in 1979, news broke that the Pope would visit Ireland that September. The Pope's visit touched something very deep in the Irish psyche. For devout Catholics, it was like three Christmases rolled into one. As thousands of pilgrims waited on Galway racecourse on a misty September Sunday morning, they laughed heartily at Bishop Eamonn Casey and Fr Michael Cleary's warm-up performance, a roller coaster of fun and frolics. Kerry footballer Mick Spillane presented an oak sapling to the Pope in

Galway, during the Papal Mass for the youth of Ireland, as part of the giving of gifts on behalf of the youth of Ireland.

Re-Joyce

Galway's Billy Joyce, sometimes known as 'Boxcar Willie', was a real character of the game. Once, before Galway played a big match in Croke Park, Billy took the squad by surprise by asking, 'Did ye ring the airport?' His team-mates didn't know what he was talking about and asked him why they would ring the airport. Billy replied, 'To tell them not to have airplanes flying over Croke Park. I'm going to be jumping so high I don't want to be in collision with them.'

Billy's midfield partner Brian Talty recalls that their disappointments in the Connacht Championship in those years were offset by victories in the Gael Linn competition.

'The prize for winning it was a trip to New York so that's why we put more into winning it than the Connacht Championship,' he says. 'We had some great times on those trips. My abiding memory is of rooming once with Billy Joyce. We were staying in the Taft Hotel. It should've been called the Daft Hotel! One day Billy was lying on the bed when one of our team-mates came rushing into the room in a state of high excitement shouting, "I've just got the news that I've won an All-Star."

'Billy coolly looked up him and said: "Didn't I tell you that you'd get one?" Our colleague beamed and said, "You did." Then modesty took over and he added, "I didn't deserve one." Billy's response was immediate: "Correct."

'When we were getting beaten in midfield by a particular player, Billy would turn to me and say, "Time to take the chopper out." The next ball that came our way, you would hear a thud and a sigh of pain.

'In the 1978 Connacht final, Billy was playing at midfield

against Roscommon's Marty McDermott, who was great fielder of the ball on an atrocious wet day. Before the throw-in Marty said to Billy, "Tis an awful day for football." Billy looked at him and said, "You don't have to worry about it. You won't be out in it very long." He was right. Billy went in for a robust challenge, on the borders of the laws of the game, and poor Marty had to be taken off.'

Tough Stuff

When the Ulster side in the 1980s gathered for their Railway Cup clash with Leinster, Nudie Hughes pretended to the hotel staff that he was the team manager and in charge of the room allocation. Nudie did a quick scout of the rooms and saw some of them had four-poster beds. Relations between the Tyrone and Down players were less than amicable at the time, so Nudie mischievously matched a Tyrone player with a Down player in these rooms. Sometimes there are games when players come off the field with black eyes, but that game was unusual because a number of the Ulster players went on to the pitch the next day with black eyes.

Dub-le Trouble

The late Mick Holden was one of the great characters of Gaelic football. Coming up to the 1983 All-Ireland final, Kevin Heffernan spoke to the Dublin team about diet and proper preparation. He told them if they had any problems sleeping before the final they should get tablets from Dr Pat O'Neill. The first person in the queue was Mick Holden. Heffo said to Mick, 'I never thought you'd have any problems sleeping.' Holden answered, 'Oh, these are not for me. I sleep like a baby. These are for my mother. She can never sleep the night before a big match.'

One Saturday morning, much to Heffo's chagrin, he was seriously late for training. The manager curtly demanded an explanation. Holden responded by saying, 'I was coming across town and I was stopped by the guards. They said I was a match for one of the guys that pulled that big bank robbery yesterday.' A bemused Heffo asked, 'Really?' Mick answered, 'No, but it sounds so much better than saying I slept it out.'

Not Free Love

One of Páidí O'Sé's stories was about a Kerry footballer of yesteryear who was in serious need of some love and affection but he had no wife nor money. So one evening he met a lady of the night in Tralee and asked her the cost of her services. When he explained he had no money, she inquired if he had anything in his pockets. He replied that he had two All-Ireland medals. As it was a slow night, she agreed to exchange her services for the two medals.

A few weeks later some Mayo footballers came to Tralee on a stag night. One of their number met the same lady of the night. The conversation unfolded as follows:

'How much do your charge?'

'Two hundred euros.'

'That's an awful lot.'

'But I'm worth it.'

'How do I know you are any good?'

'Here. Let me show you my two All-Ireland medals.'

Odd-Shaped Balls

The lush tapestry of the GAA has been greatly enhanced by its cross-fertilisation with Irish rugby. Ciaran Fitzgerald, who captained Ireland to the Triple Crown in both 1982 and

1985, played for Galway in the All-Ireland minor hurling final against Cork in 1970. His problem was that, when he played in that All-Ireland, he was marked by Martin Doherty who subsequently made it big with the Cork senior team. Big was the word for Martin. Fitzgerald would have needed a stepladder to have competed with him in the air.

At times, though, claims about the GAA's connection with rugby have been exaggerated. Former Irish out-half Mick Quinn's father was not a sporting man but he was very proud that his son played for Ireland. He seldom drank but, when he did, he really knew how to enjoy himself. Once he was having a few drinks with John Joe Whyte of *The Irish Times*. He told John Joe that Mick had acquired his ability from him and that he himself played for Monaghan in the 1928 All-Ireland Gaelic football final – not even knowing at that stage if Monaghan had played in the final that year. The next day this story appeared verbatim in *The Times*. John Joe hadn't realised he was being wound up and didn't bother to check out the facts.

Mick Galwey, (known as 'Gaillimh'), won an All-Ireland senior football medal with Kerry in 1986, before going on to play rugby for Ireland and the Lions.

In Kerry you are considered to have an inferiority complex if you only consider yourself as good as anybody else, so it comes as little surprise to discover that Gaillimh's dream team is the Kerry team of the seventies and eighties. He feels that his training as a Gaelic footballer was a big help to his rugby career, primarily in terms of having an eye for the ball. However, he feels that the primary benefit of his association with Kerry was not on the playing field. Former Irish rugby coach Mick Doyle's first love was the GAA though, when he began his secondary education as a boarder in Newbridge

College, rugby exploded into his life. He continued to trenchantly air his views about the state of Irish rugby through his weekly column in *The Sunday Independent*. His criticism was such that Moss Keane once said to him, 'Thanks be to Jaysus I don't play any more. Otherwise I'd be afraid to open the paper on Sunday because of what you'd say about me.'

Gaillimh never incurred Doyle's wrath and contends that the best help his Kerry roots has been to his rugby reputation was that Mick Doyle never wrote anything critical about him – unlike other second-row forwards that people could think of.

One Kerry fan was less than impressed by Galwey's defection to rugby saying, 'He was a great footballer until rugby destroyed him.'

Gaillimh grew up in Currow, near Castleisland, the same area as Moss Keane.

In GAA parlance, as a Gaelic footballer Moss was 'very strong'. However, he was not known for being 'fleet of foot'. According to folklore, after a less than resoundingly successful career as a Gaelic footballer with UCC, Moss's conversion to rugby came when he overheard the former GAA press officer Danny Lynch saying in a pub that, 'A farmer could make a tidy living on the space of ground it takes Moss to turn.'

When Moss went on his first tour to New Zealand with the Lions, he was the only player in the first seven weeks who the BBC had not interviewed because they did not think his strong Kerry brogue would work well with a British audience. Eventually, the Lions players said they would refuse to do any more interviews for the BBC until Nigel Starmer-Smith interviewed Moss. Nigel reluctantly agreed to this demand and asked on live television, 'Well Moss, you've been here now for two months and you've played in your first Lions Test, met the Maoris, what's been the best moment of the trip for you?'

In his thickest Kerry accent Moss replied, 'When I heard that Kerry beat Cork in the Munster final.'

It is said that Danny Lynch in his pre-Croke Park incarnation, when he worked for the Office of Public Works, went to visit Liam Mulvhill in hospital. Mulvhill had been in a car accident – with his car going through a hedge into a vegetable field. Lynch said, 'You should be used to being close to vegetables where you work.'

Mighty Meath
When Dublin faced Meath after their 1983 All-Ireland victory, Gerry McEntee said in the Meath dressing-room, 'Let's clap them on to the field. We have to do that and then let's kick the living sh*te out of them.'

Helps You Work, Rest and Play
Thanks to Lance Armstrong, the issue of drugs and sport has never been too far away from the front pages. Colm O'Rourke had an interesting revelation about his Meath team when he joked, 'Sean Boylan had us drinking herbs that could also be used for stripping paint off the gate.'

All in the Mind
Managers play all kinds of mind games. Matt Williams was back on our TV screens for the TV3 coverage of the 2015 rugby World Cup, between all their ad breaks. When he was Scottish rugby coach, he had the number twenty-seven inscribed on the training gear of all his players to signify that they eat, drink and sleep the game twenty-four hours a day, seven days a week, 365 days a year. If you add up all those individual digits, you get twenty-seven.

Matt was an abysmal failure with Scotland.

Persistent heavy defeats not only drains the confidence of a team, but it also requires some imaginative motivational ploys. A club team from Leitrim travelled 200 miles to a tournament game in Waterford. At half-time they trailed by 7-2 to 0-5. A crisis meeting was held in the middle of the pitch at half-time. Recriminations were flying until the captain called for silence and an end to the bickering and a hush descended. One player said, 'We need some positive encouragement.'

After a short delay, the manager-cum-trainer-cum-club secretary-cum groundskeeper said, 'Come on now lads. Let's go out there and show them up. It's plain to be seen. They can't score points.'

Sammon Leap
In the early 1990s, Connacht footballers were invariably free in August and September and many took the route of weekend tourist for trans-Atlantic games.

Before their glory days of 1998, Galway were knocked out early in the championship one year and a famous man in the GAA in New York, Jackie Sammon, rang Val Daly and asked him to travel over to line out for Connemara Gaels the following Sunday and to bring a couple of other good players with him. Daly rang around and persuaded former Galway full-forward Brian O'Donnell to travel with him. Brian had never played in a match in New York. The two lads flew out on the Friday evening and, on the plane, Daly briefed his colleague on how to get through the weekend. He said, 'Now Brian, they do things differently over there. It's not like at home so just enjoy the weekend, play the match and don't mind what anyone says. Whatever you do, say nothing.'

The Tribesmen enjoyed the first part of the weekend but

the match went less well. At half-time, the Connemara Gaels were seven points down. Jackie Sammon gave a team-talk and said, 'Ye're the most disgraceful shower I ever saw. Ye're a disgrace to the Connemara Gaels jersey. As for the big shots from over in Ireland, I'm sorry I brought ye out at all. Daly, you were hopeless and O'Donnell, you were even worse. You didn't even catch one ball.'

O'Donnell forgot Daly's advice and retorted, 'Sure how could ye play football out there? There wasn't a single blade of grass on the pitch.'

Sammon turned around to him and asked, 'Did you come out here to play football or to graze?'

Danger
The great American sports writer, Red Smith, said: 'I went to a fight and an ice hockey match broke out.' There's a story told about the two grasshoppers who came on to the field before an Ulster Final as the pulling and dragging started between the players on both teams. One said to the other, 'We're going to be killed here today. Do you feel the tension?'

The other replied, 'I do. Hop up here on the ball. It's the only place we'll be safe.'

Prison Break
In 1990, Nelson Mandela was freed from his years in captivity. The first thing he allegedly said after he was released was, 'Have Mayo won an All-Ireland since I was thrown into that bloody place?'

It Could Happen to a Bishop
One cleric who was much admired was Bishop Willie Walsh. He takes great pleasure from stories about posi-

tional changes. One of the things that always struck him in hurling was the strange ways positional switches were made in a match, particularly in the 1990 hurling final between Cork and Galway. After about fifteen minutes, he was wondering what the Cork selectors were going to do about Jim Cashman. Joe Cooney was destroying him and he couldn't understand why they left Jim there. They went in at half-time and Bishop Willie said in the stands, 'Well, Jim Cashman won't be centre-back in the second half', but amazingly he was and he went on to win his battle with Joe Cooney in the second half and Cork won the All-Ireland.

When Bishop Willie went back to Clare some people said to him, 'Ah, you can't beat those Cork guys. Now if that was Clare we'd have panicked and taken Jim Cashman off but the Cork guys were wise and knew what was best.' Of course, that was a bit hurtful to Bishop Willie as a Clare selector so when he went down to Cork a month later he headed straight to Dr Con Murphy and asked, 'Up front, now what happened with Jim Cashman and why didn't you change him?' Dr Con replied, 'Well, we all agreed that Jim was being beaten and we'd have to change him. The problem was that none of the selectors could agree on who we would replace him with. So we decided to do the usual thing and give him five minutes in the second half.'

Dual Stars
There have been eighteen players who have won All-Ireland medals in both hurling and football. Eleven of these are from Cork, including such luminaries as Jack Lynch, Jimmy Barry-Murphy, Brian Murphy, Ray Cummins, Denis Coughlan and famously in 1990 Teddy McCarthy.

Folklore abounds about the first Cork player to become

a dual All-Ireland medal winner: Billy Mackessy, who was also a renowned publican. An enterprising Leesider who was short of a few bob had a penchant for poaching free drink in the hostelries of the city. One day, he sauntered into Billy's pub with another chancer and, in a near whisper, asked Billy how many All-Ireland medals he had. The reply was 'two'. The quick-witted duo then went to the other end of the bar and told the bartender that they were due two drinks 'on the house'. The barman gave them a puzzled look. The resourceful drinkers then confirmed their entitlement by shouting down the pub to the owner, 'Wasn't it two you said, Mr Mackessy?'

Carlow's dual star, Paddy Quirke, hurled for the county at senior level from 1974 to 1990 and played senior football with the county from 1974 to 1987. Quirke played for the Leinster football team in both 1979 and 1981 and in four consecutive years between 1978 and 1981 for the Leinster hurling side.

Hurling was his passport to San Francisco. He played a few games out there for the All-Stars and it was really tough and physical. At one stage he put in his hurley, angled with the boss to the ground, to block an opponent, got a severe belt across the face, was taken off and rushed to hospital. He had no social security cover, but his friends who were with him decided he was Patrick Foley (a genuine holder of social security). So all of a sudden he was somebody else. The only problem was that, when he heard the name Patrick Foley being called out in the hospital, he forgot that was supposed to be him and then had to be reminded who he was.

Captain Fantastic
Some of the same fans who were throwing bouquets at Declan Darcy in 1994, after he captained Leitrim to a never-

to-be-forgotten Connacht title, were swinging cleavers when he decided to transfer to Dublin, though many of his friends and Leitrim fans wished him well.

'Once the offer was made I had to give it serious thought,' he says. 'At the time the '94 Leitrim side were disintegrating. The changes weren't to my liking. One little incident encapsulated it for me. The day before we played a Connacht Championship match, we were having lunch and were given steaks. In pretty much his last championship game, Mickey Quinn said he wouldn't eat steak. He would only eat chicken because it was the best meal for the match the next day. Here was this Leitrim legend, on his last legs, worrying about his diet but, when I went out of the hotel, I saw two of the new players – very talented guys – smoking. That was their way of preparing for the biggest game of their lives. To be honest, if Mickey was going to continue playing, I wouldn't have been able to walk away from Leitrim because I looked up to him so much and so admired his great commitment to the county.

'We came very close in 2002 when Ray Cosgrave almost equalised against Armagh but, to be honest, I believe Tommy Carr had a better team. John Bailey, then the county chairman, told us after the drawn game against Kerry in the All-Ireland quarter-final in 2001 that, no matter what happened, Tommy Carr would be staying for the next year. He actually cried with emotion as he said that but, less than a month later, he put the knife into Tommy. Players would have done anything for Tommy but we didn't do enough for him. I felt sorry for him because he was very unlucky, none more so than with the incredible Maurice Fitzgerald sideline kick that drew the match for Kerry the first day. Tommy was as honest as the day was long and was fiercely driven. There was nothing he wouldn't have done for Dublin. He was probably a better manager at the end but had more to learn and I think it's a shame he didn't get the chance.

'I have never experienced anything like Thurles those two days. I had heard about Munster finals but was not prepared for the atmosphere in the square. It was amazing and packed with people. I remember hearing the sirens as the Kerry team were arriving and it was like the Germans were coming.'

The Thurles experience did provide Darcy with the most amusing incident in his career.

'We were staying in the Horse and Jockey and I went out for a walk with one of the lads. A car pulled in beside us and my colleague said, "There's your man."

'"Who?"

'"Your man from *Star Trek*."

'It was Colm Meaney and he was walking into the car park. The next thing I knew I heard a booming voice shouting, "Hey Colm. Beam me up Scotty." It was Vinny Murphy standing at the window. He was as naked as the day he was born!

'Vinny was a character. He loved a fag. Some wag changed the sign in Parnell Park from, "No Smoking" to "No Smoking, Vinny!"'

The Demon Drink

Eugene McGee tells of a new manager who was dismayed with the drink culture in the squad. He comes up with a brainwave to illustrate the error of their ways. He summoned the team into the dressing-room and placed two glasses on the bench. He filled one with water, the other with vodka. He then dropped a worm into each glass. In the glass of water the worm lived, but in the glass of vodka the worm died. Afterwards the manager asked, 'Now lads, what can we learn from this?'

One player snapped up his hand immediately and said, 'Drink plenty – it will kill all your worms.'

The Big Apple

A Kerry county councillor is attending a junket – a fact-finding mission in New York. He checks in at the team hotel, where he is greeted at reception by a young African-American woman. His very strong Kerry accent and her Bronx accent cause a cultural clash and a major 'lost in translation' moment. The problem is accentuated when he tries to check in and is asked for his name. He says 'Geraghty'. The young woman is lost by his accent and repeatedly, to the councillor's increasing frustration, asks him to say it again. Even when he spells out 'G-E-R-A-G-H-T-Y' she is none the wiser. Finally the man gets a brainwave and says with a flourish, believing he has found the key to making her understand, 'Geraghty – as in Graham!'

The Perks of the Office

A prominent official of the Connacht Council is in Los Angeles and, from the moment he arrives, he is struck by the importance of the star system in the city. A major catastrophe ensues when he tries to check in to his hotel and discovers that his booking details are wrong. When it looks like he is not going to be checked in to the hotel his exasperated wife digs him in the ribs and whispers, 'Tell them you're from the Connacht Council.'

Motivational Speaking

Sometimes the manager can say exactly the right thing. In the 1995 Munster hurling final, when Clare trailed Cork by four points and faced the wind in the second half, Ger Loughnane defiantly told his team, 'The ship has sprung a leak but we are not going down.' They didn't.

Half-time speeches, though, can backfire just as easily. When he was Tipperary hurling manager, Babs Keating faced the problem of rallying his team even though they were trailing at half-time by eight points. After a number of inspirational words in an effort to instil confidence, he went around the team individually and asked each of them: 'Can we do it?'

To a man they replied: 'We can. We can.'

He could feel the surge of belief invading the dressing-room. Everything was going swimmingly until he turned to Joe Hayes and asked, 'Joe, can we do it?'

Joe replied, 'It's not looking great, is it, Babs?'

Babs has a history of putting his foot in his mouth. In 1990 Cork were given no chance of winning the Munster hurling final against Tipperary, the All-Ireland champions. A chance comment from Babs before the game that 'donkeys don't win derbies' galvanised the Cork team and the Leesiders claimed victory.

In the build-up to one of the early rounds of the Ulster Championship in 2004, one of the northern teams came up with an unusual motivational strategy. They put two planks across a skip and got each of the players to stand on them. One of their mentors told them that if they fell off the planks they would be rubbish and if they lost the match they would be rubbish. Did it work? No. They lost tamely.

You really have to think your motivational strategies through, lest they boomerang back to bite you. In 1997, before Clare played Kilkenny in the All-Ireland hurling semi-final, Ger Loughnane was asked in an interview what he thought of D. J. Carey. He had been absolutely brilliant in the All-Ireland quarter-final in a thrilling game against

Galway in Thurles. He practically beat the Westerners all on his own. Loughnane said, 'D. J. will prove himself to be an outstanding player when he plays really well against one of the best players in the country in a big match. Next Sunday he will be playing in a really big match against Brian Lohan and, if he plays really well against Brian Lohan, he will prove himself to be a really great player but I won't regard him as great player until he does it against somebody like Brian on the big day.'

Nicky Brennan was Kilkenny manager then. He taped the interview and played it on the bus on the way to the match. According to legend Nicky said, 'Listen to what that c*nt Loughnane said about one of our best players.' Eddie O'Connor is supposed to have piped up, 'He's f**king right!'

Positivity

Players need positive messages before big games. In 2003, in the build-up to the All-Ireland final, the late Cormac McAnallen was having problems sleeping before the match. His brother doctored a picture of Peter Canavan and produced a computer image of Peter holding the Sam Maguire trophy. Cormac hung it above his bed the week before the final. It was the first thing he noticed every morning when he woke and that put him in the right frame of mind to win his All-Ireland medal.

Gone Too Soon

Cormac McAnallen personified what the late American sports writer, Grantland Rice, meant when he wrote, 'For when the great scorer comes to write against your name, he makes not how you won or lost, but how you played the game.'

BLOOD, SWEAT, TRIUMPH AND TEARS

At the time of Cormac's death, Micheál O'Muircheartaigh read the exquisitely evocative poem 'The Beautiful Game' in tribute:

Less than a minute remains on the clock,
As I tighten my lace and turn down my sock,
One last chance, and it's all down to me,
It must be a goal, for we need all three.

I step up to the ball and look towards the posts,
Is that the crowd I hear, or is it the ghosts
Of men who before me have faced the same test,
And never once failed to give of their best.

My father he gave me the love of it all,
When he guided my feet to strike that first ball,
A hurley or football it's the same thing to me,
It's playing the game that matters you see.

From boys in a field to the crowd's great roar,
There's never been anything to excite more,
From the day I could run till the day I can't walk,
And even then, about the game I'll still talk.

The few steps to the ball now seem like a mile,
But a well-placed shot and I'll be carried in style,
On shoulders of team-mates expressing their joy,
It's a dream that consumed me since I was a boy.

My feet pound the ground, my foot sends the ball,
It sails through the air over men who are tall,

Then dipping and curling it finds the goal,
And just for the moment I'm in touch with my soul.

A whistle blows hard and I awake from the dream,
I'm watching my own son play for the team,
And maybe one day they'll announce His name,
As he steps out to play . . . The Beautiful Game.
(Author Unknown)

The Curse of Biddy Earley
A Davy Fitzgerald puckout away from Ger Loughnane's family home is Kilbarron Lake, where Biddy Earley's famous blue bottle now resides. The 'witch of Feakle' putting a curse on the hurlers of Clare and, over 100 years later, the wizard from Feakle would undo her curse. Nice story, but it might be more plausible if Biddy Earley had not died well before the GAA was founded.

Mistaken Identity
A proud father is introducing his young son to Jamesie O'Connor. The son is very shy and when the father asks, 'Who is he?' the son refuses so the father prompts him by saying, 'He's the guy you always are when you are playing in the garden.' The boy thinks deeply and finally says, 'Ollie Baker.'

When Pat Nearly Met Charlie
Páidí O'Sé captained Kerry to the All-Ireland in 1984. The following morning, Páidí brought some of the team out to meet Charlie Haughey in Kinsealy. The former Taoiseach always boasted about his great interest in Kerry football. Sadly, though, Pat Spillane missed out on his own meeting with Charlie Haughey. He came very close. He was in the Schelig

Hotel the morning after the Dingle Regatta and Charlie and his entourage were quaffing champagne. They were loud and boisterous and he heard one of them say, 'There's Pat Spillane over there.'

Charlie swanned over to the table beside him and tapped the man on the shoulder and said, 'Pat Spillane, I presume?'

The astonished guy replied, 'I wish.'

Charlie turned on his heels and walked back to his party as if nothing had happened. So much for his great knowledge of Kerry football.

Keeping it in the Family

One of the greats of ladies' football in Kerry was Katie Liston. Because she was tall, had black hair and was one of the all-time giants of the game, she was often asked by opponents if she was related to Kerry legend Eoin Bomber Liston. Although she was not related, she always said she was because her rivals found this an intimidating idea.

Pin-up Girls

A coach to a camogie club was bemused when all her players burst out laughing when she came into the dressing-room and announced, 'All the girls playing in the Saturday friendly match will be pinned to the notice-board.'

Here's to You, Mrs Robinson

During her seven years as Irish President, Mary Robinson had many visits to Croke Park. Such was the strict protocol that there was very little danger of a surprise for her. But things do not always go to plan. In the strain of an All-Ireland final in 1996 against Mayo, Colm Coyle reduced his team-mates to laughter when he asked President Robinson, as she was being introduced to the Meath team before the match, with the familiarity of intimacy, 'How are things at home?'

So Sad to Watch Good Love Go Bad

Pat Spillane's achievements on the pitch were not without a cost to his personal and romantic life.

'I used to teach in Bantry, arrive home and give my wife a break from the family bar for her dinner and I'd work the bar,' he says. 'Then I'd go and train savage hard with Dwyer in Tralee. Kerry were cost-cutting at the time so it was only sandwiches after training. When I got home from training, I would go back in to give my wife a break from working in the bar. I remember one night going upstairs, jumping into bed, knackered to the world. A few minutes later my wife slipped seductively into bed beside me. Her hand came over – that's the sort of thing that happens with newly married couples. She should have expected the right reaction from a willing partner. In this case, though, it wasn't an amorous response from a newly-wed husband but a crocked, wrecked victim of Mick O'Dwyer's training regime who proceeded to tell her, "Forget about it. I'm banjaxed. Go away. Don't even dream about it."

'With that came the quick retort, "If Mick O'Dwyer wanted you to do it, you'd do it."

'You know what. She was probably right. I told that story afterwards to Gay Byrne on *The Late Late Show* and she was sitting in the front row. Everyone who saw her afterwards said she looked mortified. She was but I was literally to pay a high price. The next day I had to take her shopping.'

How The West Was Lost

After the 1996 and 1997 All-Irelands, when Mayo let All-Ireland titles slip through their fingers, Pat Spillane poured scorn on the Mayo forwards in particular. When the county's ladies' team started winning All-Irelands and Cora Staunton emerged as a national figure, Spillane deftly used their success as a rod to beat the men's team with. 'The time has come for me to confound my critics and bravely admit that, in the last five years, Mayo have had one of the best teams I have ever seen – their ladies' football team. I can now exclusively reveal that plans are well advanced for my new series about Mayo footballers. It is to be called *Footballers' Husbands*.'

No Pat on the Back

Pat Spillane is the contradiction of John B. Keane's claim that it is harder to get a straight answer from a Kerry man than a goose egg from an Arctic tern. His candour is not to everyone's taste. In 2001, when Ireland was hit by a foot and mouth crisis, Ted Walsh said to him on RTE television, 'The real problem with the foot and mouth epidemic, Pat, is that you did not get it.'

Don't Fence Me In

In the late 1990s, Armagh took the team on a training camp to Thurles. The squad was called at 5am to go to Thurles Racecourse to go for a long run. When they got there one of the players quipped, 'Do we have to jump the fences as well?'

Basketball Star

Before becoming one of the greatest players of all time, Juliet Murphy played basketball for Ireland.

Murphy's Law

Before their first All-Ireland in 2005, the Cork team gathered in a huddle before the throw-in and looked to Juliet Murphy to say something inspirational. She took her role as spiritual leader of the team to a whole new level when she said the Our Father.

Hot Shot
Cork's ace forward Valerie Mulcahy famously wore white boots during that 2005 final.

The Boss
During the mid 2000s, the rivalry between Cork and Mayo lit up the game. Cork's manager Eamonn Ryan came up with a simple but very effective way of beating Mayo – stop their superstar Cora Staunton with a specially tailored zonal defence system to ensure that she was swarmed with defenders each time she got the ball.

The Drive for Five
In 2009, Cork won their fifth All-Ireland in a row when they beat Dublin. Their aura of invincibility was fractured in 2010 when they lost to Tyrone in the All-Ireland quarter-final. Goals from Aisling O'Keane and Sarah Connolly drove the Northerners on to victory. Normal service was resumed the following year when the Cork ladies won the first of three All-Irelands with Juliet Murphy coming out of retirement in 2013 to steer the Leesiders back to glory. They have to be considered the greatest team in the history of the GAA.

They have helped to bring ladies' football into the main-stream. This is a necessary corrective, because a man walked on the moon before a ladies' football team played in Croke Park.

You'll Never Hurl Alone
All-Ireland hurling finals always draw celebrity fans. The

2012 drawn final between Kilkenny and Galway was no exception, when Robbie Fowler and ten other Liverpool legends were appreciative fans. Their conversation was not all about hurling. Fowler tells the story of the conversation that unfolded between Rob Jones and Jason McAteer during the game.

Jones: 'I'm writing my autobiography.'

McAteer: 'What's it about?'

Jones: 'It's about my story isn't it?'

McAteer: 'Is it any good?'

Jones: 'I don't know. I haven't read it.'

Going to the Chapel, Going to Get Married
Jason Ryan's appointment as Kildare manager and the county's big victory over Louth in the Leinster Championship prompted one fan in Naas to resurrect a poster from 1998 saying, 'There's going to be a wedding: Sam Maguire is going to marry Lily White.'

A Good Walk Spoiled
After retirement, many former GAA stars turn to golf. Waterford's erstwhile hurling All-Star, Paul Flynn, went so far as to compete in the West of Ireland Amateur Championship at Rosses Point when Ireland had a white Easter in 2013. In the Arctic conditions, Flynn struggled and scored an opening round of eighty-three. When asked if the experience was tougher than facing Kilkenny in an All-Ireland final, the former sharpshooter stoically replied, 'It was a slower death anyway.'

Dan the Man
Flynn leaves the game with many happy memories of his former team-mates. A case in point is of Dan Shanahan, an

employee for Top Oil, who went into a shop one day in 2007. At that stage he had become hurling's supreme goal machine – he had just starred in Waterford's triumph over Cork in the All-Ireland hurling quarter-final and had scored eight goals and eight points in his four games that year, bringing his championship score from 2004 to an incredible nineteen goals and thirty-six points.

A little lady of mature years eyed him up slowly. Suddenly a smile of triumph came over her face. 'I know who you are now,' said the woman.

'That's good,' said Big Dan politely.

'You're the oil man,' the woman replied with a flourish.

Odds On

There is a great book to be written on GAA rumours. After being held scoreless in the 2012 Munster final, the Tipperary grapevine went into overdrive, saying that Lar Corbett had bet on himself not to score in the game. As with many great rumours, there was not a shred of truth in it. However, one of his team-mates, John O'Neill, knocked some fun out of it when he shocked his team-mates at a meeting by saying Lar suffered from poor communication skills. As Lar documents in his autobiography, with every eye on him O'Neill coolly informed Corbett that the next time he had a great tip for the Munster final he should share it with his team-mates.

Master Stroke

The night after Clare lost to Cork in the 2013 Munster Championship, Davy Fitzgerald gathered the players in the sitting room of his home in Sixmilebridge. He served them MiWadi and biscuits and for three hours they sat and dissected. They wrote down what they thought, backs in one side of the room and the forwards in the other. Davy described it as an 'unreal' event and, three months later, they won the All-Ireland.

Three in One

The 2013 All-Ireland Senior Hurling Championship was widely considered to be the best ever. In the semi-final, Limerick faced neighbours Clare and brought a massive crowd. When Ger Canning told Clare mentor Louis Mulqueen about the huge number of Limerick fans Mulqueen calmly replied, 'A huge crowd to go home disappointed, Ger.'

That Christmas RTE marked the year with a special programme on the season. It featured a group interview with Ger Loughnane, Davy Fitzgerald and Anthony Daly. Ger Canning introduced it in a theological way: 'Ger, I guess you are God the father. You (Davy) are obviously now God the son. I suppose that makes you (Dalo) the Holy Ghost.'

It's Nice to be Nice

The effect of Clare's win was so overwhelming that Ger Loughnane did the unthinkable and wished Tipperary well. In 1997 he was quoted as saying, 'If Tipperary played China in the All-Ireland final, we would be shouting for China.'

From Clare to Here

Arsenal stars Lukas Podolski and Santi Cazorla posted pictures of themselves, both armed with hurleys, and sent their best wishes to Clare before the 2013 All-Ireland final: 'Today Santi & me smashed it over the bar. Wristyhurlers.'

The same pair recruited the £42 million man Mesut Özil to join them in a photo with a poster that stated, 'G'wan Munster'. Podolski was wearing a headband which had the Munster anthem printed on it: 'Stand Up and Fight.'

Jerry Flannery, the former Munster legend who was working as a personal trainer at Arsenal at the time, is believed to be behind both tweets.

A Star is Born
Clare's All-Ireland triumph in 2013 created a new superstar in hurling in the shape of hat-trick hero and new hearthrob Shane O'Donnell. His team-mate Podge Collins described him as 'the Bieber of hurling'.

Donegal's Mark McHugh spoke for many with his prediction when he said, 'Like to wish Shane O'Donnell all the best in the next four months. He's going to enjoy some life.'

A Long Interlude
After Kevin Walsh stepped down as Sligo football manager in 2013, it was 149 days before his successor, former Westmeath manager Pat Flanagan, was appointed.

The Farmers Journal
The 2013 All-Ireland football final did produce a great moment of wisdom.

Sadly, though, the Dubs' victory produced no quip to match Keith Barr after their 1995 All-Ireland: 'There won't be a cow milked in Finglas tonight.'

Jim Gavin, at the post All-Ireland final press conference, was the clear winner in the poor mouth award: 'The minute the referee blows the final whistle, that's when the 2013 season ends. I know from speaking to other managers, they're already setting themselves up for the 2014 championship. We're probably behind now already.'

Making Mischief
Two days after the All-Ireland final, it was decided that

some of the Dublin players would have a private 'session'. Footballer of the year Michael Darragh Macauley was one of the organisers. He took a call from a member of the team looking for directions to the secret venue. His friend was well 'refreshed' as he rang the doorbell of the given address in a state of high spirits. The blood drained from his face, though, when the door was answered by Jim Gavin's wife. Macauley had deliberately sent him to the manager's home in an effort to embarrass him. He succeeded. The player's one hope was that Mrs Gavin would not recognise him. She did.

The Fab Army Four

The rich legacy of the army to the GAA was memorably illustrated in the 2014 All-Ireland hurling final when four army personnel played. Kilkenny had Corporal Eoin Larkin, Corporal Paul Murphy and Private Colin Fennelly, while Tipp had Patrick Maher of the First Infantry Batallion in Renmore, Galway.

Fast on the Draw

All-Ireland finals are always stressful for GAA-mad priests who have to make a frantic dash to Croke Park after saying all their Sunday Masses. The problem, though, has been considerably exacerbated when a county is scheduled to play in an All-Ireland hurling final replay on a Saturday evening – which of course is a direct clash with the scheduled Mass.

Fr John Littleton is a priest from Tipperary who is the director of the Priory Institute in Tallaght. As he has no permanent parish duties, he is in constant demand to provide relief for priests in his native county – particularly when Tipp are playing in Croke Park. Within the space of five minutes, immediately after Kilkenny drew with Tipperary in the All-

Ireland final in 2014, he got three texts from three different priests in different parishes asking him to provide relief so that they could attend the replay.

Donegal Versus Dublin

Former Labour Party TD Eamonn Maloney is from Donegal but represented a Dublin constituency. So when Donegal played Dublin in the 2014 All-Ireland semi-final, he was asked who he supported. Showing great political skills he replied, 'I was shouting for one team but praying for another.'

Getting Your Teeth Into It

January 2014 saw yet more allegations about biting during an inter-county match. One wag suggested that, if the trend continued, the GAA could get sponsorship from all the toothpaste companies.

Fergie Time

Alex Ferguson-style mind games are now in vogue in the GAA. Former Donegal selector Rory Gallagher aired his conspiracy theory before their 2013 All-Ireland quarter-final meeting with Mayo: 'We suspect there was a bit of collusion between Monaghan and Mayo. (James) Horan works to a premediated script and I think Kieran Shannon is behind a good bit of it.'

Newstalk's Colm Parkinson immediately described it as 'Mind James'.

All in the Name Game

Parkinson went on to describe his own mind games. He would shake hands with his opponent before a big match and deliberately call them by the wrong name just to throw them off their game, for a few minutes at least.

The Foreign Game

Sporting ecumenism is alive and well in the GAA, as is evident from the keen analysis some of our top personalities paid to the 2014 World Cup. After Germany beat hosts Brazil 7-1 in the semi-final, Monaghan's Dick Clerkin tweeted: 'If David Luiz was a house he would be a three-bed semi in Longford bought in 2007 negative equity.'

Robin van Persie's less-than-stellar performance in the other semi-final between the Netherlands and Argentina prompted Eamonn O'Hara's barb: 'Van Persie playing much better since he was taken off.'

Cavan's Michael Hannon saw the funny side of George Hamilton's commentary in the penalty shoot-out in that same game: 'The awful realisation has dawned on these (Dutch) players, it's down to Dirk Kuyt.'

Paul Galvin, though, came up with the classic comment: 'Klose beat the great Ronaldo's record. That's not right. The last time Klose dribbled past a man he was about to vomit in the men's.'

Meanwhile, Wexford's Anthony Materson was having more prosaic problems: '6.15 and still one god damn washing machine to fix. Not gonna make Parnell park now. F**K!!!.'

An Act of Faith

Going into the 2014 All-Ireland final, Kerry's James O'Donoghue was the favourite to be named Footballer of the Year. Hence the caption in Croke Park: In JOD we trust.

Footloose

After the final, as there was so little use of the foot pass in the game, one letter writer to *The Irish Times* expressed his frustration: 'Congratulations to Kerry on winning the All-Ireland Volleyball Championship.'

Different Strokes

After coming through a treacherous election process in 2014, Paul McGinley led Europe to the Ryder Cup at Gleneagles. The first Irishman to captain the European team, McGinley's hard work paid off as he tasted a sweet victory against Tom Watson's US side.

As a player, his ten-foot putt on the eighteenth hole in his match against Jim Furyk won the 2002 Ryder Cup. In the 2006 Ryder Cup at The K Club in Ireland, McGinley famously offered a handshake and conceded a twenty-foot putt for a half to J. J. Henry on the eighteenth green of his singles match because he feared his opponent might have been put off when a streaker ran across the green.

However, if it weren't for a bad knee injury, McGinley would never have become a professional golfer. McGinley had his heart set on a career in the Dublin jersey but injury ended his dreams of All-Ireland glory before he ever made the senior grade.

Tougher Than the Rest

Enda Kenny was himself an accomplished wing-back. I do not want to suggest that he was tough but, if there had been a transfer market for GAA players, the team that would want him most was the Meath team of the 1980s.

In the Psychiatrist's Chair

Since the 2016 Championship I have been diagnosed with a new condition. I am told it could be terminal. It is called PRMS – Post Roscommon Meltdown Syndrome.

FIVE

MISCHIEF MAKERS, MISCREANTS AND MAD HATTERS

The GAA has brought agony and ecstasy. This chapter snoops inside sweaty, smelly dressing-rooms and delves deep into the archives to recall its villains and victims, all of whom are part of the daily currency of Gaelic games, to consider the many controversies that offer a quirky insight into the GAA psyche.

The Ban

In 1887 Maurice Davin had called for a ban on rugby and soccer. The political leanings of the GAA had been clearly manifested in 1902 when Rule 27, 'The Ban', was introduced. It prohibited members of the GAA from playing, attending or promoting 'foreign games' such as soccer, rugby, hockey and cricket. In 1938 the GAA controversially expelled its patron, Ireland's first president Douglas Hyde, for attending an international soccer match.

The ban was clearly shown to be out of step with the times in 1963, when Waterford hurler Tom Cheasty was banned for attending a dance sponsored by his local soccer club. The ban cost him a National League medal.

Willie McGee, a Mayo great of the 1960s, had reason to be worried about being reported on another occasion.

'When I first started playing championship football the ban was still in operation, so you daren't be seen at a soccer or rugby match, or play them either,' he says. 'I vividly remember attending a soccer match in Dalymount Park one day when I heard this chant, "Burrishoole, Burrishoole!" coming from behind the goal. I'm from Burrishoole and knew it was meaning who was being identified, so I lifted my collar up to hide my face because I was scared stiff of being reported, but it was a Roscommon man and good friend of mine, Noel Carthy. I was glad to know it was him. But the ban did create that kind of climate of fear. It was as if the GAA was saying to the world, "We are not confident enough to trust our own members." Happily, that situation has changed.'

Thanks in large measure to an ongoing campaign of Dublin's Tom Woulfe, the ban on GAA players playing or even watching 'foreign' games was revoked in 1971.

The Hogan Stand
The political turmoil cast a deep shadow on the world of Gaelic games at the height of the War of Independence on Sunday, 21 November – 'Bloody Sunday', when the reviled Black and Tans shot dead thirteen people at a football match between Tipperary and Dublin in Croke Park. The Tipperary player Michael Hogan was shot, and the biggest stand in Croke Park was named in his honour.

Holy Writ
The long relationship between the GAA and the Catholic Church is rich and complex. Although culturally and, in

many respects, spiritually they were very close and the Catholic Church was to the forefront in promoting the GAA, the Church banned its priests and seminarians from actually playing inter-county football for years. Seminarians and priests had to assume a name to allow their footballing careers to continue at the highest level, despite the curious irony of men who so often preached the truth practising deception. Everybody knew who they were, including the bishop, and a blind eye was turned. It was a Jesuitical solution to a uniquely clerical problem.

In 1955, the late Michael Cleary was in line for a place on the Dublin team to play Kerry in the All-Ireland football final. The problem was that he was also attending the diocesan seminary in Clonliffe at the time. Under college regulations, there was no way he would be freed to play the match. It was a straightforward choice: which was the more important to him, to play in the final or to become a priest? He chose to become a priest but, as the final was being played, he could practically see the ball down the road in the college. After his ordination he played for Dublin under the name of Mick Casey.

Lord of the Rings

Mick Dunne spoke to me about Christy Ring's involvement in a controversy.

'In 1953 Galway hurlers, powered by the great Josie Gallagher, had beaten Kilkenny in the semi-final and qualified to play the Christy Ring-led Cork side in the All-Ireland final. Galway had the game for the winning but failed to take off Mick Burke despite his obvious concussion. What made their inaction all the more inexplicable was that Burke was marking the great Christy Ring. A large section of the Galway crowd had booed Ring throughout the game and Galway appeared to have targeted the Cork legend for "special treatment". The post-match celebration was affected by events on the field. A blow had been struck on Burke during the game. So incensed were five or six of the Galway players by this that they had an altercation with Ring that evening at the official reception and returned to the Cork hotel at breakfast the next morning to again vent their displeasure, albeit only using verbal means on that occasion.'

Float Like a Butterfly, Sting Like a Bee

One of Ireland's biggest-ever sporting occasions was held in GAA headquarters. On 19 July 1972, it took Muhammad Ali eleven rounds to defeat an ex-convict from Detroit, Al 'Blue' Lewis, at Croke Park. The fight itself was unremarkable but it was a wonderful occasion, particularly after Ali announced that his maternal great-grandfather Abe Grady had emigrated from County Clare over a century before. As part of the build-up to the fight, Ali met the Taoiseach, Jack Lynch, who informed the pugilist that, despite his busy schedule, he hoped to make it to the fight the following Wednesday. Ali replied, 'Since you're a busy man, I guess I'll get it over quickly.'

'Ah sure, that would spoil it.'

'Well in that case, I'll let Lewis stay in the ring for more than one round.'

'I might get in there for a few rounds myself and keep things going,' said Jack.

For Ali, his Irish adventure was a bit of a culture shock. On his second day in the country he rang his publicist, Harold Conrad, and said 'Hey, Hal. Where are all the ni**ers in this country?'

'Ali,' replied Conrad, 'there aren't any.'

Ali's press conferences before the fight were never less

than memorable. At one point he caught the journalists on the hop when out of the blue he asked, 'What were the last words the Lord uttered at the Last Supper?'

There was silence as the hacks present were not known for their theological expertise. Ali answered his own question, 'Let every man pick up his own check.'

Although the fight itself did not live up to the frenzied anticipation it created, one fan was heard to remark, 'After this performance, all we can do is rename the place Muhammad Alley.'

The Dirty Dozen

Former Galway star Brian Talty is uniquely qualified to give an insider's account into probably the most controversial All-Ireland football final ever.

'In 1983, I remember waking up in the morning and being very disappointed that it was such a wet and windy day because I knew it was going to spoil the match a bit,' he says. 'The game ended with us having fourteen players and Dublin only twelve but it could have been six versus six as there were so many belts flying in. Despite the extra men, we still lost because we missed so many easy chances. The Dubs manager Kevin Heffernan got his tactics right. He withdrew everyone else from the full-forward line and left Joe McNally up on his own. With the wet and windy conditions, it was the sort of day you could crowd your opponents. We didn't have the tactical variation to respond to the circumstances or even the conditions.'

The boil must be lanced. It is time to hear what really happened with Brian Mullins.

'From a personal point view, it was a massive disappointment to become embroiled in the worst controversy of my career,' says Talty. 'That was the hardest part for me, not that

Brian nearly took the top of my head off! If you look back on it on TV, you will see he really made contact with me! Brian was one of my heroes when I went to Thomond College and played with him. When I got married in 1980, Brian was at our wedding. I was on my honeymoon when he had that terrible car accident. As he started to rehabilitate, I played soccer with him so I knew at first hand how far he had to travel to get back to the level he did. Nobody else would put themselves through what he did to get back to the very top. I'm sorry that his achievement in getting back was tainted a bit by him being sent off in an All-Ireland final and especially because it was for striking me. I think what Dublin did that day was incredible but it is such a pity, for their own sake, that the controversy took away from what they did. It was heroic stuff.'

Over thirty years on, the story of what happened in the tunnel continues to be shrouded in mystery. Talty will take the full truth to his grave.

'There was a bit of pushing and shoving and I was struck,' he says. 'The real damage to me was not that one nor Brian's one but, after the sending off, I was charging through to the Dublin goal when P. J. Buckley caught me in the head. Having said that, after Brian and P. J., I could have done without the one in the tunnel! In the dressing-room Billy Joyce asked me if I was okay to continue and, while I said I was, the selectors saw it differently.'

There was unfinished business to be resolved afterwards.

Talty says, 'There was a lot of tension the next day when the two teams met up for the meal, which was the tradition at the time. A few words were exchanged! Joe McNally got up to sing 'The Fields of Athenry'. I remember thinking, "Jesus Christ, wouldn't I love to kill you!"'

'Brian and I went outside in the car park to have a conversation. What sticks in my memory is that when Brian was coming towards me I was thinking, "I hope he's not going to strike me again!" He told me and he was probably right that I was pulling and dragging out of him and that is why he reacted. To be honest, I'm not sure if the talk accomplished anything. My other vivid memory is seeing the way Galway's Stephen Kinneavy and Dublin's Mick Holden, Lord have mercy on him, blocked off the car park and nobody was going to disturb us.'

Talty is thankful for small mercies: 'Brian was teaching in Kilbarrack at the time. Before I got my teaching job in St David's Artane, I had done an interview in Brian's school but didn't get it. Imagine if I had to work with him as well while the controversy was raging!'

See No Evil
For many people the abiding memory from the 1985 semi-final between Mayo and Dublin was the infamous 'John Finn incident', in which the Mayo half-back sustained a broken jaw in an off-the-field challenge. It says a lot about John that he continued to play on. He was on the other side of the field from the ball when he was attacked. John never spoke about it so it was not hyped up for the replay, which would not have happened today. It was much later before it became common knowledge who the culprit was but, typical of the time, no action was ever taken by the GAA against the offending player.

The Keady Affair
In the late 1980s the GAA became concerned about the stream of county players, both in football and hurling, who were heading to New York for short periods during the summer to sample the delights of the Big Apple and make some money by playing with a club there. An example was made.

Tony Keady was found to have played hurling illegally in 1989 and, to the consternation of everyone in Galway, he was suspended for a year shortly before Galway's All-Ireland final fixture against Tipperary.

Sylvie Linnane explains Keady's importance to Galway: 'The 1988 All-Ireland final was one of our best games as a unit. It was very close until Noel Lane came on and scored a late goal. *The Sunday Game* had cameras live at our celebratory dinner and there was a dramatic hush when Ger Canning announced on live television, "And now the moment you have all been waiting for. *The Sunday Game* Man of the Match is . . . Tony Keady." Suddenly everybody stared around but there was no sign of Tony. We found out later that he was five miles away in a pub with Brendan Lynskey and their friends.

'Tony was Texaco Hurler of the Year that year. That was why he was such a big loss to us the following year with the infamous "Keady affair".'

Keady's team-mate Noel Lane outlines the significance of the controversy for the team: 'After he was suspended for a year, there was an appeal but he lost 20–18. Sean Tracey came in for him and he did well for us but we weren't the same tight unit of six backs as we had been when he was there. Nothing would have come through the middle with him there and he would have scored two or three points from long-range frees as he always did. Before the game and the appeal, there was a lot of discussion about whether Tony would play and that was very distracting for us. Our focus was not as good as it should have been for a team seeking three in a row. In the game itself, there were a lot of decisions given against us. Somebody made a comment to me afterwards about the referee: "He was either biased against us or he was a sh*te referee." I said he was both.

———

'I think we all felt angry about the Keady affair because there were hundreds of footballers and hurlers going to play in America at the time but Tony was the one that was made a scapegoat. Keady says that when he dies the words he wants on his tombstone are: "He should have played in '89!"'

Down Under

International rules football, sometimes called 'Compromise rules', is a hybrid code of football which was developed to facilitate international representative matches between Australian rules footballers and Gaelic footballers.

The first games played were test matches between Australia and a touring Meath Gaelic football team which took place in late 1967, after Meath had won that year's All-Ireland Senior Football Championship. Following intermittent international tests between Australia and an All-Ireland team, which began in the centenary year of the GAA in 1984, the International Rules Series really entered the popular consciousness in 1986 following a major controversy.

There was hullabaloo before the team went to Australia when the Dublin coach Kevin Heffernan was appointed as tour manager ahead of Mick O'Dwyer. Micko is the most successful Gaelic football coach of all time and he has never managed the International Rules team, which is extraordinary.

However, what really made the tour come alive was when John Todd, the manager of the Australian team, described the touring side as 'wimps' following complaints about the 'excessively robust play' of the Australian players. His remarks provoked a storm of outrage, not just among the Irish team, but back home in Ireland. It was a huge story throughout the country. It was not quite as big as Roy Keane and Mick McCarthy in Saipan, but it was pretty close. Todd's comments were taken as a slur on the Irish character and, as a result, people who had no interest in the game back home in Ireland became fascinated by the series. It became a matter of national pride for Ireland to beat the Aussies. Thankfully, the fighting Irish provided the most effective rebuttal possible to Todd's comments when they won the series.

The Hidden Truth

In 1996 after the All-Ireland semi-final, two irate Tyrone fans were loud in their condemnation of the Meath team, particularly of their alleged ill-treatment of Peter Canavan. A Meath fan made an interesting and revealing slip of the tongue in response, 'You can't make an omelette without breaking legs.'

Shape Up

The prejudices that exist towards ladies' football were apparent in the controversy in Roscommon over Malachy Byrne's opposition to a £900 grant from Roscommon VEC for the promotion of ladies' football. The controversy was fuelled further as he sought to explain himself on Shannonside radio and he said, 'I reckon that a lady or girl's body is too precious to be abused, bumped and humped playing football. Their bodies are not made for humps and bumps. They have their own natural humps and bumps.'

No Whips Please

Following Clare's victory over Tipperary in the epic Munster final in 1997, Anthony Daly made a speech in which he said, 'We're no longer the whipping boys of Munster.' A massive cheer went up from the Clare supporters when he uttered these words. To the annoyance of everyone in Clare, Liz Howard wrote in a newspaper article that the statement was 'conduct unbecoming'. Liz spent most of her youth living in Feakle, where her father was the local sergeant, so her comments hit a nerve, especially in her former home village. However, when she repeated this 'conduct unbecoming' theme two weeks later, the whole thing spiralled out of control. Other newspapers picked it up and it became a major controversy.

It is an interesting parable about the power of the media because, shortly afterwards, a man came to the door of Anthony Daly's shop in Ennis and said, 'You shouldn't have said that.'

Daly replied, 'What did I say?'

'Well, I don't know. But you shouldn't have said it.'

Straight Talking

For many people, the most memorable moment on *The Sunday Game* came the night of the 1997 All-Ireland final after Clare narrowly beat their old rivals Tipperary. Former Limerick player and manager Eamonn Cregan was one of the guests on that programme. Following Cregan's analysis, the cameras went live to Clare's celebrations at the team hotel and to the Clare manager. Ger Loughnane began his response with the comment, 'After that ten-minute whinge from Eamonn Cregan.' He then launched into an attack on Cregan. Given the intensity of Loughnane's comments, it seemed to outside observers that there must have been some history between them. Loughnane had been on the Clare team in 1983 when Cregan was training it. Loughnane did not rate him as a coach and, in his eyes, Eamonn was exactly the wrong one to come on and criticise Clare, considering he had no success there. Loughnane was standing beside Ger Canning and he sensed that the Clare crowd was aghast. Canning looked Ger straight in the eye and said, 'That's terrible isn't it?' Loughnane replied, 'Pay no heed. That's only Cregan.' Then he let fly. It is a revealing insight into Loughnane's personality that his only regret is that he didn't 'tear' into Cregan much more strongly that night.

A Flop

The Tommy Murphy Cup seemed like a good idea at the time. The weaker counties were always complaining that they did not get enough games – even though they get at least two now. What happened when they established a competition to give them more games? Only five teams entered. One of them, London, pulled out almost straight away. Sligo entered but their county manager, James Kearins, refused to train the team because he said the competition was no use. The majority of his players were not interested either. The Sligo county board had to run around and try to get an interim manager who would train the side only for this competition.

Who Fears to Speak of '98?

The year 1998 was dominated by Ger Loughnane and the many controversies that dogged his team: the clashes with officialdom and the rows with referees, as well as the unprecedented media attention. Things really ignited after the Munster final replay against Waterford, when the intense aggression began even before the match started. The man at the centre of the storm was referee Willie Barrett.

'The criticism of my performance did get to me and I wasn't appointed to any other inter-county games that year,' he says. 'I got letters from people who were very angry. I stopped answering the phone for a while and my wife started taking the calls and she got the brunt of it. Someone said to me once that it was nice to have your picture in the paper but I saw my picture every day for twelve or thirteen days in a row and it didn't add to me, I can assure you. It did affect me and I didn't know at that stage if I would have the confidence to referee a big game again. My daughter was in France at the time and I felt under siege so I brought the family to France until things settled down a bit.'

Colin Lynch was suspended for two months after the game. Resentment over the episode in Clare was compounded by the failure to take comparable action against an Offaly player. As there was no similar disciplinary measures taken against Michael Duignan, even though his blow had been captured live on television and reproduced in a photograph in the national newspapers, the feeling in Clare was that Joe McDonagh, then GAA president, had left himself open to very serious questions of partisan behaviour.

Following his retirement in March 2001, in an interview with Brian Carthy, Michael Duignan admitted that he was very lucky not to have been sent off for what he described as a 'desperate' challenge on David Forde. He generously conceded that Clare fans must have felt a great sense of injustice with the way he got off without any sanctions, whereas Colin Lynch received such a severe punishment.

Clare's All-Ireland semi-final replay against Offaly spawned a new controversy when referee Jimmy Cooney blew up the match early.

Cooney says, 'After I blew the final whistle I saw my umpire and he had his hand out with his five fingers up. I thought to myself, "Oh Jesus". All the photographers were nearly pushing themselves out of the way to get a picture of me. The umpires told me afterwards that I didn't tog in for two hours. I don't remember it but I remember my wife eventually coming into the dressing-room and she was crying, of course. We went to the Aisling Hotel. 'Twas news time and I was flashed across the screen. The waitress looked at the screen, then looked at me, before she said anything I said, "That's me." I just wanted to get home. We had a young family and I knew there could be phone calls.

'There were lots of calls. If one of the girls answered they were asked if their daddy was a referee. When they said yes they were told that their daddy was going to be killed and their house was going to be burned down and if they didn't pass on the message they would be killed as well. When I got to the phone and offered to meet the callers face-to-face they hung up quickly. It would have lasted until Christmas and after that.'

With the benefit of hindsight, Ger Loughnane looks back on 1998 with a surprising perspective: 'When we learned there had to be a second replay after the Jimmy Cooney saga I thought to myself, "Jesus, that's the last thing we want". We were beaten by Offaly in a terrific game. If ever the mental toughness of Clare was tested, it was against Offaly in that third game.

'Offaly had the hangman's noose around their necks – the next thing they found they were free. They woke up in the next world and they were alive. All of the cards were in their favour. Clare had won and were in the All-Ireland but now not in the All-Ireland. Offaly had a massive psychological advantage.

'We were devastated by injuries. P. J. O'Connell was injured. Ollie Baker was injured. Liam Doyle was injured. Brian Quinn had suffered a blackout the previous Tuesday, which I didn't know about. Barry Murphy was injured.

'I thought we'd be trounced by Offaly. What Clare produced in the second half that day was really out of the top drawer. They did everything you could do when your last ounce of energy is drained out and your back is to the wall. They fought like lions and only three great saves by the Offaly goalie and we'd be in the All-Ireland. Lucky enough we weren't because Kilkenny would have beaten us in the final, no question about it.

'It was the day I was most proud of them in every way – with all the odds stacked against them and all the media stacked against them. Their manliness and courage against tiredness and injury was something to be cherished.'

Offaly Rovers

After Offaly lost the Leinster final in 1998 to Kilkenny, Babs Keating controversially described the Offaly players as 'sheep in a heap'. Babs met with the county board and decided to stay but, the next morning, he resigned because he was 'shocked' by an interview in a newspaper with Offaly's star midfielder Johnny Pilkington, who had questioned his record with the county, stated that Babs had abandoned Offaly's tradition of ground hurling and questioned the tactics against Kilkenny. Pilkington is not someone to hide his feelings.

'It really got to me,' he says. 'Babs was manager of Offaly. We had some very bad wides on the day and we had conceded two soft goals in the last fifteen minutes. It just seemed he was passing the buck. Maybe it was the players' fault but he was the manager and he could have come down on Tuesday night and said what he had to say in the dressing-room. He always referred to Offaly as "them" – never as "us". It was a case of "they" were poor out there and "they" did things wrong.

'Michael Bond came on the scene after about a week. He just said he liked Offaly hurling and off we went training. Nobody knew who he was. Nobody knew his hurling credentials or anything. We knew he was a teacher. Someone told us he was a principal. He spoke Irish and some of his instructions were in Irish. The training sessions upped significantly. We were a group of lads who were down at the bottom of the barrel. We were after speaking out against the manager. It wasn't anyone else's responsibility to pick it up – only the thirty lads who were there. After Bond came in there was a great buzz in training and we were thinking we were great lads again. We played Kilkenny in a challenge match, though, and they gave us an even bigger beating than they had in the Leinster final. So where did that leave us?

'Loughnane took his eye off the ball before we played Clare in the All-Ireland semi-final. If they had been playing Kilkenny or Galway it would have been a different story. He took Offaly for granted.'

Not surpisingly, Babs Keating's reading of the events of '98 differs sharply from Pilkington's: 'Johnny Pilkington took great exception to my remark but one of my biggest battles at the time was to get Pilkington to train.'

Broadcaster Peter Woods offers an interesting perspective on Offaly's revived fortunes under Michael Bond: 'You could lead them with a thread but you can't drive them with an iron bar.'

Offaly captain Hubert Ringey, in his victory speech after Offaly beat Kilkenny in the All-Ireland final, said, 'We might have come in the back door, but we're going out the front door.' Offaly came through the back door, having voted against it and Offaly, true to form, voted against the back door the following year.

In the Slow Lane

Noel Lane controversially became manager of the Galway senior team, having served his apprenticeship at club level and with the county minors and under-21s. It is quickly evident that he still feels aggrieved by the manner of his treatment by the county board. Things began promisingly for Lane when Galway beat Kilkenny in the 2001 All-Ireland semi-final.

'I succeeded Mattie Murphy whether it was right or wrong,' he says. 'He was doing a good job but was only given two years. I believe that Galway should have won one or two All-Irelands in the last twenty years because the team was good enough, but there was a lack of continuity at management level. The players were the ones to suffer.

'Beating Kilkenny was a win against the head and one of the highs in my life because I had prepared a team to beat the best but I knew, for reasons unknown to me, that the knives were out for me at the county board level even when we won. It was fed back indirectly to me that the county board was not supporting me. Things had deteriorated after a league match in Tipperary. It was blatantly obvious that I was not acting as they wanted. I was doing things that I felt would help us to win, like flying the team to Croke Park for games. As manager, I had taken control of the team and I don't think that pleased them. I brought in Mike McNamara from Clare. He was a great trainer and was very good on mental toughness and mental preparation.

'The lack of support from the county board took its toll on me in the lead-up to the All-Ireland final against Tipperary. I had a huge management job outside the players with media commitments and everything else. If I got the chance again I would do things differently and put more focus on the players alone. By contrast Nicky English, the Tipp manager, had been in the job for four or five years so he had that experience to call on. The referee made some astonishing decisions that day which I felt cost us. As the co-operation from the county board wasn't there, I had to take on all the organisational details myself. I was emotionally and physically drained from the whole management of the weekend which I think meant that I didn't react sharply enough to events on the sideline during the game and, in that respect, I feel I let down the players. I lost five All-Irelands as a player but losing as a manager was worse because I felt responsible for thirty people in the squad and the back-room team. I knew straight away that the knives were out again.

'The next year we beat Cork in the quarter-final in Thurles, so I must have been doing something right. We played Clare in the semi-final in a very tight and intense game. Clare sucked us in and played the game on their terms. Colin Lynch floated a typical point to snatch the victory for them. That was when I knew the show was over. The press knew. There were long smiles on many of the county board. I felt I was just growing into the job and would have benefited from another year or two but it was very hurtful to effectively be sacked.'

Babs Speak

After Galway dished out a thrashing to his Tipp team in a league match in March 2006, Babs Keating stirred up a hornet's nest when he said, 'I saw the Galway fellas shouting at each other from goalkeeper to corner-forward – our fellas are dead only to wash them.'

When Babs let full-back Philly Maher go from the Tipperary panel, the rationale for the decision was, 'He was putting too much butter on his spuds.'

One of a Kind

The late Páidí O'Sé is probably the greatest character in the history of the GAA.

Myth and legend abound all aspects of his career. His first job was as a garda.

One time Páidí went out to a farm to check up on dog licences. He asked the farmer if he was sure he really had a dog licence. The farmer replied, 'I'm as sure of it as that you have sh*te on the tail of your shirt.'

Páidí had a few memorable run-ins with members of the public. 'How long have you been driving without a tail light?' he asked after pulling over a motorist. The driver jumped out, ran to the rear of his car and gave him a long, painful groan and put his face in his hands. He seemed so upset that Páidí was moved to ease up on him a bit.

'Come on, now,' he said, 'you don't have to take it so hard. It isn't that serious.'

'It isn't?' cried the motorist. 'Then you know what happened to my boat and trailer?'

Páidí stopped a man and his wife for speeding. Anxious to promote our national language he asked, *'Cad is ainim duit?'*

'Seán,' the man replied.

'Agus do bheann?'

'Nissan Micra.'

Another time he asked the bank clerk, who had been robbed for the third time by the same man, if he had noticed anything special about him. 'Yes,' replied the clerk. 'He was better dressed each time.'

Páidí was briefly attached to the Olympia theatre. One night shortly before an opening-night performance, there was a man sprawled out in the front row of the theatre. The usher said to him, 'You're blocking the stage.'

The man replied, 'Aaaaghh!'

The usher left and got the manager who said to the man,

'We don't allow people to put their feet on the stage. Get them down or I'll call the police.'

The man replied, 'Aaaaghhh!'

The manager got Páidí, who then told the man, 'If you don't put your f**king feet down, I'm taking you in. Where did you come from anyway?'

The man looked up and with great effort said, 'From the balcony.'

Apparently Páidí's reports on crimes were something to behold like: 'When questioned by the gardai, the accused could provide no concrete evidence that the cement mixer belonged to him.'

When Dublin played Cork in the 1978 Cardinal Cushing Games, the match was the most physically violent in living memory. A lot of old scores had to be settled and markers were put down for the championship later that year. Pat O'Neill broke Jimmy Deenihan's nose. O'Neill was very contrite and sent an apology later that night to Deenihan in the Kerry hotel. He told him he was very sorry and never intended to hurt him because he thought he was striking Páidí O'Sé.

One of the most famous tours in rugby history was that of the Lions to South Africa in 1974. On the pitch the tour saw some very physical exchanges. One of the props on the tour, Gloucester's Mike Burton, was well able to look after himself in these situations. The following year he became the first English international to be sent off in a Test match, following a clash with Australian winger Doug Osbourne. In the canon of sports' literature, Burton's autobiography *Never Stay Down* stands out. He devotes a chapter on the best punches he encountered in his career.

Páidí also had a reputation as a *fear crua*. This stemmed from his first Munster final when he was marking Cork's

Dinny Allen. Dinny started the match well and kicked two early points. He triumphantly turned to his opponent and said, 'I suppose they'll take you off soon.' Páidí's reply has become a YouTube sensation. He hit Allen with a left hook.

On another occasion, Kerry were playing the Dubs in a league match at Croke Park. Páidí was marking what he described to me as a 'prominent Dub' who turned to him in his finest city accent as they took their positions and said, 'Ye boys probably came up here on a tractor.' Páidí said nothing but he waited till the national anthem and checked that the ref was looking elsewhere and then he recalled to me, 'I bursshted him with a boxssh. He was on the ground calling for his mammy and I turned to him and said, "Jaysus Christ, you look like a lad that was knocked down by a tractor."'

As a manager, Páidí did bring a National League and under-21 All-Ireland to Kerry and two All-Irelands in 1997 and 2000. The wheels came off the wagon in the 2001 All-Ireland semi-final when Meath beat Kerry by no fewer than fifteen points. Kerry went through a twenty-nine-minute spell in the first half without scoring and then could muster only a single point from substitute Declan Quill in the second half. After the match, Marty Morrissey asked a Kerry fan, 'Where did it all go wrong in Croke Park today?'

The fan replied, 'The green bit in the middle.'

Inevitably, when a Kerry team loses by fifteen points in Croke Park serious questions were asked, particularly when Páidí refused to start Maurice Fitzgerald. Maurice's finest hour was the 1997 All-Ireland, when he regularly broke through with Mayo defenders falling around him like dying wasps and kicked incredible points from all angles.

Páidí was proved right in 2000. Maurice was most effective as an impact sub. It was a big gamble but it delivered an All-

Ireland. Páidí's autobiography was the perfect opportunity for him to finally tell us what his problem with Maurice was, but on the single issue that most exercised Kerry people he said absolutely nothing. Ronan Keating was wrong. You do not say it best when you say nothing at all.

In 2002 it was joked that Páidí was the greatest magician of all time. He made Kerry disappear for the entire second half of the 2002 All-Ireland final against Armagh. An old joke was revisited. 'Why aren't the Kerry team allowed to own a dog?'

'Because they can't hold on to a lead.'

This match was a classic case of *nouveau riche* versus old money. At half-time in the 2002 All-Ireland final, Pat Spillane was dismissive of Armagh's chances of beating Kerry. He caused consternation among Armagh fans when he said, 'My mother has arthritis, but even she has more pace than the Armagh full-back line.' In the second half, Spillane was left looking a right idiot and understandably one banner featured prominently in the subsequent media coverage. Against a backdrop of the Armagh colours it said simply, 'Are you watching, Pat Spillane?'

Three days later, when Armagh played Louth in the GOAL challenge, a large man dressed up in drag in the Kerry colours and wearing a placard stating, 'Pat Spillane's Ma', challenged each of the full-back line to an individual race. 'She' won each time.

Most people thought that Kerry had underachieved in the previous two years but that 2003 was going to be the year that Kerry made up for lost time and reclaimed the Sam Maguire trophy. Fate was destined to booby-trap Kerry once again that summer. When the going got tough for Kerry in Croke Park in successive years against Meath, Armagh and Tyrone respectively, Páidí was unable to come up with a Plan B to reverse the situation.

Páidí's year of the U-turn was 2003. He gave an interview with *The Sunday Independent* in January and famously said, 'Being the Kerry manager is probably the hardest job in the world because Kerry people, I'd say, are the roughest type of f**king animals you could deal with. And you can print that.'

A short time later he was forced to meekly apologise, 'I regret very much if I have offended all or some of my Kerry supporters who have been very loyal to me.'

The two big controversies of Páidí's reign – the Maurice and animals controversy – were played out in the full glare of the media. He was unlucky insofar as the animals contro-versy blew up at a very quiet time of the year when there was nothing else for GAA journalists to write about and paper never refuses ink.

A lot of Páidí's most vocal critics were people with agendas. His interview in South Africa was ill-advised. It was not good for Kerry football to have its dirty linen washed in public nor to have colleagues and former colleagues on opposite sides. There were no winners in that situation and it left a bitter legacy and a sour taste.

No Blood on Their Hands
I had hundreds of conversations with Dermot Earley on the phone, in the course of a close friendship of twenty years, but three stand out – two during his illness and one the morning after he was sacked as Roscommon manager.

Results were disappointing during his two-year tenure and a significant number of Roscommon fans were vocif-erous in their criticism of his performance. Things came to a head with the defeat to John O'Mahony's Leitrim by a point in the Connacht Championship in 1994. Although Leitrim went on to win only their second provincial title that year, the rumblings of discontent among Roscommon fans grew to a crescendo.

The day after Dermot's death, in the course of an effusive tribute Shannonside radio's leading personality Joe Finnegan recalled on his morning show, 'His playing days with Roscommon were unforgettable but afterwards his time as manager, he'd probably be the first to admit himself, didn't go well. I couldn't get over the treatment he got in certain quarters. Some of it was vicious and they couldn't get rid of him fast enough. I remember thinking at the time, "My God, if they can do this to Dermot Earley what will they do to somebody else?"'

Some weeks after the Leitrim game, Dermot met up with two senior officials on the Roscommon County Board to review his stewardship of the team. As attention to detail was his mantra, Dermot had prepared a detailed plan for the coming year. When he was asked at the start of the meeting what he thought about things, Dermot launched into his plan with his customary enthusiasm but he quickly noticed that the two men did not seem to be really listening and were looking at each other rather than at him. He came to an abrupt halt and asked them bluntly, 'Do you want me to resign?'

One replied: 'Well, would you?'

Thus ended his managerial career with the county he loved so well.

Knowing about the meeting, I rang him the next morning. It was not like a Roy Keane and Alex Ferguson situation after United let Keano go. There was no bitterness or rancour. However, the conversation was memorable for the number of uncharacteristic pauses and because it was the only time I ever heard him sounding clearly hurt. Not even during his illness was there a hint of that tone. Nobody likes getting rejected and dumped by one of the few great loves of their life.

Ours is an age when the currency is a loyalty bonus. Dermot never sought such a bonus, but instead wanted to give the bonus of loyalty to Roscommon.

The way the meeting had been conducted was not the way he would have handled it himself. Over twenty years on his summary sentence, said not in anger but in a soft whisper of resignation, remains indelibly carved on my memory. 'They wanted my head on a plate but they didn't want my blood on their hands.'

Power to All Our Friends

In his latter years, Dermot Earley developed an unexpected admiration for Ger Loughnane. In 2006 Loughnane began an unsuccessful two years as Galway manager, where he had a jaundiced view, both of some of the county's hurling officials, and of the training facilities.

'I was on the Hurling Development Committee, which tried to persuade Galway to come into the Leinster Championship,' he says. 'When we met them, one official fell asleep at the end of the table. That's a fact. Another official's only concern was that the kitchen was closing at 9pm, so the meeting had to be over then, so that he'd get his meal. They weren't the slightest bit interested.

'Ballinasloe is like a sheep field. Loughrea is an absolute disgrace – a tiny, cabbage garden of a field. Athenry is the worst of all. I asked myself what were these people doing in the 1980s when they had all this success? It was Pearse Stadium they concentrated on – the stand, not the pitch. Because the pitch is like something left over from Famine times, there are so many ridges in it.'

190

Dermot hoped that Loughnane's comments might be the catalyst for some serious debate about the role of county boards: 'I wouldn't have put it as colourfully as Ger. In fact there is probably no topic I would put as colourfully as Ger. The GAA is a magnificent organisation. I doubt if there is any other amateur sporting body in the world to match it. I have the height of admiration for the many fine people I have met down the years who gave so much to their county board – people like the late Michael O'Callaghan in Roscommon and, likewise, some incredibly dedicated people in Kildare and elsewhere. That does not mean, though, that there are not some serious questions to be raised.

'Ger is pointing to the fact that there are many people with their own agenda and let's be honest about it for some of them, living high on Mount Ego, their main achievement is their own advancement. Local and often petty politics, egos and the desire to be in control is sometimes more important than the issues that should really be at the centre, like coaching kids and developing a coherent strategy for the future to ensure that teenagers, girls as well as boys, see Gaelic games rather than sports like rugby as their natural home.

'Just take one example. Outside Roscommon and Kildare, the county I would most like to see winning an All-Ireland is Mayo. People often forget that I was born in Castlebar. In 1989, John O'Mahony guided Mayo to contest a thrilling All-Ireland final against Cork. If Anthony Finnerty's kick had not gone a foot wide they would probably have won. In 1991 the Mayo County Board told John that he could not appoint his own selectors. John had no option but to resign. What happened? The next year the senior team was in disarray. There was a bad vibe all year and, even though they won the Connacht final against Roscommon, there was a sense in

191

the camp that things were not going well. Probably the most memorable incident in that game was that Enon Gavin broke the crossbar in Castlebar and the match had to be delayed.

'Things got ugly after that. It was probably an early example of player power. The players said that if there wasn't a change of management, a lot of them would walk away. As everybody knows, they spent a training session pushing cars in the Dunnes Stores car park in Castlebar. John O'Mahony is known for his meticulous preparation and his attention to detail. Does anybody think John would have the Mayo players pushing cars in a car park? Yet Mayo should have beaten Donegal in that semi-final and Donegal beat the hotly fancied Dubs in the final. I don't usually do "what ifs" but I've often wondered, if John was in charge that year, would Mayo have won the All-Ireland?

'What did John do? He managed a Leitrim team that beat Mayo in the Connacht final in 1994. Then he went to Roscommon and woke the sleeping giant that was Saint Brigid's and led them to their first county title in twenty-eight years and set them on a journey to become a dominant force in Connacht club football. Then he went on to lead Galway to two senior All-Irelands, playing football the way it should be played at its very best. I wonder if the county board officals who gave John his P45 had their own positions questioned. I could pick myriad other examples from other counties to cast doubt on the competence of some county boards across a whole range of issues, from wrong appointments, to structures, to planning, or more accurately the lack of it, to financial mismanagement.

'In the last few years we have had scandals in the Church, the banks, the medical profession, politics and business and, as a result, there have been many calls for accountability and transparency. County boards have huge power but who are

192

they answerable to? I hope maybe Ger's comments could be the spark to start some serious questions in the long-term interests of the Association about the role of county boards. Maybe we should get Ger to lead an audit of all county boards.

'There are some county boards that must be doing a good job. The evidence suggests they are in Kilkenny, for the hurlers at least. I sometimes think, though, that county teams often enjoy interludes of success, not because of their county boards, but in spite of them.'

Despite the irrepressible benignity of his nature, there was one species that really frustrated Dermot.

He said, 'I don't want to generalise, but I find it hard at times to stomach the minority of GAA officials who are so eager to climb the ladder that they won't do anything to rock the boat. You need people in county boards who dream big dreams and have serious moral courage, not people who are terrified to offend. Those who try to be all things to all men inevitably end up being very little to very few.'

Puke Football

After the 2004 All-Ireland final when Kerry beat Mayo, Tommy Lyons sent a text to Pat Spillane saying, 'Football is coming home.' Spillane had been the most high-profile critic of the blanket defence tactics employed by both Armagh and Tyrone in their march to their respective first All-Irelands in 2002 and 2003. Spillane had provoked consternation the previous year when he described Tyrone's performance against Kerry as 'puke football'.

Joe Brolly is more understanding of Tyrone: 'I think in 2003 they just wanted to win an All-Ireland. They didn't care whether it was pretty or not and that's why they used the swarm defence. They played against a great Kerry team and nobody will ever forget the image of Darragh O'Sé with five Tyrone men around him. He was like a Nigerian woman holding a food parcel she had grabbed off a lorry over her head because neighbours were trying to steal it off her. Kerry were caught on the hop. Armagh had won the All-Ireland the previous year playing a defensive brand of football but there was something to admire about it, something heroic about it. Even Armagh couldn't cope that year with Tyrone's play. In Tyrone, the individual was anonymous. Peter Canavan was able to play in that final, kicking on only one leg. People started to ask, "Is that football at all?" But they won their All-Ireland.'

Another Fine Mess

The chaos and confusion after the Kilkenny–Clare All-Ireland hurling quarter-final in 2004 was another GAA fiasco. After the match was drawn, the teams were exchanging jerseys and the crowd was leaving Croke Park when an announcement was made over the public address system that extra-time would be played. Mass head-scratching took place. There would be extra-time. No there would not. Nobody knew what was happening. Players, team management, match commentators, fans and the national television audience were completely in the dark. GAA officials were spotted running around like headless chickens. Eventually, another announcement was made that a replay would take place. The shambles was captured live on television. What was the problem? The *clár an lae* said there would be extra-time.

Claregate

If a week is a long time in politics, eleven years is a long time in hurling and, in 2006, a bizarre series of events involving an

194

overheard phone conversation and a complaint to the guards created a virtual civil war in Clare hurling that entered the vernacular as 'Claregate'. At its core was a row between Ger Loughnane and what he terms 'the Clare hurling establishment'. How does Loughnane reflect on the bitter controversy?

'I believe there is an element in charge of hurling in Clare who want to rewrite the history of what happened in '95 and '97 because they want to keep things in their own hands. Essentially they were bypassed in our glory years and they don't want that situation to be repeated – even if it means we are not successful as a county.'

The controversy reheated itself in 2007, when Loughnane weighed in to back his old friend Tony Considine who was experiencing a turbulent time as Clare manager. What raised most eyebrows was the timing of his comments – shortly before his Galway team were playing Clare in a crunch game. Loughnane was bemused by the hullabaloo.

'I threw a pebble and everyone thought it was an earthquake,' he says.

Loughnane sparked an even bigger controversy that summer when he complained that Kilkenny's tactics crossed the line on occasions.

'Christ I got such criticism, some of it for words I never actually used, that I thought at one stage I was going to be blamed for global warming,' he says. 'I sometimes laugh when I turn on the radio and listen to sports shows and find they are talking about something I said as if it was more newsworthy than the Gettysburg Address. What makes it all the more laughable is that they invite journalists on to interpret what I have said and they talk about "Ger" as if they knew me well. Some of these guys are people I have rarely, if ever, spoken with in any meaningful way and often they know as much about me as I know about synchronised swimming.'

Croke Park

The GAA showed real leadership in revoking Rule 42 and opening up Croke Park to rugby and soccer. Nobody will ever forget the atmosphere and the sense of history in 2007 when Ireland beat England in Croke Park. It was a defining moment for many people and it meant so much to everybody in the country.

For an amateur organisation, it is a staggering achievement to have created an incredible stadium like Croke Park especially in the middle of Dublin. They have shown incredible leadership.

There was much controversy beforehand though. In 2003, Eire Og delegate Pat Daly at the GAA Convention in Cork said, 'It's about time the GAA woke up. The ban has been gone since 1973 – if Frank Sinatra can play in Croke Park, then why not the Irish international rugby team?' However, Munster Council Treasurer Dan Hoare went for an 'out, out, out' approach, 'I would not let anybody into the car park, not to mention into Croke Park.'

A delegate at the Wicklow GAA County Convention said, 'We are being asked to wake up some morning and see the English soccer team playing in Croke Park. Just eighty years ago the English came to Croke Park and shot Gaelic players.'

Ulster Council Secretary Danny Murphy suggested that, unless there was a clear case for change, then there were definite reasons not to change. The then Ulster Council President Michael Greenan weighed in with a real beauty. He said the GAA were not in the business of housing the homeless. On *Prime Time*, the Cork representative who appeared on the programme argued that the GAA should keep the ban in place as a result of what happened in Croke Park on Bloody Sunday.

Some fans were frustrated that the GAA were so concerned to protect our 'cultural purity' yet they had been more than willing to take the shilling when those well-known champions of Irish culture, Sir Elton O'Sean, Billy O'Joel agus Neil O'Diamond had sold their wares in Croke Park. Even more amazingly, the GAA had been happy to host an American football match there in 1997. Did that seem consistent?

Not the Eye of the Tiger

To much fanfare, Hawkeye was introduced to Croke Park in 2013. Newstalk radio station even had its own 'Hawkeye correspondent'. Immediately, umpiring controversies abated and all was well with the world. Then there was the dreaded glitch in the system and Limerick were deprived of a place in the All-Ireland minor hurling final. A campaign, with no thought for political correctness, began in Limerick to demand that Hawkeye be renamed as 'the Stevie Wonder'.

I Don't Thank You for the Music

A Donegal All-Ireland winner in 2012 was the victim of a clever but embarrassing prank. He was to be interviewed live on BBC television. A 'good' friend, though, changed his ring tone and rang him while he was doing the live interview. The Donegal player's blood visibly drained from his face when he heard his new ring tone. The Wolfe Tones were blaring out 'A Nation Once Again'.

The Sound of Silence

The spat of the year in 2013 was between Ger Loughnane and John Mullane. That January, Mullane anounced his retirement from the Waterford team. After Waterford lost to Kilkenny, Loughnane appeared to blame Mullane for retiring and for 'letting his county down'. Asked on Newstalk's *Off the Ball* about Loughnane's remarks, Mullane appeared to be the bigger man when he replied, 'He's entitled to his own opinion. But I'm not going to comment on that.' However, he couldn't resisit saying, 'I think if you're dealing with ignorant people, the only way you can deal with it is to ignore it.'

Up His Own Ass

The film *Four Weddings and a Funeral* made Hugh Grant a star. It also spawned one of the biggest selling songs of all time with Wet Wet Wet's cover of 'Love is All Around'. On Valentine's Day in 2014, love was all around again – well almost. It was the day Ger Loughnane chose to write in his column in *The Star* that Offaly were the 'only team in the modern era with fat legs, bellies and ars*s'.

Twitter went into meltdown. Daithi Regan had a response that raised an intriguing biological question, 'Someone give Ger a replica Liam McCarthy Cup, stamp it 1998 "winners" then he might crawl back up his ass.'

The Sky Deal

Liveline went into meltdown after it was announced that the GAA had done a deal with Sky television in 2014 which meant that some crucial games would no longer be available on terrestrial television. Asked for his view, Pat Spillane was uncharacteristically phlegmatic, 'My wife left me during the week so it's a case of no woman, no sky.'

Six

Simply The Best

Gaelic games have a long and storied history and, in the process, have produced many fabled heroes. This chapter pays homage to some of the brightest and the best, encompassing notable feats and epic encounters of famous sons and daughters of the GAA.

Over the Bar Said Lory Meagher

Real Madrid star Cristiano Ronaldo says he wants to 'live like a king' after retiring and credits playing success to tough teenage years where 'I had to do my own ironing'. GAA stars are cut from a different cloth.

Kilkenny have produced some of the greatest hurlers of all time, such as Eddie Keher, D. J. Carey and Henry Shefflin. There was one, though, who blazed a trail for others to follow.

A regular feature of Kilkenny's matches throughout the 1920s and 1930s was Lory Meagher wearing a blood-stained jersey or head bandage making scything tackles, immune to the threat to his own safety. As his only protective gear was a peak cap he collected many stitches, mostly facial, in his inter-county career and lost enough blood to keep Dracula going for months. The message to his opponents was loud and clear: 'The black and amber will not be beaten.'

Kilkenny's Lorenzo Ignatius Meagher was perhaps the first true star of hurling. Meagher could not have chosen a better or more nurturing environment to begin his career. Over the next decade, he would both feed off and fuel the fires of passion in one of hurling's greatest shrines. The obsession created in Kilkenny is the envy of nearly every hurling side in the country and Lory was always quick to acknowledge the debt of gratitude owed to the most benevolent of patrons. He was to hurling aficionados in the county what Nureyev was to the ballet enthusiast.

He won three All-Irelands in the 1930s and entered the club of GAA immortals on foot of his towering performance in dreadful weather in midfield when Kilkenny beat the hot favourites and reigning champions Limerick in the 1935 All-Ireland, having previously won All-Irelands in 1932 and '33.

On that wet September day in 1935, Meagher answered all the questions with an outstanding exhibition from midfield. Nine years earlier, he had lost an All-Ireland final to Cork when his brothers Willie and Henry were also playing for Kilkenny.

In his later years, Meagher would delight in recalling an amusing postscript from the 1935 final, 'A few days later a stranger approached me and said, "Well, Lory, boy, you did alright on Sunday."'

Lory was brought up in a very nationalistic family. As a boy he was inculcated into the beliefs of Michael Davitt, the driving force behind the Land League in the later part of the nineteenth century. One of Meagher's favourite passages was Davitt's comments that: ' . . . old men have forgotten the miseries of the Famine and had their youth renewed by the sights and sounds that were invoked by the thrilling music of the camán.' Meagher did make magnificent music with the camán whenever he lined out in the black and amber.

Lory embodied the incomparable appeal of hurling, the blood-stirring excitement and democracy of ambitions which takes ten of thousands to Croke Park buoyed by the certainty that they are about to share not only hurling's greatest event, but one of the most enjoyable experiences the entire sporting calendar can offer. Lory was a great reader of the game and one of the few hurlers of his time who could actually side-step, whereas many of his peers seemed content when they got the ball just to drive into their opponent.

Such was his status within the game that, when he died in 1973, he had a funeral fit for a prince. For years young Kilkenny hurlers chanted, 'Over the bar said Lory Meagher', when they scored in training sessions. His legacy is commemorated in the Lory Meagher Heritage Centre, which was opened by former president Mary Robinson in 1994.

Apart from his genius on the field, Meagher is renowned for his modesty off it. This character trait was most vividly illustrated when a journalist met him on the roadside one day and asked where he might track down Lory Meagher. The Kilkenny ace's reply was, 'You've just missed him. He passed up this way a few minutes ago. If you hurry you've a good chance of catching him.'

The Green and Red of Mayo
The first Connacht team to win an All-Ireland was Galway in 1934. Two years later, Mayo won their first All-Ireland. The star of the Mayo team was Henry Kenny, father of Taoiseach Enda Kenny.

Enda says, 'A mythology developed in the county about the '36 team, not least because they went fifty-three games without defeat. People thought they could jump over telegraph poles.

'My father went to teacher training college in De La Salle Waterford. Times were very tough and the food was so scarce there that my father said you needed to have the plates nailed to the tables! After he qualified, he went to teach in Connemara and cycled sixteen miles to train for the club team and sixty miles to Castlebar to play for Mayo. One of his team-mates was Paddy Moclair, who was the first bank official to play county football and he cycled from Clare. I've seen telegrams from the time from the Mayo County Board and they were told, "Train yourself, you've been selected to play".

'My father was particularly famous for his fielding of the ball. He grew up on the same street with Patsy Flannelly, another of the stars of the '36 team. They had no football as kids so they went to the butcher's shop and got pig's bladders from him to use instead of footballs. Dad always said, "If you could catch those you could catch anything."

'The other thing he was noted for was his ability, after he caught the ball in the air, to turn before his feet touched the ground. When my brothers and I started playing his advice to us was always, "Be moving before the ball comes." He found a big change in the way the game was played, especially when they started wearing lighter boots like the soccer players. When he saw a pair of them he said, "These boots are like slippers." He didn't have much time for the solo runs and that's why he called it "the tippy toe". He said he would "beat the solo runner with his cap".

'Dad had great admiration for athletes. That's probably why the player he admired most was Kildare's Larry Stanley who, of course, holds a unique distinction of winning All-Irelands with Kildare (1919) and Dublin (1923) and of representing Ireland in the Olympics (in the high jump at the 1924 Games in Paris).

'In 1936, Seamus O'Malley captained the Mayo team to the All-Ireland. He travelled to Dublin by train the evening before the match. On the day of the match he announced that he could not stay for the celebrations and got a lift back to Mayo after the match. The Sam Maguire Cup was put in the boot of the car. He had to go to his work as a teacher the next morning. He left for work by bicycle with the Sam Maguire Cup strapped on his back! The times have changed.'

Tom McNicholas was the last survivor of the 1936 Mayo team. He retained vivid memories of that team: 'There wasn't the same cult of personality back then but there was no question that the star of our team was Henry. He was wonderful at catching balls in the air. He had great duels with the mighty Kerry midfielder Paddy Kennedy and was probably one of the very few players, if not the only footballer, who could hold his own with Kennedy. This was particularly the case in the All-Ireland semi-final in Roscommon when we beat Kerry 1-5 to 0-6 in 1936, when Kennedy was the new star in the game.

'Henry was known as "the man with the magic hands". He had big hands and he could hold the ball in one hand. Now our game has become more like basketball as there is so much hand-passing. Back then, though, it was a game of catch and kick and nobody did it better than Henry. I don't think any of our team would believe the way the game has changed, especially the emphasis on stopping teams from playing and, above all, the number of times people pass the

ball backwards. We believed in positive football and playing
your own game rather than the opposition's.'

The Playboy of the Southern World

> *Grant me, O Lord, a hurler's skill,*
> *With strength of arm and speed of limb,*
> *Unerring eye for the flying ball,*
> *And courage to match whatever befall.*
> *May my stroke be steady and my aim be true,*
> *My actions manly and my misses few;*
> *No matter what way the game may go,*
> *May I rest in friendship with every foe.*
> *When the final whistle for me has blown,*
> *And I stand at last before God's judgement throne,*
> *May the great referee when He calls my name*
> *Say, You hurled like a man, you played the game.*

Nobody embodied the spirit of 'The Hurler's Prayer' better
than Mick Mackey.

Unlike rugby, nicknames are not part of the culture in the
GAA. There is no question that this is a good thing. What
makes Mick Mackey unique among the giants of Gaelic
games was that he had three nicknames. He was often
described as 'The Laughing Cavalier', occasionally as 'The
King of the Solo Run' but most often as 'The Playboy of the
Southern World'. He always seemed to have a smile on his
face – both on and off the field. He was one of those exceptional talents who made the crowd come alive because of his
swashbuckling style and the higher the stakes, the better he
performed, which is a sure sign of greatness.

He was also renowned for his shrewdness. In a senior

hurling game between his club Ahane and Thurles Sarsfields, the established practice was for a prominent clergyman to throw in the ball to start the game. Sometimes it served as the real throw-in and the match started but, at other times, it was merely ceremonial. For this match, the local parish priest was given the honour of throwing in the ball. With typical mischievousness Mick shouted, 'Go easy there lads. This is not the real throw-in.' The opposing team fell for the trick and made no attempt to go for the ball, allowing Mackey to swoop in unchallenged and race for goal with one of his trademark solos and secure the opening point.

One of his finest performances came in the 1936 Munster final against Tipperary. He had suffered a bad knee injury before the game and, knowing he was likely to 'have it tested' by his opponents, wore a massive bandage – on his healthy knee. He scored five goals and three points that day. In the heady aftermath of their triumph, the Limerick fans were ready to acclaim a new hero, a player who reached his zenith on that occasion. They were enthralled by his irresistible aggression, which mixed almost animal drive with a keenly appreciated mastery of the fine skills. His armoury included seemingly lightening speed on the solo run, staying power and limitless heart.

He captained Limerick to the All-Ireland title that year, defeating Kilkenny in the final by 5-6 to 1-5, and again in 1940, having won his first All-Ireland in 1934. He made his debut for Limerick in 1930 and, over his seventeen-year career, he also won five National League medals and eight Railway Cups, many in the company of his brother John. He also won fifteen county senior hurling championships with Ahane and five county football medals. One of those football titles came in 1939, when Ahane won by a single point.

Nothing unusual in that at first glance but what made that point unique was that it was the only score in that match.

One of his finest hours came in the 1944 Munster final, which has gone down in history as 'the Bicycle Final' because it occurred during 'the Emergency' when private cars were off the road because of rationing during the war effort led by Seán Lemass. People arrived in Thurles in their droves on their bicycles. The fact that it was against old rivals Cork added to the lustre of the occasion. One of Mackey's most valuable contributions was to temporarily challenge the traditional established order in Munster between Cork and Tipperary and the 'big three' on a national scale with Kilkenny added to the mix.

From a Jack to a Ring

Jack Lynch was first elected to the Dáil in 1948, having initially been approached to contest the election by Clann na Poblachta. He was appointed Parliamentary Secretary to the Government in 1951 with responsibility for the Gaeltacht. In 1957 he became Minister for Education and, two years later, he replaced Seán Lemass as Minister for Industry and Commerce. He was appointed Minister for Finance in 1965 and, the following year, he reluctantly allowed his name to go forward for the leadership of Fianna Fail when Lemass announced his retirement. He won and became the first Taoiseach of the post-civil war generation. His finest hour came in 1977 when he led Fianna Fail to a General Election victory, with a twenty-seat majority.

When you ask someone who held the unique distinction of winning six senior All-Ireland medals in consecutive years (1941–46) what his favourite personal sporting memory is, the last thing you expect to be told about is an All-Ireland final he lost. Yet such was the case with Jack Lynch.

'It may be paradoxical, but the games of which I have the most vivid memories are of the ones we lost,' he said. 'Of these I remember best the first All-Ireland hurling final in which I played. It was Cork versus Kilkenny on 3 September 1939. I was captain of the team and hopeful of leading Cork out of a comparatively long barren spell. Cork had not won a final since 1931, when they beat Kilkenny in the second replay of the final.

'The match I refer to has since been known as the "Thunder and Lightning Final". We had all kinds of weather, including sunshine and hailstones. It was played on the day that the Second World War commenced. I missed at least two scorable chances – of a goal and a point. I was marking one of the greatest half-backs of all time, Paddy Phelan, and we were beaten by a point scored literally with the last puck of the game. I can remember more facets of that game than almost any other in which I played.

'Although I was lucky enough to play in many All-Ireland finals, all the Munster finals were special. It was always about more than sport. It was a social occasion where men drank in manly moderation but, probably more than any other moment in the calendar, it defined our identity. Looking back, there were a lot of hardships in those days with rationing and so on. To take one example, both Tipperary and Kilkenny were excluded from the 1941 hurling championship because of an outbreak of foot and mouth disease. Yet no matter how bad things were, like at Christmas, the Munster final was always guaranteed to put a smile on people's faces.'

The Wizard of Cloyne
Following his retirement, Jack Lynch noted a minor revolution in the game of hurling. 'Hurling certainly has changed

over the past fifty years, in some respects for the better but overall it has not improved as a spectacle. There is not the flow in the game as there was in my day, similarly with pulling on ground balls. There is now a tendency to catch an overhead ball, which admittedly can look so spectacular but like overindulging in trying to pick every ball into the hand from the ground instead of pulling on it, it slows up the game and leads to crowding and scrambling.'

When asked of his opinion of himself as a hurler, Lynch was understandably reticent. 'I would prefer to leave this assessment to people I played with or against or saw me play.'

However, he was much more forthcoming about his opinion of other great players. Inevitably the analysis began with Christy Ring.

'Christy Ring was the greatest hurler that I knew,' he says. 'I know there are some who will contend that others were better – Mick Mackey, for example. I think Mick Mackey was the most effective hurler that I played against. Mackey was great but, in my opinion, Ring's hurling repertoire was greater. He was totally committed to hurling, perhaps more so than any player I have ever met. He analysed games in prospect and in retrospect. In essence, he thought and lived hurling.

'I conclude with the observation that Christy Ring made in his article in *The Spirit of the Glen*, which depicts the hurlers Glen Rovers 1916–1973: "My hurling days are over – let no-one say the best hurlers belong to the past. They are with us now and better yet to come." Typical of Ring's brilliant mind.'

The Ring of Fire
Nobody did more to transform our national game in to our national soap opera than Christy Ring. Such was his legend that it was said he could shoot the eye out of your head from

two fields away. His epic deeds were evocatively conveyed in a poem in his honour:

> *Now Cork is bate,*
> *The hay is saved,*
> *The thousands wildly sing.*
> *They speak too soon,*
> *My sweet garsun,*
> *Cos here comes Christy Ring.*

The late Bill O'Herlihy often saw Ring at close quarters growing up in Cork in the 1940s and 1950s.

'My generation was very lucky because we grew up at a time when sport in Cork was terrific,' he said. 'Cork hurling was the best hurling in the country at the time by a distance. In Cork City, you had Glen Rovers, Sarsfields, Blackrock and St Finbarrs, which was in my parish. They had unbelievable teams and there was unbelievable tribalism involved. Ring was the greatest hurler I've ever seen and I saw a lot of him, because my father, God rest his soul, loved hurling and brought me to a lot of games. But you would have an extraordinary attitude to Ring. When he was playing for Glen Rovers you hated him because you were from the Barrs, but if he was playing for Cork you thought he was a god. He was a very nice man but he had this aura about him and he wasn't the easiest man I've ever talked to. He was difficult because he was shy, not because he was rude.'

Jim Fives, who played for both Waterford and Galway, was chosen at right full-back on the Centenary team of the greatest players never to have won an All-Ireland medal. He had the unenviable task of marking Ring on a number of occasions.

'My favourite character in the game was Kilkenny's "Diamond" Hayden,' he says. 'He was a great believer in psychological warfare. He would do everything and anything to put you off your game. He was always talking himself up, always trying to get you to think that you would be much better off trying to find someone else to mark. I believe Christy Ring played those sort of mind games as well, though he never did on me. He probably felt that he didn't need to.

'Ring was the best player I ever saw. I marked him in Railway Cup matches. It was a very trying experience as a back because you never knew what he was going to do. A lot of the time you never knew where he was. He just ghosted into positions. One minute you were right beside him, the next he was gone and you were left for dead.'

Dublin's former All-Star Mick Birmingham got up close and personal with Ring.

'I first got to know him when he was working in Dublin and he used to go training in Islandbridge,' he says. 'I was fifteen and he was in the autumn of his career. My uncle played against him in the Railway Cup final in 1947, so that gave me the courage to go up and speak to him. We pucked a few balls together.

'I got to know him better when I played with him later in the Cardinal Cushing Games in America. He was very intense. There were no shortcuts with him. It was a great education to watch him. He had great anticipation and was a master of judging the flight of the sliotar. I learned a lot about how to play corner-forward from him. If he got a score he'd dance a little jig to annoy his opponent and straight away won the psychological battle. I always tried to out-think my opponent and, as a result, I never stood still in a match.'

Clare legend Jimmy Smyth came up against Ring often.

'Nicky Rackard was the third best hurler of all time behind Mick Mackey but the greatest of all was Christy Ring,' he said. 'Forward play has deteriorated since my time but back play has come on a lot. They mark forwards so tightly now that you can hardly do anything. I just wonder how Ring would cope now. He would still get a lot of scores but I don't think he would have got quite so many.

'Ring was like Muhammad Ali. He once said: "Modesty is knowing where you stand." He always knew. If he thought he had played below his own high standards, he would be the first to say so. He was well aware of his own ability and didn't believe in concealing the fact that he knew. I remember we were playing in a Railway Cup match once and he said to me, "When I get the ball you run in for the pass. And remember. I don't miss."'

Jack Lynch was amused by one aspect of Ring's impact on Cork hurling.

He said, 'A few days before the 1972 Munster final between Cork and Clare, Cork dual-star Denis Coughlan pulled in for petrol and who should pull in beside him but Christy Ring? Christy started to talk to him about the match and asked Denis to show him his hurley. Christy decided to take a few swings with it but somehow broke it. The blood drained from Christy's face but, when he recovered his composure, he told Coughlan not to worry. He pulled out a hurley from the boot of the car. It was the one he used in three of his greatest All-Ireland triumphs. It was too heavy for Denis, though, so Christy called back to him a few hours later with a hurley that was a ringer for the one he broke. "That will bring you luck," said Christy. With Cork leading comfortably, Denis was sent off for the only time in his career.'

From a Jack to a King

Jack Lynch won five All-Ireland hurling medals with Cork. He also won an All-Ireland football medal. His football career left him with one enduring memory from the 1945 All-Ireland football final. Lynch took mischievous pleasure in recalling Frank O'Connor's claim that Cork had a mental age of seventeen. 'You had to leave at seventeen if you were to be happy and stimulated whereas Dublin had a mental age of twenty-one.'

Lynch said, 'Having completed my law examinations I was in digs on the southside of Dublin in Rathgar. I met the Cork team at Kingsbridge Station on the Saturday evening and I told the selection committee I would not be at the hotel the next morning as there was a bus route near my digs which passed by Croke Park and that I would go straight there. I was waiting in a queue about twenty yards long. Bus after bus passed, each taking only a couple of people at a time. At one stage, I barged to the head of the queue. The conductor told me to go back and await my turn. I pointed to my bag of togs and said I was playing in the All-Ireland football final in Croke Park within the hour. The conductor said sarcastically that this was the best reason for breaking a queue that he ever heard but let me stay on. I alighted from the bus at the junction of Drumcondra and Conyngham Roads and ran around to the back of the Cusack Stand where the dressing-rooms were then located. About fifteen minutes to the throw-in, I knocked at the Cork dressing-room door to be greeted by an ominous silence except the sound of footsteps slowly and deliberately pacing the floor. The door opened. It was Jim Hurley, former Cork hurling midfielder, then secretary of UCC and chairman of the Cork Selection Committee. I expected to be bawled out. Instead I got, "Hello Jack Lynch, you were great to come." I had missed the president at the time, Sean T. O'Ceallaigh, coming into the dressing-room to wish the team well. I regretted that because he had been in the GPO in the 1916 Rising. I think I escaped any nasty recriminations afterwards when I was involved in the movement that set up the winning goal.'

Lynch also made his mark in a club football match

'The star-laden Clonakilty side were playing Saint Nicholas in Bandon,' he said. 'It was during the winter and the river adjacent to the pitch was flooded. Mick Finn deliberately belted it into the river because Clonakilty were losing and there was only one football and he hoped the match would have to be abandoned. I jumped into the river and swam out to retrieve the ball. The Clonakilty lads never forgave me for it.'

Rackard Royalty

Liam Griffin put it memorably: 'In a land without royalty, the Rackards were king.'

Few families have had the impact on the game as the Rackards. Nicky's status as the greatest full-forward in the history of the game is reflected in his selection in that position on both the team of the century and team of the millennium, while his brother Bobby was picked at right corner-back on both teams. Meanwhile, their younger brother Billy won three All-Ireland medals. Traditionally, only Christy Ring and Mick Mackey have been placed ahead of Nicky Rackard in hurling's hierarchy of greats.

Rackard was one of the most colourful characters hurling has ever known. He changed the whole sporting and social structure of Wexford. He went to St Kieran's College in Kilkenny and developed a love for hurling which he brought home to his brothers and to his club, Rathnure. Wexford had traditionally been a football power going back to their famous four-in-a-row side of 1915–18. But Nicky Rackard turned Wexford, almost overnight, into a recognised hurling bastion. He was crucial to Wexford's two All-Irelands in 1955 and 1956. In the 1954 All-Ireland semi-final against Antrim, he scored an incredible seven goals and seven points.

The 1956 final between Cork and Wexford was one of Rackard's happiest memories and is acknowledged as one of the greatest hurling finals of them all. It had been history in the making as Christy Ring was seeking a record ninth All-Ireland medal. The game will always be remembered, above all, for Art Foley's save from Ring.

It was a match that captured the imagination like few others. Tradition favoured Cork. Going into the game they had won twenty-two titles against Wexford's two. Such was the interest in Wexford that two funerals scheduled for the day of the final had to be postponed until the following day because the hearses were needed to transport people to the match. More than 83,000 people attended. The final had to be delayed until 23 September because of a polio scare in Cork. The authorities did not want a huge crowd assembling in one place.

The crucial contest was between Christy Ring, playing at left-corner forward, and Bobby Rackard. It was the Wexford man who would win out in every sense.

Wexford had the advantage of a whirlwind start with a goal from Padge Keogh after only three minutes. Two minutes later, Ring registered Cork's first score with a point from a twenty-one-yard free. Wexford went on to win by 2-14 to 2-8.

Significantly, that Wexford team had a special place in Christy Ring's affections: 'I always loved our clashes with Wexford in Croke Park. It's a different climate in Croke Park because you didn't have the pressure of the Munster Championship on your back. It was the same for Wexford. They

214

didn't have the pressure of beating Kilkenny on them. Both of us could relax a bit.'

Success bred jealously and the full glare of media intrusion. Mercifully, Nicky was no paragon. There were times when he sought solace in the bottom of a bottle. After his playing days had ended, Nicky went through a turbulent time with alcoholism but, true to form, he rallied and drew on his own darkness to bring light to others when he became a counsellor with AA to those with the same condition. He died in 1975 at the age of fifty-three. The knowledge that we had lost him too early generated a sense of loss, which far exceeded anything that would have been felt for any politician or media personality.

The Queen of the Ash
Camogie's most famous star is Kilkenny's Angela Downey. During an All-Ireland final against Cork, Angela was goal bound when her opponent, Liz O'Neill, made a despairing lunge at her which caused Angela's skirt to end up on the ground. Undeterred, Angela kept on running and, even when the Cork goalie Marian McCarthy whisked the hurley from her hands, she palmed the ball into the net and then calmly returned to collect her skirt. Even more telling was her subsequent comment: 'Even if she had pulled off all my clothes, I was going to score a goal first.'

As a girl, Angela always had a hurley stick in her hand and her theatre of dreams was her backyard. As a teenager, there was not much to do other than camogie: no discos, no cinemas locally – although she did cross-country running for Kilkenny City Harriers. She practised by hitting stones on the roof of the slaughterhouse at her father's butcher-shop. Her heroes included Liz Neary and Helen O'Neill. She made the senior county team when she was fifteen and won her first All-Ireland at seventeen. The Kilkenny team were trained by Tom Ryan, who often came to training in his Wellingtons.

Not surprisingly, she has been immortalised in folklore and is to camogie what Christy Ring is to hurling. Hurling was in her genes. Her father was the legendary Shem Downey, who starred for the black and amber in the 1940s and 1950s, with an All-Ireland medal in 1947 in Kilkenny's classic triumph over Cork. Shem brought the passion he exhibited in the black and amber on to the sidelines when he watched his daughters on the camogie field.

Angela played in her first senior All-Ireland final with Kilkenny in 1972, against Cork, when she was just fifteen. It was to be a rare reversal for the young player but all present that day remember their first acquaintance with Angela and knew intuitively that something special had arrived on the sporting scene. In the coming years they were destined to often see her glide through bedraggled defenders, making a feast from a famine of poor possession. She appealed to the finer side of the imagination, with memory cherishing not only what she did in Croke Park and elsewhere, but how she did it – with panache and elegance. Although she would be defeated in '72, she went on to win seven consecutive All-Irelands for Kilkenny, in a team trained by Tom Ryan, from 1985 to 1991. In total, she would win twelve All-Irelands. The first would come after a replay against Cork in 1974. Only Dublin's Una O'Connor, with thirteen, and the late Dublin star Kathleen Mills, with fifteen, have surpassed that achievement. She captained the county to All-Ireland success in 1977, 1988 and 1991. In 1986, Angela became only the third camogie player to be given a Texaco award.

To add to Angela's joy, all her All-Ireland medals were

won with her twin sister Ann. In 2010, both were jointly presented with the Lifetime Achievement Award in *The Irish Times* Sportswoman of the Year Awards.

The definitive tribute to Angela and Ann Downey comes from 'the Star of the County Down', Máirín McAleenan: 'Angela and Ann Downey of Kilkenny made a fantastic contribution to camogie in the 1980s and 1990s. Their longevity at the highest level is amazing and I believe will never be equaled, never mind surpassed. Ann is fiery, strong, tough and was a non-stop runner. Angela was like lightening and skilful beyond belief. Camogie owes a great deal to the Downeys. *Go raibh míle maith agaibh.*'

Angela was also keenly appreciative of the importance of the club, in her case St Paul's and later Lisdowney. To add to Angela's medal haul, she won an incredible twenty-two county titles and six All-Ireland club titles.

A geography teacher at Grennan College in Thomastown, Angela's career witnessed two controversies. In 1988, just before her club faced Glenamaddy in the All-Ireland final, Angela was sensationally suspended for six months. Appropriately, St Paul's united in the face of what they saw as an injustice against Angela and won by a point with the last puck of the ball.

In February 2004, Angela boycotted the presentation of the Team of the Century in protest at the absence of her twin sister, Ann, from the team. When asked to clarify her absence, Angela said, 'I don't like singling out individuals because Gaelic games are team-based and it is teams who win and lose matches and being part of a team always appealed to me. Ann gave twenty-five years to camogie, has twelve All-Irelands and actually one more club title than me because I was suspended for one final.'

Footballing Artist

Offaly's Matt Connor will be forever imprinted into GAA immortality because of his scoring feats. He was Ireland's top marksman for five consecutive years from 1979 to 1983 and scored a remarkable eighty-two goals and 606 points in 161 matches for Offaly. His silky skills on the ball, his free-taking ability, his power on the ball and his speed of movement and thought made him stand out from everybody else. He scored a stunning 2-9 (2-3 from play) in the All-Ireland semi-final in 1980 against Kerry, when the final score was 4-15 to 4-10 in Kerry's favour.

A football career is measured in moments rather than in days. One vignette that typifies his career came for his club Walsh Island (whom he steered to six consecutive county titles between 1978 and 1983) in Newbridge, in a Leinster Club match. His side was under pressure and needed a score. Matt collected the ball twenty-five yards out from his own goal and went the length of the field on a solo run. In his green and white hooped jersey he left everybody that came to tackle him behind, stretched on the ground, without any of them even touching him, where he swerved, feinted, sold a dummy, slowed up or accelerated to lose his man. As the ball went over the bar, some of the players he had beaten were still on the ground, some were picking themselves up and one or two were on one knee. All were pictures of dejection, beaten by superior skills.

Dublin's status as kingpins of Leinster was abruptly ended by Offaly in the 1980 Leinster final. Offaly's manager Eugene McGee was to mastermind one of the biggest upsets in football history when his Offaly team beat a Kerry team seeking five-in-a-row in the 1982 All-Ireland final. The undisputed star of that team was Matt Connor, who scored seven points that day and his points when Offaly were under pressure enabled the team to claw their way back.

'The build-up in 1982 suited us very well because all the pressure was on Kerry. They were probably the best football team ever,' says Connor. 'They had a lethal forward line, an extremely good back line and a great midfield. They really had no weakness. We had to work hard on the day and never give up. One very important thing was that our manager Eugene McGee put my brother Richie in at centre-forward. That was a key decision on that day because the year before Tim Kennelly had absolutely cleaned up at centre-back. He was going to make sure that the main reason we were beaten in 1981 wasn't going to happen again. He put Richie as a kind of stopper and a playmaker at centre-forward and that worked a treat. Another thing was that Eoin Liston was the key man in the Kerry forward line and we had to stop him and stop the supply of ball to him. Liam (O'Connor – Matt's cousin) did quite a good job in that sense on the day and the players out on the field did a lot of hard work and hard grafting to stop the ball going into the Kerry full-forward line.'

A sadness so deep that no tears would come fell over football fans everywhere, devoted to the flickering images of a rich history, two years later with the news that, at the age of twenty-five, Matt Connor's career had come to a premature end.

'I was going home from Tullamore on Christmas Day to my Christmas dinner,' he explains. 'My car went out of control and I was thrown out of the car and landed on my back. I damaged my spine and I suffered paraplegia from that accident. That finished my football career. When I had the accident I suppose football wasn't the main priority at that stage. It was just a complete change of life that I was not able to walk again.'

Seldom has one man brought so much pleasure to so many. Former Donegal star Seamus Bonner is one of Matt's many admirers. He says, 'Matt Connor was the best player I ever saw. He had it all: brilliant from frees and brilliant from play and could do it with either foot. I know him well through working in the gardai together. It was such a shame that his career ended so early.'

Runaround Sue

Along with Mayo's Cora Staunton and Cork's Juliet Murphy, Sue Ramsbottom is recognised as one of the greats of the modern game of ladies' Gaelic football. She has gone boldly where no female has gone before. What made her Laois under-twelve county championship medal unique was that she won it playing with the parish boys' team.

'I played in my first senior inter-county All-Ireland against Kerry when I was fourteen,' she says. 'It was the first ladies' football final played in Croke Park and, partly because of that, it got great coverage in the local papers. I scored so that was a big thrill, even though we lost. It's a great stage and to be playing in an All-Ireland final at fourteen is fabulous. I got my first All-Star that year so that was great.'

The teenage years are notorious for their fads, prompting many a frustrated parent to say, usually more in hope than in confidence, 'It's just a phase they're going through.' When most of her contemporaries were besotted with the fresh faces of Jason Donovan and Bros (there were many who said the band should have been called Dross) Sue's two heroes were less likely pin-up material – Barney Rock and Colm O'Rourke.

'I went through a huge phase of being Barney Rock,' she says. 'I used to think I was him taking frees. I had him off to a tee with the seven steps back routine. When Barney retired and Charlie Redmond took his place, I experimented with his technique at frees for a while. When I was playing, though, I was always Colm O'Rourke. He was the ultimate footballer. In 1996 I was chosen as *The Sunday Game*'s Player of the Match for the All-Ireland final. It would have been a great honour for me in any circumstances, but what made it one of the highlights of my career was that the selection was made by Colm O'Rourke.'

In fact Sue found herself in the exalted company of such top players as O'Rourke and Mickey Linden when, in an imaginative effort to increase the profile of Gaelic games among children, the GAA introduced a collection of cards featuring the photos of top players. Sue became part of many families' breakfast throughout the country when she was one of the few ladies featured in multiple boxes of Kellogg's. Despite her admiration for O'Rourke, however, he has to take second place in Sue's hierarchy of GAA greats.

'One of the most special moments in my life came after one of the All-Irelands when I was approached by Micheál O'Muircheartaigh and he drove me out to RTE for an interview,' she says. 'Just to be in his company meant an awful lot but the fact that they went to such trouble for me really made my day.'

Sue is a natural athlete. Apart from winning All-Ireland medals in basketball and volleyball, she was also an international rugby player.

Does she not find it surprising that the overwhelming majority of coaches in ladies' football are men?

'You need a strong character to manage a team and most men learn to adapt,' she says. 'Our club coach, for example, was Pat Critchley who trained the Carlow men's team.

He knows that you have to modify your style a bit when coaching ladies but many of the principles are the same, like knowing how to coach different players in different ways. Some need to have the pressure put on them, others need lots of encouragement. Some things, though, that might work well with men don't work as well with women.

'I think back to one of our All-Ireland finals. We were losing at half-time and when we got back to the dressing-room one of our mentors, who is a lovely, considerate woman, said, "I've put the kettle on and we'll have a cup of tea." Our manager immediately thumped the table ferociously and everything on it went flying all over the place. Then he yelled (in less polite language), "How the hell could you think of tea at a time like this?" To be honest I find that kind of thumping on the desk approach to motivation more funny than inspirational. I think, though, it's time now for us to have more female coaches.'

Would Sue consider a coaching career herself?

'Give me some men's county team and I'd get them into shape,' she says. 'There'd be some shock wouldn't there? Pat Spillane would have something to say then!'

How would Sue like to see the game marketed?

'People like Helen O'Rourke are doing a great job on that front. We have so many great players in the game and I think they are the best promotion for it.'

The long awaited All-Ireland senior medal finally came Sue's way in 2001 when Laois beat Mayo in the final. However, her memories of that famous win are tinged with sadness because of the premature death of her team-mate – the great Lulu Carroll.

'It was her persistence and nagging of our teacher, Mr Sayers, that led the way for girls to play on a boys' national schools team,' says Sue. 'Lulu got a great kick out of saving boys' penalties and would taunt them with, "Ah you couldn't score a goal on a girl." Lulu dreamed of playing in Croke Park on All-Ireland final day – which she did in 1988 against Kerry.

'Lulu played in the forwards, midfields, backs and goals. Many people have done this before and many will do this in the future, but the difference is Lulu was brilliant in all these positions with All-Stars and replacement All-Stars to prove it. We had a wonderful time together on that journey to get an All-Ireland medal. Girls came and went but Lulu's steely determination, focus and energy made sure her dream was realised.

'The year 1996 was great for Lulu as the sports commentators commented that she was "the Liam McHale of ladies' football with her long, tanned legs". It was also on the day of the final that Lulu got that marvellous equalising goal for Laois in the last seconds so we could have another bite at the cherry.

'It was in 2001 that the Laois Ladies won that famous All-Ireland. Not many people remember that Lulu got Player of the Match in the 2001 Leinster final. This was the hardest game Laois faced and played en route to the All-Ireland in 2001. While all her team-mates lay down, Lulu rose everybody else that day and ensured the dream was kept alive. Lulu was a real hero and, but for her, there would be no All-Ireland medal in Laois.

'Lulu was a proud Timahoe and Laois woman and wore her jerseys with pride. When she finished playing for Timahoe, she enjoyed coaching and passing on her skills and knowledge to the new kids on the block. She had eight county medals to her credit. I know the last county medal she won the year she died meant so much to her. The Timahoe club owes a great deal of gratitude to Lulu as a player and a manager, helping it to the dizzy heights of reaching a club All-Ireland in 2000.

'Lulu was the epicentre and the heart and soul of every team she played on. We will all play again some day with Lulu in the great pitch called Heaven. The best of things come in ones: one great friend, one Croke Park, one All-Ireland medal and one Lulu.'

Primrose and Blue

January 2016 saw the death of Gerry O'Malley, one of Roscommon's greatest icons. As a boy, O'Malley's footballing skills had been honed in a field at home in Brideswell called 'the Grandstand' because it was filled with kids playing football every evening.

O'Malley was the star of the Roscommon team that caused a sensation in 1952 when they beat the great Mayo team led by Seán Flanagan which famously won All-Irelands in 1950 and 1951. Because of a national newspaper strike, many people around the country only heard the result on the Tuesday after the game and, when they did, most thought it was a mistake.

Given his stature in the game, all neutrals wanted the 1962 All-Ireland final to be 'Gerry O'Malley's All-Ireland', only for Roscommon's star player to be injured in the game and Kerry to beat the men in primrose and blue by 1-6 to 1-12. The passage of time allowed O'Malley to see the black humour in the occasion.

'I had to be taken to hospital after the All-Ireland and I was in a bed beside a man I had never met before,' he said. 'My "neighbour" knew who I was and we got to talking, the way

224

you do. The next day a fella came in with the newspapers. He didn't recognise me from Adam and my new friend asked him, "How did the papers say O'Malley played?"

'"Brutal," came the instant reply, and it certainly left me feeling even more brutal.'

Earlier that year, Roscommon had been involved in an incident that has become part of GAA folklore. In the 1962 Connacht final, Roscommon trailed Galway by five points with less than ten minutes to go and looked like a beaten side. A Galway forward took a shot and put his team six points up. As the ball was cutting like a bullet over the crossbar, the Roscommon goalie, the late Aidan Brady – a big man – jumped up and hung on to the crossbar and it broke. There was a lengthy delay until a new crossbar was found. The delay disrupted the Galway players' rhythm and allowed Roscommon to snatch victory from the jaws of defeat thanks to a vintage display from O'Malley, ably assisted by his St Brigid's colleagues, the Feeley brothers.

O'Malley recalled with relish the way in which the breaking of the crossbar disrupted the Galway players' rhythm and allowed Roscommon to snatch victory from the jaws of defeat.

'I remember talking to Seán Purcell while we were waiting for them to fix the crossbar. I said to him, "It's probably gone from us. We can't turn it around now. Then I thought to myself "maybe not". I went up to Eamonn Curley, who was playing at midfield, and told him to swap positions. Fortunately we got two goals to tie things up. When we equalised I ran over to the Roscommon fans on the sideline and asked them how much time was left. They said that time was up. Luckily, I won the ball and put Des Feeley through for the winning point.'

The late Jimmy Murray was often asked to compare the respective merits of Gerry O'Malley and Dermot Earley in terms of their place in the hierarchy of Roscommon greats. He answered with typical diplomacy.

He said: 'When Gerry retired it was a huge blow for Roscommon and I suppose many of us felt we would never see his like again but, luckily enough, within a couple of years we discovered another great star in Dermot Earley. I don't really think you can or should compare players from different eras and it's not fair to either Gerry or Dermot to compare one against the other. Both were superb players over a long number of years and both had tremendous dedication.'

In marked contrast, Dermot Earley had no such reservations: 'Gerry O'Malley was Roscommon's greatest ever footballer.'

One of O'Malley's most attractive qualities was his ability to tell stories against himself. Gerry was also a wonderful hurler. At one stage he played for Connacht against Munster in a Railway Cup match. At the time, the balance of power in hurling was heavily weighted towards Munster but Connacht ran them close enough. On the way home, he stopped off for a drink with the legendary Galway hurler, Inky Flaherty. Given the interest in hurling in the Banner County, the barman recognised Inky straight away and said, 'Ye did very well.'

'Not too bad,' replied Inky.

'I suppose if it wasn't for O'Malley you would have won,' speculated the barman.

Flaherty answered back, 'Here he is beside me. Ask him yourself.'

SEVEN

WIRED FOR SOUND

Despite all the incredible advances in technology, television is not everything. Most people, given the chance, prefer to 'be there'. From its earliest days, sport was a great spectator attraction. The great Roman architects laid out their stadia not just for the Russell Crowes and Charlton Hestons of their time as gladiators and chariot-racers to showcase their talents, but to create 'atmosphere'. Sport is so popular now that only a tiny fraction that would like to get the opportunity to attend All-Ireland finals or rugby internationals can get tickets. Hence, the importance of television. It is now the medium through which the vast majority of people have access to their favourite sports. Indeed, sports such as snooker owe their popularity almost entirely to television exposure. New satellite technology brings even more opportunities.

George Bernard Shaw once said, 'Men trifle with their business and their politics; but never trifle with their games. It brings truth home to them.' From the earliest times, there were people who reported on sporting events. Greek and Roman writers recorded many sporting events. In *The Iliad*,

Homer recorded in considerable detail the games organised at the funeral of Patroclus. The attraction of sport is that it provides drama, tension, excitement, winners and losers, pain, laughter and sometimes even tragedy. It is uncertain, often to the very finish, (remember the 1982 All-Ireland?) and it is intensely human. It makes headlines, it provides a good read and it makes great pictures.

Television creates heroes and anti-heroes. Muhammad Ali was the first true world star of the TV age. Paul Gascoigne's fame soared after the 1990 World Cup, not because of his skills, but because he struck an emotional chord in the massive worldwide TV audience for shedding tears on the pitch when it looked as if a yellow card from the referee might rule him out of the World Cup final. Within months, he was endorsing a wide range of products, many outside football: board games, deodorants, jewellery, calendars, school lunch boxes, to name just a handful. He also had a hit record, even though he has a dreadful voice. Mind you, that's not a unique achievement. Even losers can find temporary fame and sometimes fortune through the universal appeal of sport, as the disastrous British ski jumper Eddie 'the Eagle' Edwards has shown in recent times. Incredibly, in 2016 Edwards was the subject of a major Hollywood film starring Hugh Jackman.

Sports stars have been used to endorse products since 1947, when the English cricketer Denis Compton, a kind of James Bond figure, became the face of Brylcreem. His face and slicked-down hair became one of the best-known pictures in Britain, used in magazines and on billboards all over the country.

Every rose has its thorn. Television has created its own problems for sport. Back in 1983 Sir Dennis Follows, chairman of the British Olympic Association, observed, 'We have now reached a stage where sport at top level has become almost completely show business with everything that one associates with showbiz: the cult of the individual, high salaries, the desire to present a game as a spectacle – with more money, less sportsmanship, more emphasis on winning. All this has come through television.' The following year Jack Nicklaus observed, 'Television controls the game of golf. It's a matter of the tail wagging the dog.'

Sport is vicarious living. It is tense, immediate and glamorous. Television generally (Gaelic games is something of an exception) pays large sums of money to bring the drama and entertainment of the major sports events into our homes. Sport is so popular with television companies because they are acutely aware that nothing stops the world in its tracks more effectively. In relative terms, compared with many other forms of entertainment, such as film, it is cheap. The bustling cities of Ireland were a ghost town when the boys in green were playing in the World Cup finals during Italia '90. Scarcely a bus moved on the streets. Sport is so important to television companies because it generates a large viewing audience. As such, it is a powerful weapon in the ratings war. An example serves to illustrate.

It was not until 1964 that the BBC initiated what was to become the hallmark of British soccer coverage for an entire generation: recorded highlights on *Match of the Day*. ITV was quick to respond and initiated *The Big Match* on Sunday afternoons, featuring recorded highlights of one of the previous day's top games. For the first time, British viewers were given the benefit of expert analysis to complement the action. The BBC had the advantage of having no commercial breaks. To give them an advantage over the Beeb, ITV invested £60,000

– a massive sum in the 1960s – in a slow-motion machine.

By the World Cup of 1970, when national interest was high and England's chances of retaining the trophy supposedly even higher, ITV boldly announced it had discovered 'the formula'. A panel of provocative experts would enliven half-time and post-match discussions through a combination of informed comment, passionate debate and full-scale abuse. Malcolm Allison, Bob McNab, Pat Crerand and Derek Dougan, 'the two goodies and the two baddies', sought to establish ITV's credentials as a legitimate alternative to the BBC in bringing soccer to the television audience. The science, using the term loosely, of football punditry was born.

The Odd Couple
Those RTE viewers who lived in single-channel land were first introduced to football analysis via *Match of the Day*, which was shown after *The Late Late Show* on Saturday nights. RTE has always been good at spotting a good idea and, after a few tentative steps, by the 1978 World Cup in Argentina the channel was fast catching up with the stations across the water in the punditry stakes. It was the 1982 World Cup, though, that really showed a star was born in the way Eamon Dunphy went against the tide of virtual universal euphoria about the Brazil team. He claimed that the stylish Brazilians were flawed because they couldn't defend properly. Italy went on to prove Eamon right.

In the European Championships in 1984, Eamon was at it again. This time he consistently claimed that French superstar Michel Platini was 'a good player but not a great player'. This time, however, Platini proved Eamon wrong. The point, though, was that everyone was talking about Eamon and that is what a television station prays for. Mind you, Eamon himself took umbrage when the late, great Dermot Morgan did a sketch on him after one of the games and Eamon went off in a huff.

A good quality in any pundit is irreverence. Dunphy scores highly in this category. In 2002, when speculation was rife as to who would replace Mick McCarthy, Dunphy was asked if he'd like the job. He replied, 'I'd love to do it but I couldn't afford the wage cut.'

Eamon is probably better at football analysis than at self-analysis. People were more than a little surprised to hear him describe himself: 'I'm the simplest, most clean-living guy in this country.'

With Dunphy and his co-panellist John Giles (until his retirement after Euro 2016), there's no danger of banalities. Giles and Dunphy became two of the most famous people in Ireland during the glory days of Jack Charlton's reign as Ireland manager. In that period, they served one of the key functions of an analyst, which is to provoke controversy. Ray Houghton's goal gave Ireland a 1-0 victory over the 'old enemy' England at Euro '88. The RTE switchboard was jammed following Ireland's victory with irate callers complaining, in particular, about John Giles' less-than-glowing assessment of the Irish performance.

Ireland went to the European Championships in 1988 with a reputation, at least in certain quarters, for playing a Wimbledon-type game – in this perspective, the only tactic they were allegedly capable of was the long ball. The game against Russia gave lie to this notion as Ireland outplayed their opponents with the most stylish football they had played under Charlton's stewardship, culminating in a stunning goal from a Ronnie Whelan volley. An apparently blatant penalty was denied the Irish in the second half when

Tony Galvin was fouled in the box. Sadly, despite their superiority, Ireland failed to book their place in the semi-finals when the Russians equalised totally against the run of play on the counter-attack with only six minutes remaining.

In the post-match analysis, another chapter in what was becoming a familiar theme began when John Giles and Eamon Dunphy once again drew attention to Mick McCarthy's inadequacies as centre-half. The 'McCarthy debate' raged throughout the country with some 'pundits' passionately defending him and others equally vociferously claiming that Dave O'Leary should be in the team. The debate inevitably seemed at times to be somewhat personalised but, from an RTE perspective, the important thing was that everyone was reacting to the analysts' comments.

Father Ted

One of the most important qualities any pundit can have is accessibility: to be able to speak in a way the punters can easily understand. We are lucky to have a few masters of this art on RTE television – none more so than Ted Walsh.

Ted has an empathetic relationship with every Irish racing fan because he is someone with whom even the most beleaguered punter can have a rapport. This was illustrated in his comment at the Cheltenham Festival: 'Conor O'Dwyer is as nice a fella as ever pulled his breeches over his knees.'

Seasons of Sundays

Gaelic games have been at the heart of broadcasting in Ireland from its earliest days. On New Year's Day 1926, 2RN, Ireland's national radio station, began its transmission. On 29 August that year, a Gaelic game was transmitted live for the first time. The All-Ireland hurling semi-final between Kilkenny and Galway was the first radio commentary outside America of a field game. When RTE television came on air in 1961–62, the GAA initially adopted a cautious approach, restricting this coverage annually to the two All-Ireland finals, the two football semi-finals and the Railway Cup finals on St Patrick's Day. Over the years, the GAA has spotted that television is not a threat, but a useful ally in attracting people to our national games.

The year 1979 will be forever remembered for the Pope coming to Ireland. It also marked the first transmission of *The Sunday Game,* a rare programme then devoted exclusively to Gaelic games. Popular Galway-based journalist Jim Carney and Seán Og O'Ceallacháin were the first presenters. Seán Og's contribution to Gaelic games was well known because of his varied career as a Dublin county footballer and hurler, referee and sports commentator and reporter. In fact, so associated was he in the popular mind with Gaelic games that people had great difficulty thinking that he had an interest in any other sports. This was memorably demonstrated when a caller to RTE Radio Sport rang to ask about Manchester United. The conversation went as follows:

'Is this Seán Og?'

'It is indeed.'

'Seán Og O'Ceallacháin?'

'The one and the same.'

'Off the radio?'

'That's me!'

'Sure what the f**k would you know about soccer?'

Seán Og had a good team behind him at RTE with Maurice Reidy as the editor and John D. O'Brien as director. They made the brave decision to have Liz Howard as one of their main analysts. Liz was an All-Ireland camogie player brought up in a hurling household. Her father was the great Limerick All-Ireland star Garrett Howard. For years she was PRO for the Tipperary County Board.

In 1979, Liz hit the headlines following her comments about the Leinster football final on *The Sunday Game*. Legendary Dublin full-forward Jimmy Keaveney was sent off for an elbow offence on Offaly defender Ollie Minnock. Liz was in no doubt that the sending off was very harsh. The next day, *The Irish Press* carried the headline 'TV personality supports Jimmy Keaveney' over a front page story. Keaveney was asked to attend a meeting of the Leinster Council Disciplinary Committee to explain his actions. The Dublin County Board invited Liz to attend the meeting and give evidence in support of Jimmy. She did and so did Ollie Minnock, who pleaded for leniency on Keaveney's behalf. Their pleas for mercy fell on deaf ears and Keaveney was suspended for a month, ruling him out of the All-Ireland semi-final against Roscommon. On the day of the match, Liz was going into Croke Park when she was accosted by a big Dublin fan who shouted at the top of his voice, 'Look at her. She's the wan who shafted Jimmy Keaveney.' It shows the hazards of being an analyst. You just can't win.

In the Beginning

Initially the chief football analyst on *The Sunday Game* was the late Enda Colleran, who was a key part of the Galway three-in-a-row All-Ireland-winning side 1964–66, captaining the side in the latter two years. He was selected at right full-back on both the Team of the Century and the Team of the Millennium. He used the knowledge he acquired to telling effect as an analyst and blazed the trail for others to follow.

In Seán Og's two years as a presenter, many players, both

active and retired, were called on to give their opinions. The hurling guest analysts included Limerick's Eamonn Cregan and Pat Hartigan; Kilkenny's Pat Henderson, Eddie Keher and Phil 'Fan' Larkin; Clare's Jackie O'Gorman and Johnny Callinan; Tipperary's John Doyle and Cork's Jimmy Brohan. The football guests were equally distinguished and included Kerry's Mick O'Connell and Mick O'Dwyer; Dublin's Kevin Heffernan; Antrim's Kevin Armstrong; Cork's Eamon Young; Mayo's Seán Flanagan; Cavan's Jim McDonnell; and Down's Sean O'Neill and Joe Lennon.

Down through the years, the programme has evolved and become indelibly imprinted in the national psyche, with Michael Lyster becoming the main presenter. *The Sunday Game* does not happen in a vacuum with the match and analysis. There is a complex and highly professional packaging operation designed to convey a more attractive and seductive context for the event. The packaging begins from the first minute with sophisticated graphics, evocative and carefully chosen music, with judiciously chosen and lively filmed images. These establish a mood of anticipation of an exciting programme to come. Powerful and dramatic opening sequences will almost certainly attract marginal viewers to certain sports.

One of the reasons the programme has prospered is that the production team are always on the lookout for new analytical talent. On the hurling side, they brought in the greatest manager of the 1980s, Cyril Farrell. Some people in Galway were disappointed that he continued to work as an analyst with the programme during his second coming as Galway manager in the mid 1990s. Their point was that it is hard to hunt with the hare and hunt with the hounds. Donal O'Grady, Thomas Mulcahy, Pete Finnerty and Michael

235

Duignan are among a number of former great players who have made an invaluable contribution to the programme.

For media bosses, the temptation to plunder the thoughts of former star players and successful managers and benefit from their judgements is overwhelming, particularly when, like Ger Loughnane's, their name has become the touchstone for controversy. After the famous Loughnane interview on Clare FM in 1998 at the height of the Colin Lynch controversy, someone remarked that Loughnane cost Irish industry £25 million because workers were constantly talking about him when they should have been doing their jobs.

Loughnane brings some of the qualities he showed as a player to his job as a pundit. In the 1976 League final replay, Eddie Keher got a head injury and the blood was pumping out of him, necessitating a long delay while he got attention. Loughnane, ever helpful and compassionate, went up to him and said, 'Jaysus, Keher, would you ever get up and get on with it. Sure there's nothing wrong with you.'

The Earley Years
Few current players act as analysts now compared to previous times. In the late 1980s, for example, Paul Earley was a regular analyst on *The Sunday Game* even though he was still playing for Roscommon and had been an All-Star a few years before. He worked well because he matched his deep knowledge of the game with a bit of humour.

One of his best moments came after the 1988 All-Ireland semi-final when Mayo, managed by John O'Mahony, put up a credible showing before losing to mighty Meath. At the end Michael Lyster asked Earley, 'Will Mayo be back?' Quick as a flash Earley replied, 'I hope not.'

Colm O'Rourke has been an analyst since 1991, when he

was still the best player in the country. In his autobiography, Liam Hayes deals with the ripples of discord created on the Meath panel back in 1991 but O'Rourke has been an inspired choice and, to this day, is one of the best pundits you will find anywhere. His mind is as agile as an Olympic gymnast. When he talks about football he nearly always seems, quite simply, to hit the right note. You can't ask any more of an analyst than that. Colm also comes up with some good one-liners. In 2003, as Armagh's focus and obsessive will to win a second All-Ireland looked all-consuming, O'Rourke's incisive observation was, 'If Adam was an Armagh footballer, Eve would have no chance. Instead of an apple, he would have looked for a banana, as this is on the diet sheet.'

Former players and managers like Martin Carney, Kevin McStay, John Maughan, Bernard Flynn, Ciaran Whelan and Tommy Lyons have all played their part.

For those personalities who have retired, media involvement affords them the platform to continue their happy addiction to the small and large dramas created by players when they suspend accepted reality in favour of a private, if heightened, version of it on the pitch. As a television pundit, their task is to inform, enthuse and to entertain, drawing on the depth and authenticity of their experiences. In recent years, one pundit has stolen the show in the world of Gaelic games.

There is No Show Like a Joe Show
As a player, Joe Brolly was famous for blowing kisses when he scored a goal. The Derry manager Eamonn Coleman was away after they won their only All-Ireland in 1993. His deputy, Harry Cribbin, was in charge and he didn't select Joe to start. He thought Brolly was too big for his boots. By his

own admission, Joe would have been 'as cocky as anything'. There was a massive crowd because it was such a big deal for an Ulster team back then to have won an All-Ireland. With fifteen minutes to go, Derry were struggling and Brolly was brought on. The first ball he got, he put over the bar. The second ball he put over the bar. The score was tied and a high ball came in over the top. The Down defender thought he could get it and was backpedaling but he missed it. Brolly caught it, the Down goalie came out to him and he lobbed the ball into the far corner. The crowd were really animated. Brolly ran down the length of the field blowing kisses by way of saying, 'Harry, you dirty b*stard for not picking me.' One of the subs told Brolly that Harry Gribbin said, 'Oh that wee b*stard's trying to sicken me.' It was the talk of the place and everyone really enjoyed it.

Down's heads went down after the celebration and Brolly could see after that it became a sort of psychological weapon. It became a thing that, if he scored a goal in the Ulster Championship, it had a demoralising effect on the opposition. Fergal Lohan told him that he had said to the Tyrone team when he was captain: 'The key thing is to stop that f**ker from scoring a goal.' Ten minutes into the second half, Brolly scored a goal. It deflated Tyrone.

His flamboyant celebrations were not universally popular among opposing players, though. He had his nose broken twice after scoring goals.

One time he lobbed the Meath keeper in Celtic Park. He was a big, tall man and Brolly popped it over his head. Colm Coyle came charging over to Brolly as he began his celebrations and drove his boot into him. Joe needed about thirteen stitches. Brian Mullins was managing Derry at the time and said to Brolly, 'You deserve that you wee bollix.'

One of Brolly's favourite memories is of marking Kevin Foley. A high ball came in between them, Brolly fielded it and, in his own words, he 'danced around' Foley and blasted the ball over the bar. A second high ball came in between them with exactly the same result. Brolly, though, was aware that the Meath crowd had gone very quiet and noticed Foley and Liam Harnan exchanging signals. The next ball that came in, Brolly was aware of both Foley and Harnan coming at him at top speed so he ducked, causing Harnan to catch Foley with his elbow. Foley was stretchered off unconscious. Brolly became a hero in Derry not because of any score he ever got, but because he was the man who 'floored' Kevin Foley.

Some pundits, like Michael Owen, use implication: 'I'm not saying Benteke is lazy – but he could work harder.' Brolly favours the more direct approach. Nobody watching will ever forget his comment after a tackle on Monaghan's Conor McManus in 2013, when Tyrone's star midfielder cynically took down his opponent as he chased in on goal: 'He's a brilliant footballer but you can forget about Sean Cavanagh as a man.'

In November 2015, this writer organised a conference where Joe was the keynote speaker. At one stage, he was about to relate a tale that could not be committed to paper. He asked if there were any journalists present. Mags Gargan put up her hand. Joe said a more colourful version of, 'You write what I say and I will come after you with all I have.' Mags nodded assent but obviously not sufficiently for Joe, so he added, 'Do not f**k with me.' Then, wondering if she was a tabloid journalist, Joe asked her what paper she wrote for. Mags got the laugh of the day when she replied, '*The Irish Catholic.*' Nobody laughed harder than Brolly at her answer.

One of Joe's topics was the banality of 'managerspeak' and 'playerspeak' – which quickly descends into the clutter of common cliché and which creates 'a conformist freak show'. He illustrated it with a fictional conversation between a random top player or manager and his good friend Marty Morrissey.

Marty: 'You've got Leitrim in the qualifiers today. It will be little more than a run out for you?'

Random player/manager: 'Well, Marty, Leitrim are a great team and we've got the greatest respect for them'

Marty: 'But they lost to Mayo by thirty-four points in Connacht.'

Randomer: 'Well, Marty, we watched the video of that and they certainly didn't do themselves justice. Seven of those goals came from uncharacteristic mistakes and fourteen of the frees they conceded were unfortunate. They are a great team and I've no doubt that they will have learned from those errors. We are under no illusions that this is a huge challenge for us today.'

Marty: 'But seven of their first team, including their left-footed free taker, right-footed free taker, goalie, midfielders, full-back and centre-forward have gone to America since the Mayo game. We're hearing that the bus driver has had to tog out today.'

Randomer: 'Well, that is right, Marty. But the under-21s and the three minors they've brought in are all quality players and the bus driver is extremely experienced. We know that, if we're not at the top of our game, we'll not come through this challenge – so we are under no illusions that this is a huge challenge today.'

Marty: 'And, of course, the game is in Croke Park, where this Leitrim team have never played.'

Randomer: 'Well, Marty, the fact is Croke Park puts all pressure on us. Leitrim are a great team and they haven't come here to make up the numbers, so it is a huge challenge for our players and we're under no illusions that this is a huge challenge.'

Brolly went on to bemoan the fact that the only time today's top inter-county players make themselves available for interviews is when a commercial company hires them for promotional work – a practice he stated was 'as tacky as the child in the beauty pageant'. That was just his polite warm-up for his criticism of the GPA (Gaelic Players Association), which he described as 'a nasty, money-grabbing little cartel that has come to dominate the county game'.

Before Brolly gave his lecture, the previous speaker was former Roscommon star Karol Mannion, who spoke courageously about his two experiences of concussion playing football. Karol spoke publicly for the first time about the reasons he retired from the inter-county game a little earlier than might have been expected. He felt he had lost the enjoyment playing the game at the highest level and that it was taking the players' lives from them. When he began with Roscommon they were a vibrant, imaginative team playing free-flowing football in Division One of the National League. He described playing top inter-county football then 'as part of a healthy, balanced lifestyle'. They were able to socialise and share a drink together.

Bare-faced Cheek
Brolly intervened to remind Karol that, on one famous occasion, some of his team-mates got naked in a hotel in Derry after a challenge match, walking casually through the place in the nip. The hotel manager went to the games room and

saw a new vision of ball games when two prominent players were calmly playing snooker, stark naked.

Brolly contrasted this attitude with how the fixation of winning has taken hold and, as a consequence, 'elitism has replaced participation and a once-healthy ethos has been corrupted'. Such elitism, he argued, created a focus on a minority and this created an 'unhealthy pressure' on players.

He reported that he had been shown earlier that year a weekly diary of an Ulster squad. Each week, the players were given a timetable containing minute detail. One vignette serves to illustrate this. 'Tuesday morning: Out of bed by 8am. Eat breakfast at home' – before prescribing exactly what that breakfast should be. Brolly found the mere suggestion ludicrous that any player should have to be told to eat breakfast at home.

He contrasted the strict emphasis on diet with a memory of staying in the Slieve Russell Hotel with the Derry squad when his team were in their prime after winning what he calls their 'one-in-a-row' All-Ireland in 1993. A waitress asked Tony Scullion if he wanted the continental breakfast and he and Brian McGilligan almost fell on the floor, they were laughing so hard. Within minutes, the squad were scoffing huge Ulster fries.

As it was the week after the Rugby World Cup final, he spoke of the Australian manager Michael Cheika's description of his team as 'a mixture of lovers and fighters' who socialise together after every game and who have a balanced lifestyle. Brolly cited the example of Cheika's number eight, David Pocock, universally recognised as one of the world's greatest players. He is co-founder of EightyTwenty Vision, a rural development programme in poverty-stricken Zimbabwe. His training load is less than any senior inter-county player. Pocock spends much of his free time on his farm in Canberra with his partner, Emma, where they have nine chickens and their garden provides their fruit and veg. He is also studying Ecological Agricultural Systems, his passion. He is also heavily involved with the climate change movement. He was arrested by police when he chained himself to a master digger to prevent the desecration of an ecologically important site. Brolly asked if an inter-county player would ever be seen to do that? He answered his own question by saying that the only time leading GAA players came into sight was when they were endorsing products.

The Winner Takes It All

Brolly's next target was the win-at-all-costs mentality which had been imported from soccer. He quoted the then Chelsea manager Jose Mourinho who, in happier times with the club, had announced after losing to Sunderland that he was suspending his attempts to play good football. He said, 'I don't want to do this. I want to play proper football that everyone else can enjoy. But if I have eleven robots playing my system, I can win 1-0 every time. It's one of the easiest things in football. It's not difficult because you don't give players the chance to express themselves. There are few risks.'

Brolly cited the example of this trend infecting the GAA in the under-ten St Brigid's footballers he coached, who had reached the final of an important Mid-Ulster tournament. As the game looked destined for extra time, the opposing midfielder launched a long ball, which bounced on the fourteen and went over the bar. The referee blew the final whistle. His charges sunk to the ground. Half of them were crying and meant it. The other half were crying because it seemed the appropriate thing to do. Their man of the match, Oisin McDonnell, was weeping inconsolably. Brolly went to him, tousled his hair and said, 'Ozzie, you have nothing to cry about. You covered yourself in glory out there today.' The boy replied, 'F**k off, Joe.'

The problem is exacerbated by the role of officialdom. 'County boards throw good money after bad to get absolutely nowhere,' says Brolly.

So what was his solution? He described how, in the 1920s, German philosopher Eugen Herrigel visited Japan to study Zen philosophy. He started with archery. What he discovered surprised him. The point of archery was not to hit the target or defeat the opponent. The point was to become deeply absorbed in the activity itself. Winning or losing was merely a by-product. The fascinating thing was that those who were able to absorb themselves fully in the contest were also the ones most likely to win. Classic examples of this have been Jim Gavin's Dublin, Tony McEntee's Crossmaglen or any Kerry senior team.

Brothers in Arms
No pundit can touch Brolly for gems such as: 'It is, only you wouldn't see Kasparov taking Karpov and dragging him across the table and down to the turf as he was about to checkmate him.' This was as he dismissed Pat Spillane's analysis of the Dublin versus Cork All-Ireland quarter-final as a chess match in 2013.

There was also: 'Sweet mother of all the Brollys.' This was his reaction to the suggestion that Galway might have beaten Mayo in the 2013 Connacht Championship.

Brolly also provides memorable analogies, such as, 'The GAA is powerful. It's like the Masons without the handshakes.'

He does not have it all his own way, though. Armagh manager Paul Grimley swiped back at Brolly's criticism after Armagh's defeat by Cavan in 2013, saying, 'One thing my brothers didn't do was go around Croke Park or any other park blowing kisses to the crowd.'

The Boxer

Brolly has been involved in some strange conversations.

Colm O'Rourke: 'I think this is a Mayo team made up of different steel.'

Joe Brolly: 'But Dublin are the Amir Khan of Gaelic football – dazzling attack, dodgy defence.'

Michael Lyster: 'Not being a cricket fan, Amir Khan . . . '

Joe: 'He's a boxer.'

Pat Spillane: 'You were thinking of Imran.'

Michael: 'I was thinking of Imran.'

Brolly: 'How much is the national broadcaster paying you for this?'

Spat Spillane

Brolly often spars with Pat Spillane on *The Sunday Game*. Spillane's introduction to TV work came when he was invited by RTE to compete in their Sports Superstars Championship, to be recorded early in 1979.

Those programmes brought huge ratings for RTE. They asked big sporting names like Limerick hurler Pat Hartigan, Dave O'Leary, swimmer David Cummins, Formula One driver Derek Daly, athlete Noel Carroll, Dublin footballer Jimmy Keaveney, boxer Mick Dowling and Cork's Jimmy Barry-Murphy, to participate. To give a light touch to the proceedings, the sports personalities were divided into teams each made up of two 'superathletes': one female athlete, one personality and one politician. Personalities who agreed to take part included Fr Michael Cleary, Frank Kelly and Dickie Rock.

After he won the competition, Spillane took part in the World Superstars competition in the Bahamas. He did not know much about protecting himself from the sun and, as a result of his pink visage and body, a new phrase entered popular currency: 'Pat Spillane tan.'

Radio Daze

In 2002, Spillane presented *Sportscall* for much of the summer. His preparation beforehand was not what he expected.

'When I was invited to present the *Sportscall* programme on RTE I went up early in the morning,' he says. 'I was certain I was going to be well trained before the programme started on studio control and on how to use all the gadgetry and technology and voice projection and all that.

'My preparation for prime-time radio involved the following:

* With ten minutes to go to air I am sitting on a studio chair not knowing what is going on.

* With eight minutes to air a woman walks into the studio. She looks at the computer. It is not on. She hits it and eventually something comes up on the screen.

* Five minutes to air a sound man comes in and says, "Press that button and shout into it." I pressed the button and said a few sentences. I now know that's what's known in the business as a soundcheck.

* Three minutes to go on air. The producer comes in and tells me that there are no phone calls in yet but that I should keep talking and eventually something will come up on the screen.

'That was my introduction to *Sportscall*, a prime-time programme on national radio.'

Dunne In

In 1979, after Kilkenny beat Galway in the All-Ireland hurling final, Fan Larkin rushed off the field and into the dressing-room to tog in. A clearly startled Mick Dunne went into the Kilkenny room just minutes after the match to prepare later for a live interview, only to see Fan already fully clothed. Clearly Fan had missed the presentation. Dunne asked him why was he in the dressing-room so quickly?

'I have to go to Mass, Mick,' replied Fan in a matter-of-fact voice.

Power to the People

After he stepped down as manager of the Clare team, there were strong rumours that Ger Loughnane would be interested in getting involved in politics. Subsequently, he was courted by Fine Gael and the Progressive Democrats. Loughnane's mischievous streak may have been a contributory factor to this round of speculation. In 1999, he agreed to a request from Clare FM to take part in an April Fool's Day joke. The local elections were coming up, so he announced on Clare FM that he was resigning from the Clare team and was going to stand for the county council. He stated that there were things more important than hurling and that he was going to stand as an independent, and that a lot of the Clare team were going to campaign for him. He launched into a passionate tirade about the need to improve the roads in east Clare. So convincing was he that many people swallowed the story hook, line and sinker and the station was inundated with phone calls. Such was the reaction that the station had to issue a statement that evening to admit that it was all a joke. The only time an April Fool's joke elicited such a reaction was almost ten years previously, when David Norris very persuasively declared on RTE radio that he was going to get married.

Nothing But The Truth

Former Laois star Colm Parkinson was being interviewed on Newstalk radio and remarked that, whenever there was a controversy, it was always branded a 'scandal' in the county. The interviewer Ger Gilroy asked, 'Why is that?' Parkinson calmly replied, 'Probably because we were always drinking.'

Parkinson was also characteristically candid when asked about his own evaluation of his performance for Ireland against Australia in the Compromise Rules series, when he was marking a player who had a big physical advantage over him. 'The first time I tried to tackle this big fella I was holding on to his jersey and he started to run down the pitch,' he said. 'I don't think he even noticed I was holding on to him.'

The Faithful Left Faithless

The first live GAA match on Sky Sports was on Saturday, 7 June 2014 when Kilkenny beat Offaly by 5-32 to 1-18 (fifty-six scores in all) in a windswept Nowlan Park. The presenters were Rachel Wyse and Brian Carney. The tagline for their coverage was: 'More than just sport. It's a way of life.'

A total of 32,000 watched the match on Sky TV. However, only 18,000 viewers tuned into Sky Sports for their second game: Wexford versus Dublin hurling in the Leinster Championship.

Up For The Match

Every year, one of RTE's institutions is *Up for The Match*, where Grainne Seoige and Des Cahill reach out to a very different audience than with programmes such as *Love Hate*. The fact that the audience collapses into mirth when it emerges that two people who come from different counties have done the apparently unthinkable and married one another seems to be a mystery for young viewers. One tweeted, 'What the fock is this focking thing?'

Tipp Topped

The rivalry between Kilkenny and Tipperary down the decades has produced many great quips. On RTE's *Up for The Match* All-Ireland preview in 2014, former Tipperary captain Declan Carr said he could never sleep the night before an All-Ireland final and suggested that if you could sleep you were not properly up for the game.

Former Kilkenny great Michael Kavanagh was immediately asked if he slept the night before a final. He replied, 'It depended on who we were playing. If we were playing Tipperary, I slept like a baby.'

EIGHT

MORE THAN WORDS

One of the most endearing features of the GAA is the perennial humour of many of its characters. Witness this collection of Freudian slips, true confessions, double entendres which demonstrates that GAA foot-in-mouth disease is far more rampant than mad cow disease.

> *'The modern game is like those infamous pictures of Kim Kardashian's ass covered in oil – not a pretty sight.'*
> Pat Spillane

> *'Every man, woman and monkey is nearly writing them off in Mayo.'*
> David Brady

> *'I know some fellas who were brilliant footballers but who were quiet and introspective and couldn't handle criticism. You have to handle these fellas differently than to some lad who was a messer and who you knew needed to get a good kick up the hole every now and then.'*
> Shane Curran

'He's just a contrary, cantankerous hoor.'
Shane Curran on Frankie Dolan

'I've never seen a stout guy move so quick.'
Padraig Harrington on marking Dessie Farrell as a schoolboy

'I'd wear a pink G-string for Mayo to win the All-Ireland.'
David Brady

'I'm not bleedin' Dumbledore ... I can't wave a magic wand and produce a footballer out of nothing.'
Johnny Magee reacts to criticism of Wicklow's league campaign in April 2015

'It's not a police state ... this is not North Korea.'
Joe Brolly argues against Tyrone's Tiernan being banned for the hair-ruffling incident that saw Monaghan's Darren Hughes sent off in the 2015 All-Ireland quarter-final

'If I get all these accusations against me and I win an All-Ireland, I don't give a sh*t to be honest.'
Philly McMahon

'I don't want to say Pat Spillane went down easily – but watching him in the 1980 All-Ireland final I threw a paper napkin at him on the telly and he fell over.
Cavan fan

'I'm not saying it was really cold but I did hear a fan observing, "There's a wind out there that would blow an elephant off his Missus".'
Down fan

'It's a cage where twenty-five or thirty men are stripped down to their bare bollocks while rattling inside with fear and anxiety and insecurity.'
Shane Curran on the dressing-room

———

BLOOD, SWEAT, TRIUMPH AND TEARS

'Jamie Clarke is the Messi of Ulster football.'
Pat Spillane

'We had to work very hard for this – it took 119 years for us to get it.'
Tyrone boss Mickey Harte after winning the 2003 All-Ireland

'Did you ever hear "One day at a time, sweet Jesus?" Before yesterday there were no All-Irelands in Tyrone, now there's one.'
Mickey Harte when asked about the possibility of two-in-a-row

'While there are many claims that managers are being paid under the table, the GAA couldn't even find the tables.'
Former GAA president Peter Quinn

'They said we were like the British Army, that we lose our power when we cross the border, but we've proved we have power today.'
Peter Canavan as he lifted the Sam Maguire Cup

'It's not a North-South thing, sure we're all the same – it's six of one and twenty-six of the others.'
Tyrone comic Kevin McAleer on the 2003 All-Ireland final

'The midfield area was like New York City, going down Times Square, crazy.'
Seamus Moynihan after Kerry lost to Tyrone in 2003

'A late tackle in Monaghan is one that comes the day after the match.'
Anon

'The Down forward line couldn't strike a match.'
Donegal fan after the demolition job in the Ulster Championship in 2002

'How would you know a Cork footballer? He's the one who thinks that oral sex is just talking about it.'
John B. Keane

'Somebody should check his birth cert because I don't think he was born, I think he's a creation of God.'
Colm O'Rourke on the apparently divine Colm 'Gooch' Cooper

'The first time I got the ball I passed it to a team-mate and raced on to take the return pass but instead he booted the ball two miles in the air.'
Iggy Jones on his Tyrone debut

'Those guys are going to be bleeding all over us.'
Cork player responds to the sight of a very heavily bandaged Willie Joe Padden in the 1989 All-Ireland final

'Don't be so modest (Padraic) Joyce. You're not that great.'
Westmeath fan during their shock defeat of Galway in 2006

'Jaysus, if Lee Harvey Oswald was from Mayo, JFK would still be alive.'
Mayo fan

'Even Iarnrod Eireann don't carry as many passengers as we saw today.'
Colm O'Rourke's verdict on the Dublin and Offaly forwards in the 2007 Leinster semi-final

'If Dublin win, it's over-hyped; if Dublin lose, it's over-hyped.'
Ciaran Whelan

'I used to think it was great being a wee, nippy corner forward, but it's better now being a big, burly one.'
Former Meath All-Star Ollie Murphy

'*Keep your high balls low into the wind.*'
Advice to a young John B. Keane

'*He'll regret this to his dying day, if he lives that long.*'
Dubs fan after Charlie Redmond missed a penalty in the 1994
All-Ireland final

'*Referees are like wives – you can never tell how they're going to turn out.*'
John B. Keane

A young boy's parents were being divorced. The judge asked him 'Would you like to live with your father?' 'No, he beats me.' 'So you would like to live with your mother?' 'No, she beats me.' 'Well, who would you like to live with?' 'The Kilkenny football team – they can beat nobody!'

'*Hurry up and make a decision, ref. I have to go home to bale the hay.*'
The late Michael Young during a club game in Derry as the ref dithered about whether to award a penalty

'*He simply wished us well for the second half and hoped the awful weather would improve.*'
Denis Allen's edited version of what Micky Kearins said to him and Dublin captain Gerry Hargan when he pulled the captains aside before the start of the second half and instructed them to warn their players about their behaviour in the 1989 All-Ireland semi-final after a very physical first half

'*Now listen lads, I'm not happy with our tackling. We're hurting them but they keep getting up.*'
John B. Keane ventures into coaching

'Football and sex are so utterly different. One involves sensuality, passion, emotion, commitment, selflessness, the speechless admiration of sheer heart-stopping beauty, rushes of breathtaking, ecstatic excitement, followed by shattering, toe-curling, orgasmic pleasure. And the other is sex.'
Joe O'Connor

'Last guys don't finish nice.'
Frustrated Leitrim fan

'Is it any wonder we never won anything? The men on the county board were so incompetent they couldn't even pick their own noses.'
Former Wicklow star Gerry O'Reilly

'Mayo always had a big problem coping with being favourites and never lost it.'
Former Mayo star Willie McGee

'Why did they not take off their pyjamas?'
A young boy to his father in 1960 watching Down became the first inter-county team to wear tracksuits

'Kerry would have won if Meath hadn't turned up.'
A Kerry fan reflects on the All-Ireland semi-final defeat in 2001

'Meath are like Dracula. They're never dead till there's a stake through their heart.'
Martin Carney

'Behind every Galway player there is another Galway player.'
Meath fan at the 2001 All-Ireland final

'When Joe Brolly is winning, he's objectionable. When he's blowing kisses, he's highly objectionable.'
Cavan fan

'Joe Brolly always talked a great game. The problem was that he didn't always play a great one.'
Colm O'Rourke responds to a Joe Brolly after-dinner speech, which had a few digs at the Meath team O'Rourke starred on

'He (the referee) wouldn't see a foul in a henhouse.'
Frustrated Sligo fan

'There are two things in Ireland that would drive you to drink. GAA referees would drive you to drink and the price of drink would drive you to drink.'
Another Sligo fan at the same match

'You get more contact in an old-time waltz at an old folks' home than in a National League final.'
Pat Spillane

'They (Cavan) have a forward line that couldn't punch holes in a paper bag.'
Pat Spillane

'The first half was even, the second half was even worse.'
Pat Spillane reflects on an Ulster Championship clash

'Meath players like to get their retaliation in first.'
Cork fan in 1988

'Micky Joe made his championship debut in such a way that he will never be asked to make it again.'
John B. Keane

'Meath make football a colourful game – you get all black and blue.'
A Cork fan

'Karl O'Dwyer will go down in history as the rat who joined the sinking ship.'
Kerry fan

'Frankie goes to Hollywood.'
Mayo fan's reaction to Frankie Dolan's 'theatricals' which 'caused' a Mayo player to be sent off in the Connacht final in 2001

Anxious corner-forward before club match in Sligo: 'Do you think I need gloves?'
Mentor: 'For all the ball you'll get, it's not going to matter.'

'That's the first time I've seen anybody limping off with a sore finger.'
Armagh's Gene Morgan to 'injured' team-mate Pat Campbell

'We're taking you off but we're not bothering to put on a sub. Just having you off will improve our situation.'
Mentor to club player in Derry

'Well you can't blame me. I never got near the ball.'
A corner-forward disclaims responsibility for a heavy defeat in a club game in Mayo

'The fire happened on a Saturday night and, when the fire brigade came, one of the firemen jumped off and asked me, "Is the ball safe?" As I was watching my business go up in smoke, the ball wasn't my main priority.'
Jimmy Murray after his pub-cum-grocery, which was home to the football from the 1944 All-Ireland final, was destroyed in a fire

———

BLOOD, SWEAT, TRIUMPH AND TEARS

'I was the non-playing captain.'
Dinny Allen after he captained the Cork team to win the All-Ireland in 1989. A lot of hurlers on the ditch alleged that Allen hadn't contributed much to winning Sam

'Kevin, keep close to the goal today. I didn't bring any oxygen.'
Billy Morgan expressing concern about the fitness of his full-back, Kevin Kehilly

'He was a man mountain – he would catch aeroplanes if it helped Kerry.'
John B. Keane on Mick O'Connell

'I warned the boys they couldn't go through the league unbeaten and, unfortunately, they appear to have listened to me.'
Tyrone manager Art McRory after his side's defeat by Donegal

'In terms of the Richter scale, this defeat was a force eight gale.'
Meath fan after the 2001 All-Ireland final

'The grub in the hotel was the only good thing about the day.'
Nemo Rangers fan after the 2002 All-Ireland club final

'I'm going to tape The Angelus over this.'
Meath fan on receiving the video recording of the 2001 All-Ireland final

'John O'Mahony has given up football. He's just become Kildare manager.'
Waspish Galway fan

'Poor Mayo, with no real method up front, resembled a fire engine hurrying to the wrong fire.'
Spectator at the infamous 1993 All-Ireland semi-final against Cork

---

'Lovely piece of whole-hearted fielding. Mick O'Connell stretched like Nureyev for a one-handed catch.'
Micheál O'Hehir

'The rules of Meath football are basically simple – if it moves, kick it; if it doesn't move, kick it until it does.'
Tyrone fan after controversial 1996 All-Ireland semi-final

Jack Mahon: 'I played at centre half-back on the Galway team in 1956.'
Fan: 'Gosh, that's shocking.'
Jack: *'Why?'*
Fan: 'Because I've just discovered my dad's a liar. He's always said that when Galway won that All-Ireland they never had a centre-back.'

'Whenever a team loses there's always a row at half-time but when they win it's an inspirational speech.'
John O'Mahony

'Gaelic football is like a love affair: If you don't take it seriously, it's no fun; if you do take it seriously, it breaks your heart.'
Patrick Kavanagh

'What they say about Cork footballers being ignorant is rubbish. I spoke to a couple yesterday and they were quite intelligent.'
Brendan Kennelly

'Life isn't all beer and football – some of us haven't touched a football in months.'
A Kerry player during the league campaign in the early 1980s

Kilmore player trying to trick Tony McManus: 'Tony, Tony, pass the ball to me.'

BLOOD, SWEAT, TRIUMPH AND TEARS

Tony McManus: 'Even if I was playing with you, I wouldn't pass you the ball.'

'It gives a whole new meaning to "powder your nose".'
Fan's reaction to a rumour that a player was reacting to pressure by taking cocaine

'My dad told me you were the man that lost the All-Ireland for Tyrone.'
Young fan to Iggy Jones

Journalist: 'How's the leg, Kevin?'
Kevin Moran: 'It's very fuc . . . it's very sore.'
After the 1978 All-Ireland final

Gravedigger pointing to the graves of all the famous Kerry footballers: 'It's a very impressive collection, isn't it?'
Jack Bootham: 'Tis indeed but, the way things are going at the moment, you'll have to dig them all up again if Kerry are ever going to win anything.'

'He (Colin Corkery) is as useless as a back pocket in a vest.'
Kerry fan

'Colin Corkery is deceptive. He's slower than he looks.'
Kerry fan

'He [Micheál O'Muircheartaigh] can take the ball from one end of the field to the other with just the players' occupations.'
Jack O'Shea

'Padraic Joyce sold more dummies than Mothercare.'
Willie Hegarty

'The current Galway under-21 team has more bite than Luis Suarez.'
Willie Hegarty in the wake of Galway under-21's victory over
Cork in the All-Ireland final and Luis Suarez's bite on Branislav
Ivanovic in 2013

'I think Mickey Whelan believes tactics are a new kind of piles on your bum.'
Disgruntled Dubs fan

'Brian, in years to come GAA people will be sitting around their fires and they'll be talking about the great wing-backs of all time and you know something Brian, when they do, you won't even get a mention.'
Jimmy Magee giving the team-talk to boost morale before a
Jimmy Magee's All-Stars to his wing-back, Fr Brian Darcy

'And here comes Nudie Hughes for Nudie reason.'
Micheál O'Hehir

'Every year we had a different trainer. In fact we had more trainers than Sheik Mohammed.'
Kildare's Pat Mangan

'Fermanagh has such a small playing base. Half is made up of water and the remaining half are Protestants.'
Fermanagh fan bemoans the paucity of talent

The Clash of the Ash

'Football is a game for those not good enough to play hurling.'
Tony Wall

'It's f***king bullsh*t, as you can see yourself.'
Galway's Johnny Glynn responds to suggestions that Galway
had only Joe Canning in attack

'Frank Murphy knows as much about high performance sport as I know about the sleeping habits of the Ayatollah.'
Donal Og Cusack after Cork's hurling and football teams exit the championship on the same weekend in July 2015

'There's a level of a lot of politics in hurling. I don't think Henry Kissinger would have lasted a week on the Munster Council.'
Ger Loughnane

'To be a great goalie, you need a big heart, big hands and a big bottom.'
Comment about a former Antrim goalie

'Ger Loughnane was fair, he treated us all the same during training – like dogs.'
Anon Clare player

'If you put monkeys on to play they'd still pack Croke Park on All-Ireland final day.'
Anon

'I said to the manager, "This is supposed to be a five-star hotel and there's a bloody hole in the roof." He turned around and said, "That's where you can see the five stars from."'
Player on All-Stars tour

'I love Cork so much that if I caught one of their hurlers in bed with my missus I'd tiptoe downstairs and make him a cup of tea.'
Joe Lynch

'A fan is a person who, when you have made an idiot of yourself on the pitch, doesn't think you've done a permanent job.'
Jack Lynch

'*Remember, postcards only, please. The winner will be the first one opened.*'
The late RTE commentator Liam Campbell

'*Pessimists see a cup that is half-empty. Optimists see a cup that is half-full. But we haven't even seen the cup.*'
Sligo hurling fan

'*Jesus saves – but Jimmy Barry-Murphy scores on the rebound.*'
Graffiti

'*We've got grounds which are state of the art and administration which is state of the Ark.*'
Ger Loughnane

'*Any chance of an autograph? It's for the wife. She really hates you.*'
Tipp fan to Ger Loughnane

'*I'm not giving away any secrets like that to Tipperary. If I had my way, I wouldn't even tell them the time of the throw-in.*'
Ger Loughnane on his controversial selection policy

'*I say nothing but I never stop talking.*'
Ger Loughnane on his media interviews before the 1995 All-Ireland

'*Never watch a Gaelic football match before hurling as it slows the mental reflexes.*'
Mentor to Cork team in the 1960s

'*My definition of a foreigner is someone who doesn't understand hurling.*'
A unique contribution to the asylum seekers discussion

'*Cork hurling games are like sex films – they relieve frustration and tension.*'
Joe Lynch

'*Broken marriages, conflicts of loyalty – the problems of everyday life fall away as one faces up to D. J. Carey.*'
Anon Wexford player

BLOOD, SWEAT, TRIUMPH AND TEARS

'He [Nicky English] spoilt the game – he got too many scores.'
Antrim fan at the 1989 All-Ireland final

'A referee should be a man. They are for the most part old women.'
Nicky Rackard

'The GAA is an amateur association run by professionals. The FAI is a professional body run by amateurs.'
Fan during the Roy Keane 2002 World Cup saga

'Cork are like the mushrooms – they can come overnight.'
Jim 'Tough' Barry

'Is the ref going to blow his whistle? No, he's going to blow his nose.'
Commentator on Kilkenny FM

'A forward's usefulness to his side varies as to the square of his distance from the ball.'
Galway fan during the 2001 All-Ireland

Nicky English shortly before the end of the 1988 All-Ireland: 'How much time left, ref?'
The ever-helpful Sylvie Linnane: 'At least another year for Tipperary.'

'When Sylvie Linnane is good, he's great. When he's bad, he's better.'
Galway fan

'I think of myself as a socialist hurler. I'm not too bothered who scores – as long as we win.'
'The Viking', Cormac Bonnar

―――――――

'Ger Loughnane is paranoid. He's the Woody Allen of hurling.'
Tipp fan

'You should play every game as if it's your last, but make sure you perform well enough to ensure it's not.'
Jack Lynch

'There's only one head bigger than Ger Loughnane's and that's Birkenhead.'
Limerick fan

'If Babs Keating wrote a book on humility he'd be raging if it wasn't displayed in the shop window.'
Offaly fan in 1998

'Babs Keating "resigned" as coach because of illness and fatigue. The players were sick and tired of him.'
Offaly fan in 1998

'Babs Keating has about as much personality as a tennis racquet.'
Offaly fan in 1998

'I didn't get Christy Ring's autograph. He trod on my toe, though.'
Anon

Fan: 'Do you hear that, Christy? They reckon here that you're past it.'
Christy Ring: 'Huh! Past it! I'll be hurling when I'm f**king ninety.'

'Hurling – it's all a matter of inches: those between your ears.'
Kevin Armstrong

'Everyone knows which comes first when it's a question of hurling or sex – all discerning people recognise that.'
Tipp fan

'The only time in my playing days I heard anybody talking about hamstrings was when they were hanging outside a butcher's shop.'
Mick 'Rattler' Byrne

Mick 'Rattler' Byrne: 'Don't be worrying, Tommy. There are two parachutes under the seat, you put one on, jump out, count to ten, press the button and you jump to safety. What could be simpler?'

A nervous Tommy Doyle on a flight to New York: 'But what happens if the parachute doesn't open?'
Mick: 'That's easy. You just jump back up and get the spare one.'

Rattler Byrne: 'By God, Christy, we'll have to shoot you.'
Christy Ring: 'Ye might as well. Ye've tried everything else.'

'To tell you the truth, I'd rather he had won a Munster medal.'
Former Tipperary star Billy Quinn in 1990 to a journalist when he was asked if he was proud of his son, Niall, who scored the goal against Holland at Italia '90

'I was only doing Babs Keating.'
A ten-year-old Niall Quinn after shattering his kitchen window to smithereens with his sliotar when practicing his frees

An irate county board official: 'Where's your pass?'
Christy Ring (jumping over the stile instead of displaying his pass as he went into a match): 'I don't have it.'

———

Board official: 'But Christy, you ought to have. You won no fewer than eight All-Ireland medals.'
Christy: 'And if I hadn't been carrying passengers like you, I'd have won at least eight more.'

'Sylvie Linnane would start a riot in a graveyard.'
Tipp fan

'Sylvie may not be sugar but he adds plenty of spice.'
Galway fan

'As a Clare minor, my first introduction was under the late Paddy 'Duggie' Duggan who gave a most amazing speech in the dressing-room in Limerick. While whacking a hurley off a table and as his false teeth did three laps of his mouth, he called on the team to kill and maim the opposition before saying an Our Father and three Hail Marys.
Ger Loughnane

'A Munster final is not a funeral, though both can be very sad affairs.'
Ger Loughnane

'Hurling and sex are the only two things you can enjoy without being good at.'
Jimmy Deane

Fan: 'How bad was the pitch?'
Jimmy Doyle: 'Well, the grass was so long a hare rose at half time.'

Garret Fitzgerald on the canvas trail in 1981, when he posed for a photo opportunity swinging A hurley: 'I've always wanted to play hurling so I thought it would be a good thing to learn the rudiments of the game.'

BLOOD, SWEAT, TRIUMPH AND TEARS

Interviewer: 'So have you learned much?'
Garret (attributed): 'Yes I have. How to swing a cue.'

'I never knew Solidarity had such popular support in Cork.'
Remark attributed to Garret Fitzgerald when he arrived in Cork on a Sunday and saw hordes of people swathed in red and white, at a time when the Solidarity movement in Poland was at its zenith, not realising they were on their way to a Munster Championship match

Pat Carroll: 'My hurley was stolen this morning.'
Friend: 'That's terrible – where did you lose it?'
Pat: 'In the car park.'
Friend: 'Did the thieves damage your car much?'
Pat: 'I don't know – they stole that too.'

'Funny game hurling, especially the way Kerry play it.'
Cocky Cork fan

'Frank Murphy. The comb-over who rules the world.'
Tom Humphries

'The toughest match I ever heard of was the 1935 All-Ireland semi-final. After six minutes, the ball ricocheted off the post and went into the stand. The pulling continued relentlessly and it was twenty-two minutes before any of the players noticed the ball was missing.'
Michael Smith

'And as for you, you're not even good enough to play for this shower of useless no-hopers.'
Former Clare mentor to one of his subs after a heavy defeat

'Why are Limerick magic? Because they can disappear for five minutes.'
Offaly hurling fan after the dramatic 1994 All-Ireland final

'There is nothing even vaguely intellectual about a Munster hurling final, yet a proper enjoyment of the game presupposes a sophisticated appreciation of the finer things.'
David Hanly

'The Kilkenny players took their sleeping pills too late because they hadn't fully woken up until after the match.'
Dejected fan in 1966 after red-hot favourites Kilkenny surprisingly lost the All-Ireland to Cork

'Hurling is cavemen's lacrosse.'
 A British Sunday newspaper

'Rugby is a sport for ruffians played by gentlemen, Gaelic football is a sport for gentlemen played by ruffians, but hurling is a sport for gentlemen played by gentlemen.'
Anon

'They wouldn't bate dust off a carpet.'
Kilkenny fan prematurely dismisses Galway's chances before the 2001 All-Ireland semi-final

'Babs Keating has been arrested in Nenagh for shaking a cigarette machine, but the gardai let him off when he said he only wanted to borrow twenty players.'
Waterford fan after Babs had predicted a heavy defeat for Waterford in the 2002 Munster final
'They haven't come to see you umpiring, they have come to see me hurl.'
Christy Ring after a clash with an umpire

'F-f-f-f**k you Lynch. Try that again an' there'll be a f-f-f-f**kin by-election.'

Tony Reddin. Reddin had something of a speech impediment and during the white heat of a Cork versus Tipp clash, Lynch charged into Reddin and in the process bundled both of them into the net

'If I had the ball they have today I'd drive it to f**kin Doora.'
Former Clare goalie bemoaning the demise of the old sliotar

'Ah sure, Daly you can't score a point and what's worse you can't f**ken even pull a pint.'
Limerick fan after publican and legendary Clare player Anthony Daly missed a long-range free

'Let's pick the team first and we'll sort out the terms of reference later.'
A journalist's approach to the selection process for the All-Stars team

'Winning the All-Ireland without beating Cork or Kilkenny is an empty experience but, as empty experiences go, it's one of the best.'
Tipperary fan in 2001

'In Kilkenny an unscrupulous shopkeeper will try to slip you an All-Ireland medal for a euro, they have so many to spare.'
Ger Loughnane

'The referee is so cautious that he plays extra time before the game starts in case of fog.'
Ger Loughnane

'Born at a very young age. I've never been a millionaire but I know I'd be unreal at it.'
Opening line of Shane McGrath's Twitter account

The Voice
Micheál O'Muircheartaigh was one broadcaster who is
universally loved. Micheál has left an indelible mark on the
GAA landscape with a series of classic comments. This is a
baker's dozen of his magic moments:

1. 'I see John O'Donnell dispensing water on the sideline.
   Tipperary, sponsored by a water company. Cork sponsored
   by a *tae* company. I wonder will they meet later for afternoon
   tae.'
2. 'He kicks the ball *lan san aer*, could've been a goal, could've
   been a point . . . it went wide.'
3. 'Colin Corkery on the forty-five lets go with the right boot.
   It's over the bar. This man shouldn't be playing football. He's
   made an almost Lazarus-like recovery. Lazarus was a great
   man but he couldn't kick points like Colin Corkery.'
4. 'Stephen Byrne with the puck out for Offaly . . . Stephen,
   one of twelve . . . all but one are here today. The one that's
   missing is Mary, she's at home minding the house . . . and the
   ball is dropping in Lar na Pairce . . . '
5. 'Pat Fox has it on his hurl and is motoring well now . . . but
   here comes Joe Rabbitte hot on his tail . . . I've seen it all now,
   a rabbit chasing a fox around Croke Park.'
6. 'Pat Fox out to the forty and grabs the sliotar . . . I bought a
   dog from his father last week, sprints for goal . . . the dog ran a
   great race last Tuesday in Limerick . . . Fox to the twenty-one,
   fires a shot, goes wide and left . . . and the dog lost as well.'
7. 'Danny "The Yank" Culloty. He came down from the moun-
   tains and hasn't he done well?'
8. 'Teddy looks at the ball, the ball looks at Teddy.'
9. 'In the first half they played with the wind. In the second half
   they played with the ball.'
10. '1-5 to 0-8, well from Lapland to the Antarctic, that's level
    scores in any man's language.'

11. 'I saw a few Sligo people at Mass in Gardiner Street this morning and the omens seem to be good for them. The priest was wearing the same colours as the Sligo jersey. Forty yards out on the Hogan stand side of the field, Ciaran Whelan goes on a rampage, it's a goal. So much for religion.'

12. 'Brian Dooher is down injured. And while he is down I'll tell ye a little story. I was in Times Square in New York last week, and I was missing the Championship back home and I said, "I suppose ye wouldn't have The Kerryman would ye?" To which, the Egyptian behind the counter turned to me he said, "Do you want the North Kerry edition or the South Kerry edition?" He had both, so I bought both. Dooher is back on his feet.'

13. 'David Beggy will be able to fly back to Scotland without an airplane, he'll be so high after this.'

Riddle Me This

Q: What's the difference between Philly McMahon and Kylie Minogue?

A: Philly marks tighter than Kylie's famous hotpants.

Q: 'What do Mayo footballers have in common with a Wonderbra?'

A: 'Lots of support but no cup.'

Q: 'What do you say to a Laois man in Croke Park on All-Ireland final day?'

A: 'Two packets of crisps please.'

Q: 'Why did Derek McGrath climb the Eiffel Tower?'

A: 'He was looking for forwards.'

Q: 'How many Cavan footballers does it take to change a light bulb?'

A: 'Are you paying with Visa or American Express?' (Monaghan fan)

Q: 'What do Kerry footballers use for contraception?'

A: 'Their personalities.' (Cork fan)

Q: 'What's the difference between Paddy Cullen and a turn-stile?'

A: 'A turnstile only lets in one at a time.' (Kerry fan after Cullen conceded five goals in the 1978 All-Ireland final)

Q: 'What's the difference between Paddy Cullen and Cinder-ella?'

A: 'At least Cinderella got to the ball.'

Q: 'Who were the last two Westmeath men to play midfield in the All-Ireland final?'

A: 'Foster and Allen.'

Q: 'How many intelligent Cork fans does it take to screw in a light bulb?'

A: 'Both of them.'

Q: 'What's the difference between God and Pat Spillane?'

A: 'God doesn't think he's Pat Spillane.'

Q: 'What's the signature tune of the Armagh team?'

A: 'You'll Never Walk Again.'

Q: 'When do you know a Meath player is feeling generous?'

A: 'He wears iodine on his studs.'

Q: 'What's the difference between the Pope and Sam Maguire?'

A: 'The Pope has come to Mayo more often than Sam Maguire since 1951.'

Q: 'What's the difference between the Fermanagh team and Kit Kat?'

A: 'Kit Kat has more silver.'

Q: 'What's the difference between tennis players and the Tyrone hurlers?'

A: 'Sometimes tennis players put the ball in the net.'

CONCLUSION

In 2009 the GAA celebrated its 125th anniversary. Fr Harry Bohan stated, 'All through its existence, the GAA has been bound up with a sense of place, belonging and a sense of community. This has bonded people together and given people stability. Today we live in a cloud of instability and confusion. We have witnessed a loss of trust in institutions, spiralling unemployment, the continuing collapse of culture shaped by consumerism and borrowing. If we are to bring stability and security to our own lives, we will need to rediscover a sense of place and take pride in who we are and the culture that shapes us. Without a vision, people die.'

Love it, hate it or try to be indifferent to it, Gaelic games subtly shape Irish social history and everyday life. It permeates the media, sets the mood of Monday's post-match workplace and dominates pub-talk. For many, life and death still run second to major GAA events. Almost every young boy, and an ever-increasing number of girls, dream of playing in Croke Park.

Gaelic games offer us a group identity, a spiritual home to belong, a sacred space where we can be among our people and therefore be ourselves. There is something innocent, something mysterious about Gaelic games's hold on our identity, which is completely removed from analysis. This is its power. To shamelessly borrow from Don McLean, something touches us deep inside. We all crave it, the sense of connection, the thought we can be better than we are, even if better only through someone else – our fifteen representatives. The surging runs of Henry Shefflin or the intricate footwork of Colm Cooper take us to a higher power, altered for a moment, alive in another's body and mind. That's the reason we need our own heroes, so that we too can be elevated.

The past isn't dead and buried – it is not even dead. There is a need, to quote John McGahern, to 'rescue the past from forgetfulness'. Institutional memory is a prized asset in all walks of life today. Memory rescues experience from total disappearance. The lamp of memory holds traces and vestiges of everything that has ever happened to us. Nothing is ever lost or forgotten. It is important that the great players and personalities and the classic victories and thrilling contests of the last generations of the GAA be stored in the popular imagination.

For generations, the GAA has been the one fixed point in a fast-changing age. Those years have not been without their troubles but, even when the storm clouds gathered, the people's organisation has not withered before their blast and a greener, better, stronger movement lay in the sunshine when the tempest was past.

Our economic system values measurable outcomes but what is deepest about us, transcends what can be said and outstrips what can be analysed. It is not given to us to peer into the mysteries of the future but we can safely predict that, in the coming years, Gaelic games will continue to reach to something profound within us. For what, we may not always be sure. Except that there are moments when we know that there is more to life – and to us – than the grim and grasping existence of seeking and striving and succeeding. There are moments of wonder, hope and grace that give us hints of ecstasy and lift us out of ourselves. They are, in Yeats's phrase, the soul's monuments of its own magnificence. These moments take us to the heart of the deep mystery of being a person, the subterranean stirrings of the spirit, the rapid rhythms of the human heart. They have to do with remembering who we are, enlarging our perspective and seeing ourselves whole.

Thanks for the memories and for those still to come.

As the two All-Ireland hurling semi-finals and replay, and the epic All-Ireland football semi-final between Kerry and Dublin showed in 2016, we can still feel great optimism about our national treasures.

The best is yet to come.